Sampling Normal and Schizophrenic Inner Experience

EMOTIONS, PERSONALITY, AND PSYCHOTHERAPY

Series Editors:
Carroll E. Izard, *University of Delaware, Newark, Delaware*
and
Jerome L. Singer, *Yale University, New Haven, Connecticut*

Current volumes in the series

THE COGNITIVE FOUNDATIONS OF PERSONALITY TRAITS
Shulamith Kreitler and Hans Kreitler

THE EMOTIONAL BRAIN: Physiology, Neuroanatomy, Psychology, and Emotion
P. V. Simonov

EMOTIONS IN PERSONALITY AND PSYCHOPATHOLOGY
Carroll E. Izard, ed.

FREUD AND MODERN PSYCHOLOGY
Volume 1: The Emotional Basis of Mental Illness
Volume 2: The Emotional Basis of Human Behavior
Helen Block Lewis

GUIDED AFFECTIVE IMAGERY WITH CHILDREN AND ADOLESCENTS
Hanscarl Leuner, Günther Horn, and Edda Klessmann

LANGUAGE IN PSYCHOTHERAPY: Strategies of Discovery
Robert L. Russell, ed.

THE POWER OF HUMAN IMAGINATION: New Methods in Psychotherapy
Jerome L. Singer and Kenneth S. Pope, eds.

THE PSYCHOBIOLOGY OF EMOTIONS
Jack George Thompson

SAMPLING NORMAL AND SCHIZOPHRENIC INNER EXPERIENCE
Russell T. Hurlburt

SHYNESS: Perspectives on Research and Treatment
Warren H. Jones, Jonathan M. Cheek, and Stephen R. Briggs, eds.

THE TRANSFORMED SELF: The Psychology of Religious Conversion
Chana Ullman

Sampling Normal and Schizophrenic Inner Experience

Russell T. Hurlburt
University of Nevada, Las Vegas
Las Vegas, Nevada

Plenum Press • New York and London

Library of Congress Cataloging in Publication Data

Hurlburt, Russell T.
Sampling normal and schizophrenic inner experience / Russell T. Hurlburt.
p. cm.—(Emotions, personality, and psychotherapy)
Includes bibliographical references.
ISBN 978-1-4757-0291-0 ISBN 978-1-4757-0289-7 (eBook)
DOI 10.1007/978-1-4757-0289-7
1. Schizophrenics—Case studies. 2. Introspection—Case studies. I. Title. II. Series.
RC514.H87 1989 89-22848
616.89′8209—dc20 CIP

Softcover reprint of the hardcover 1st edition 1990
A Division of Plenum Publishing Corporation
233 Spring Street, New York, N.Y. 10013

To my wife

Foreword

What are the basic data of psychology? In the early years of experimental psychology, they were reports of "brighter" or "heavier" or other estimates of the magnitude of differences between the sensory stimuli presented in psychophysical experiments. Introspective accounts of the experience of seeing colored lights or shapes were important sources of psychological data in the laboratories of Cornell, Harvard, Leipzig, or Würzburg around the turn of the century. In 1910, John B. Watson called for the objectification of psychological research, even parodying the typical subjective introspective reports that emerged from Edward Bradford Titchener's laboratory. For almost fifty years psychologists largely eschewed subjective information and turned their attention to observable behavior. Rats running mazes or pigeons pecking away on varied schedules of reinforcement became the scientific prototypes for those psychologists who viewed themselves as "doing science."

Psychoanalysts and clinical psychologists sustained interest in the personal reports of patients or clients as valuable sources of data for research. For the psychologists, questionnaires and projective tests that allowed for quantitative analysis and psychometrics seemed to circumvent the problem of subjectivity. Sigmund Freud's introduction of ongoing free association became the basis for psychoanalysis as a therapy and as a means of learning about human psychology. Slips-of-the-tongue, thought intrusions, fantasies, hesitations, and sudden emotional expressions became the data employed by psychoanalysts in formulating hypotheses about resistance, memory, transference, and a host of presumed human wishes and conflicts.

While these sources of data continue to be useful, there are reasons to seek other ways of learning about human thought. William James had early identified the phenomenon of the stream of thought, but he carried out little research on the process. Actually it is from the astute observations of writers in the stream-of-consciousness genre—James Joyce, Virginia Woolf, Dorothy Richardson, William Faulkner, and Saul Bellow—that we obtain some sense of the complexities and variety of ongoing thought. In the late 1950s, John Antrobus and I sought to capture some of this data by systematically interrupting individuals for reports while they engaged in vigilance and signal detection experiments under carefully controlled laboratory conditions. Such a procedure permitted us to identify Task-Irrelevant Thought and Imagery (TUITs) and to determine under what conditions of external stimulation such TUITs were enhanced or reduced, how such thought was related to predetermining conditions (e.g., stress), or to more general personality characteristics.

Russell Hurlburt, however, pioneered in the use of electronic paging devices that could be carried by subjects during normal daily activities, who—when beeped on random schedule—could write down and categorize their ongoing thought. This method allowed for systematic quantifiable analysis and met reasonable conditions of rigor. Important theoretical analyses by Eric Klinger were tested using variations of Hurlburt's method. The work of Mihalyi Csikszentmihalyi and his collaborators at the University of Chicago demonstrated that large-scale studies could be carried out employing the thought sampling procedures. A large number of high school students carried paging devices for a month and a useful picture adolescent life emerged. Research by Dan McAdams has shown that persons who show need for intimacy and affiliation as measured by Thematic Apperception Test stories also prove to have more thoughts reflecting affiliative needs when interrupted by paging devices during the day's activities.

Now Hurlburt has moved further in providing extremely detailed data on the ongoing thought available for the scrutiny of researchers. The present volume provides us the basic data we need about the naturally occurring thought of normal and emotionally distressed persons. The data come to us in their rich variety and dynamic fluidity. But we also see that methods for analysis of such data within and across individuals are available. This volume provides important clues to the naturally occurring thought of some ordinary people going about their regular activities; but we also obtain some startling insights about the thought world of depressed or schizophrenic persons. The poverty of associations and fragmented quality of the thought reports from schizophrenics confirms more directly what had been inferred from Rorschach or Thematic Apperception Test studies. To talk of schizophrenics as living in a "complex but private world" simply does not hold up, at least for the persons sampled in this book.

Ultimately we may get important clues about brain functioning from this new data source that is being tapped by Hurlburt. The method is labor-intensive, yes, but if social science research is to be funded sometime at a level even partially commensurate with natural science, we will be able to accumulate these data. It can be matched against the various new brain-imaging devices with great profit. A comparable method has already been fruitfully employed in cardiovascular research where patients can carry halter monitors, and silent ischemic painless responses on the EKG can be matched to samples of concurrent ongoing thought reports.

I began by asking what are the basic data of psychology. Clearly overt acts, questionnaire responses, choices made under laboratory conditions—all are necessary sources of information for scientific evaluation. Now we have a new version of the introspective data that once were derided as "armchair" psychology. The introspective reports obtained by Hurlburt's procedure are free of the explanations and attributions that have been criticized as "after the fact" or unpredictive of behavior by social psychologists. Instead, they are the raw material of spontaneous emotion and imagery or interior monologue that can lend themselves to potentially deep analyses of ordinary thought. What they may lack in the literary attractiveness of a monologue written by James Joyce they make up in their undoubted authenticity. We have the beginnings here of an exciting means for capturing the flow of natural human thought, critical data indeed for a full understanding of human psychology.

Jerome L. Singer
Department of Psychology
Yale University
New Haven, Connecticut

Preface

This book is the result of a very simple intention: to understand directly people's inner experiences. Acting on this intention has proven to be simultaneously both simple and complex: simple in the sense that all that needed to be done was to get in a favorable position to observe inner experience and then report what was seen; complex in the sense that providing ourselves and the reader with assurance that we had done just that is a difficult task in the context of modern psychology. Perhaps studying inner experience has always had this lure of the simple but the disappointment of the complex, because even after several millennia of attempts, thinking has remained stubbornly resistant to adequate description. The present study is the result of yet another attempt to outmaneuver that stubbornness, undertaken because it seems surprising that our era, with its burgeoning interest in things psychological, has remained relatively silent about the very activity that pervasively occupies our lives.

There are many people who contributed greatly to this work, both individuals who participated with me in earlier attempts at thought-sampling and authors who have written about topics directly or indirectly related to the course of this research. They are not explicitly cited here, even though I freely acknowledge their influence. The decision to omit citations is much more an indication of the breadth of influence than a paucity.

The final manuscript for this volume benefited greatly from critical comments on earlier versions. I thank Eric Klinger, Jerome Singer, Donald Diener, and especially Susan Melancon.

Contents

Preliminary Comments Designed to Suspend the Introspection Controversy 1

1. Introduction 9

2. Method 17

Phase 1: The Pre-Sampling Retrospective General Account of the Subject's Inner Experience 19
Phase 2: The Sampling Itself 21
Phase 3: Writing the Descriptions 26
Phase 4: Reviewing Each Sampled Thought 28
Phase 5: Comparing Sampled Thought Descriptions to the Pre-Sampling Generalizations 28
Phase 6: The Follow-Up Sample 28

3. Method Considerations 31

I. THE NORMAL SUBJECTS 39

4. A College Freshman 41

with Susan M. Melancon

Images 41
Daydreaming 42

Problem-Solving Images ... 45
Comparison of Images with External Reality ... 48
Revisualizations of External Details ... 50
Inner Hearing ... 51
Inner Speech ... 53
Wordless Speech and Imageless Seeing ... 54
Wordless Speech ... 54
Imageless Seeing ... 55
Paying Particular Attention ... 56
Feelings ... 58
Discussion ... 59

5. A Professional Potter ... 61

Feelings ... 62
Images ... 65
Noticing Characteristics ... 69
Just Doing ... 71
Body Sense ... 72
Verbal Thought ... 72
Discussion ... 73

6. A Record Store Manager ... 77

with Susan M. Melancon

Unsymbolized Thinking ... 78
Feelings ... 81
Verbal Thought ... 84
Inner Speech ... 84
Inner Hearing ... 85
Speaking Aloud ... 86
Visual Thought ... 88
Images ... 88
Altered States ... 89
No Thought ... 92
Discussion ... 93

7. A Medical Doctor ... 95

Verbal Inner Experience ... 96
Inner Speech ... 96
Inner Hearing ... 99

The Use of a Foreign Language 99
Partially Wordless Speech 100
Wordless Verbalization 101
Reading 102
Word Repetitions 103
Absorbed in Speaking 103
Paying Attention 103
Nonverbal Inner Experience 104
Feelings 104
Unsymbolized Thinking 106
Visual Experience 107
Images 107
Imageless Seeing 108
Other Characteristics of Helen's Inner Experience 108
Multiple Experiences 108

8. A Graduate Student 111

Sonja Smith

Word Repetition 111
Self-Aware Thoughts 113
Images 116
Reverie 116
Taking in Quality of Objects 118
Actions: Doing, Reading, Listening, Talking 119
Comparison with Sonja's Pre-Sampling Expectations 119
The Follow-Up Study 122
Discussion 122

9. A Research Associate 125

Susan M. Melancon

Verbal Thought 125
Inner Speech 125
Inner Hearing 127
Unsymbolized Thinking 131
Images 132
Observing Characteristics 136
Speaking Aloud 137
Active Listening to Other Persons Speaking 138
No Thought 139

Comparison with Sue's Pre-Sampling Expectations 139
The Follow-Up Study 141
Discussion 141

10. Characteristics of Normal Inner Experience 143

Inner Verbal Experience 143
Images 147
Meaning without Words or Images 149
Other Observations 151

II. THE SCHIZOPHRENIC SUBJECTS 153

11. A Schizophrenic Woman with "Goofed-Up" Images 157

with Susan M. Melancon

Visual Experience 159
Images 159
Images of External Reality 160
Images Related to Current Activities 162
Daydreams 163
Images of Written Words 166
Distortions in Images 168
Role of Color and Movement 171
Verbal Thought 176
Feelings 179
Unsymbolized Thinking 181
No Thought or Forgotten Thought 182
Comments on the Sampling Procedure 183
Discussion 190

12. A Schizophrenic Man with (Perhaps) No Inner Experience 193

with Susan M. Melancon

The Experience of the Beep 196
Being the Beeper 201
The Question of Inner Experience 204
Discussion 224

13. A Decompensating Schizophrenic 227

with Leny Meertens

The Symptom-Free Period 228
Feelings 228
Visual Experience 231
Verbal Inner Experience 233
The Decompensating Period 234
Discussion 239

14. A Schizophrenic Woman Who Heard Voices of the Gods .. 243

The Voices of the Gods 244
Visual Experiences 248
Images 248
Verbal Inner Experience 250
Feelings 251
Discussion 251

15. Implications for Understanding Schizophrenia 253

16. Discussion 265

17. A Look at Depression and Beyond 281

Index 283

Sampling Normal and Schizophrenic Inner Experience

Preliminary Comments Designed to Suspend the Introspection Controversy

This book describes in detail people's inner experiences; shows how schizophrenia may be more a disorganization of inner images than of association; and suggests that depression may be due to a lack of words and images in the thinking process rather than to negative self-thoughts. These observations are based on a new method of eliciting careful self-reports of inner experience, which some readers may unfortunately characterize as "introspective" and then dismiss because they accept the conclusion that accurate introspection is impossible. This introductory section shows such skeptical readers that the present study is different from, and quite possibly much better than, previous studies that have been labeled introspective.

We will take the "Nisbett and Wilson *versus* Ericsson and Simon debate regarding the validity of verbal reports" (Grover, 1982, p. 205) as typical of the present polarized positions on introspection. Nisbett and Wilson (1977) argued against the possibility of accurate introspection, concluding that "the evidence reviewed is then consistent with the most pessimistic view concerning people's ability to report accurately about their cognitive processes" (p. 247), and ". . . there is by now enough evidence discrediting introspective reports to allow us to ignore any argument based on introspection" (p. 255). On the other hand, Ericsson and Simon (1984) argued in favor: "It is now time for verbal reports to reassume their position as a rich source of data, combinable with other data, that can be of the greatest value in providing an integrated and full account of cognitive processes and structures" (p. 373). We will comment on both positions in turn.

Nisbett and Wilson's (1977) article cited a wide variety of reports, mostly from the social psychology literature on cognitive dissonance and attribution theory, where subjects were unable to describe accurately their own inner processes. We will summarize two of these studies here to give a typical flavor of the kinds that Nisbett and Wilson reviewed.

In our first example, Bem and McConnell (1970) asked each subject in an experimental group to write an essay that took a position in opposition to their own opinion on a topic. Subjects in a control group wrote no such counter-attitudinal essay. Comparisons between the groups showed that the subjects in the experimental group had changed their attitudes as a result of writing the counter-attitudinal essay, a result typical of the cognitive dissonance literature. However, Bem and McConnell found that none of the individual subjects in the experimental group detected any change in their own attitude. Nisbett and Wilson concluded, "Thus subjects apparently changed their attitudes in the absence of any subjective experience of change" (p. 236).

In our second example, Storms and Nisbett (1970) gave insomniac subjects in an experimental group placebo pills to take before bedtime, with a deceptive explanation that the pills would cause breathing irregularities, rapid heart rate, etc.—in short, the symptoms of insomnia. The subjects then reported the amount of time necessary to fall asleep on a series of nights. As expected, the subjects reported getting to sleep faster on the nights they took placebo pills.

At the conclusion of their participation in the study, subjects were asked to explain their ability to get to sleep faster on the nights they took the pills. None of the subjects thought that the pill had affected their ability to sleep; they gave instead a variety of plausible but incorrect explanations. As Nisbett and Wilson summarized, "the explanations that subjects offer for their behavior in [these] experiments are so removed from the process that investigators presume to have occurred as to give grounds for considerable doubt that there is direct access to these processes" (p. 238).

After reviewing these two and many other studies, Nisbett and Wilson concluded: "In summary, it would appear that people may have little ability to report accurately on their cognitive processes" (p. 246). Our own evaluation of Nisbett and Wilson's conclusion is that it is too broad: Nisbett and Wilson reviewed studies in the insufficient-justification, attribution, subliminal perception, and creativity paradigms and found *in those paradigms* that subjects were unable to report accurately their cognitive processes. However, the cognitive processes associated with these paradigms are but a subset of the total category "cognitive processes"; so Nisbett and Wilson's conclusion is an overgeneralization from their review. Perhaps a better summary statement would have been that people have little ability to report accurately on *some* (or even many) of their cognitive processes.

Nisbett and Wilson were aware that their review did not allow complete generalization: "We also wish to acknowledge that the studies do not suffice to show that people *could never* be accurate about the processes involved. To do so would require ecologically meaningless but theoretically interesting procedures such as interrupting a process at the very moment it was occurring, alerting subjects to pay careful attention to their cognitive processes, coaching them in introspective procedures, and so on" (p. 246, italics in original).

The method that we are using in the present book satisfies all three of these requirements: it *does* interrupt processes at the moment they occur; it *does* alert subjects to pay careful attention to their cognitive processes, and it *does* coach them on the procedures. There are thus two conclusions to be drawn: First, it would seem that Nisbett and Wilson rather specifically exempted our present method from their sweeping anti-introspection generalization because it meets the three requirements stated above; second, Nisbett and Wilson specifically acknowledged that a study that meets their three requirements (as does ours) *could* provide accurate reports about cognitive processes. (As an aside, we have no idea why Nisbett and Wilson would consider such a method to be "ecologically meaningless.")

Ericsson and Simon (1984) provided an opposing position to that of Nisbett and Wilson, and concluded that verbal reports of cognitive processes are deserving of a prominent place in cognitive science. Their argument can be summarized as follows. It is commonly understood that verbal reports have for much of this century been excluded from scientific psychology; but this view rests on the mistaken assumption that yes/no responses or response latencies, which have been acceptable to psychology, are not themselves types of verbal response. Once we recognize that such responses are in fact verbal responses, then the question becomes not *whether* verbal responses should be accepted but rather *under what circumstances* they should be accepted. Ericsson and Simon then present an information-processing model of cognition to evaluate which kinds of verbal reports are likely to be accurate.

Their information-processing model predicts that

> Two forms of verbal reports can claim to being the closest reflection of the cognitive processes. Foremost are *concurrent verbal reports*—'talk aloud' and 'think aloud' reports—where the cognitive processes . . . are verbalized di-

> rectly. . . . We claim that cognitive processes are not modified by these verbal reports. . . . [The] second type is the *retrospective report*." (p. 16, italics in original)
>
> In the ideal case the retrospective report is given by the subject immediately after the task is completed while much information is still in STM [short-term memory] and can be directly reported or used as retrieval cues. . . . In this particular case, the subject will still retain the necessary retrieval cues in STM when a general instruction is given "to report everything you can remember about your thoughts during the last problem." This form of retrospective verbal report should give us the closest approximation to the actual memory structures. (p. 19)

Thus, Ericsson and Simon's model predicts that there are two kinds of "ideal" verbal reports: concurrent (think-aloud) reports and retrospective reports given immediately. We will evaluate each in turn by asking whether Ericsson and Simon could possibly have considered our kind of data when arriving at their ideals.

First, Ericsson and Simon claimed that think-aloud reports are the "closest reflection" of cognitive processes, and that these "cognitive processes are not modified by" the think-aloud procedures. The richness of our own data, as will be seen, makes it impossible for us to accept such claims. It is premature to summarize all of our results (see Chapters 10 and 15), but a few observations will make evident why thinking aloud cannot possibly accurately reflect inner experience as our subjects described it.

First, our subjects may take as long as 30 *minutes* to describe a one-*second* experience, indicating that the nuances of experience do not translate easily into words. Second, our subjects frequently report multiple simultaneous cognitive processes: visual images simultaneous with words, etc. Third, verbal thoughts themselves are not experienced simply as "strings of phonemes," as Ericsson and Simon stated (p. 63), but are instead complex processes, where, for example, the rhythm of a phoneme sequence may be present but the phonemes themselves absent. Fourth, inner verbal experience sometimes involves visual representations of the words simultaneous with their phonetic utterance, and the simultaneous visualized words may be different from the internally spoken words.

We will cite other examples in Chapters 15 and 16, but the conclusion is clear: Thinking aloud cannot provide an adequate rendering even of inner *verbal* experience, much less of inner cognitive experience in general. Thinking aloud is at best only a one-dimensional representation of a process that is multidimensional. That Ericsson and Simon could make the claim that thinking aloud represents the "closest reflection" of cognitive processes, and that "cognitive processes are not modified by [thinking aloud] verbal reports," indicates to us that they must not have included our kind of data in their analysis.

Ericsson and Simon's second "ideal case [is] the retrospective report given by the subject immediately after the task is completed while much information is still in STM" (p. 19). Now it happens that our own method of thought sampling asks for "reports on the immediately preceding cognitive activity," and so seems to qualify as an "ideal case" under Ericsson and Simon's analysis. But a further analysis shows that our subjects may have *better* access to their cognitions than did any of the subjects in the studies reviewed by Ericsson and Simon. Consider Ericsson and Simon's above-quoted "ideal . . . retrospective . . . instruction: 'Report everything you can remember about your thoughts during the last problem'" (p. 19). According to Ericsson and Simon, this is an "ideal case" because the *retrieval cues* are present in STM when the general instruction is given. The thoughts themselves which the subjects are to recall are clearly not in STM, because the problem during which the thoughts occurred may have required several minutes to complete.

By contrast, we will see that in our own study subjects were trained to use a clear, unambiguous beep as a signal to report everything they can about their experience that was occurring at the moment of that same beep. Thus, the *entire experience* which our subjects were to describe, not merely the retrieval cues, has just occurred when the subject begins to report, and so it would appear that our own subjects' reports may be better, perhaps much better, than the "retrospective ideal" described by Ericsson and Simon.

We conclude our review of Ericsson and Simon's analysis with a summary of our two conclusions: First, Ericsson and Simon were not including studies such as ours in their analysis; and second, a study such as ours may provide even more accurate data on cognition than Ericsson and Simon's "ideal" study.

We reached essentially the same two conclusions when reviewing Nisbett and Wilson's analysis as we did when reviewing Ericsson and Simon's. That may seem surprising given that Nisbett and Wilson and Ericsson and Simon are seen to be on opposing sides of the introspection debate. The explanation for the similarity of conclusion is that both Nisbett and Wilson and Ericsson and Simon were interested in the same kinds of verbal reports. Ericsson and Simon were more supportive of introspection because their information-processing model identifies some cognitions as being more accessible than others. For example, an introspection of a cognition that demands a search of long-term memory but provides inadequate retrieval cues is more difficult than an immediate retrospection (the "ideal" discussed above) where the retrieval cues are already present in short-term memory. Thus Ericsson and Simon supported the adequacy of *some* verbal reports because they identify some introspective tasks as easier than others.

We have seen that neither Ericsson and Simon nor Nisbett and Wilson directly considered the detailed descriptions of moments of inner experience such as are provided in the present book, and we have shown that such descriptions may provide a more accurate view of cognition than any of the studies called "introspective" by either Nisbett and Wilson or Ericsson and Simon. The present book explores that possibility of accurate reporting of cognition by instructing our subjects to "describe what you experience at this particular moment." We do not ask them to explain *why* they are having that particular experience. We do not ask them to tell us what particular environmental events *are responsible* for that experience. In fact, we do not even ask them to tell us whether that experience is *typical* for them or not.

In short, we ask them to report only those experiences for which they have direct (not inferred) access: We simply ask them to describe what they are aware of at some particular moment in time, and at that particular moment when the experience is as fresh as it can possibly be. No introspective study has used a method like this, and we have seen that there is reason to believe that such a method may produce relatively accurate descriptions of inner experience.

Of course, the fact that Nisbett and Wilson and Ericsson and Simon can be interpreted as supporting the possible existence of a method of accurate introspection does not make the present method necessarily accurate. The present study can be viewed as a *test* of the premise that subjects can give accurate responses to our simple descriptive request. We ask that the reader suspend for the moment any biases about introspection and decide for him or herself whether this study provides accurate, useful descriptions of inner experience, evaluating this study on its own merits rather than on preexisting beliefs about introspection.

REFERENCES

Bem, D. J., & McConnell, H. K. (1970). Testing the self-perception explanation of dissonance phenomena: On the salience of premanipulation attitudes. *Journal of Personality and Social Psychology, 14*, 23–31.

Ericsson, K. A., & Simon, H. A. (1984). *Protocol analysis: Verbal reports as data*. Cambridge, Massachusetts: The MIT Press.

Grover, S. C. (1982). A re-evaluation of the introspection controversy: Additional considerations. *The Journal of General Psychology, 106*, 205–212.

Nisbett, R. E., & Wilson, T. D. (1977). Telling more than we know: Verbal reports on mental processes. *Psychological Review, 84,* 231–259.

Storms, M. D., & Nisbett, R. E. (1970). Insomnia and the attribution process. *Journal of Personality and Social Psychology, 2,* 319–328.

1

Introduction

What is thinking like? Chances are good that you don't have a very clear answer to that general question. You might take a stab at a response: "It's like people talking to themselves"; or, "It's how problems are solved." But you are not likely to consider either of these answers to be satisfactory, so let us take an easier question. What is *your* thinking like? That should be an easy one, because it asks for a description of something that you have been doing almost every waking minute of your entire life; certainly you should be able to describe that. But once again, this turns out to be a difficult question, no easier to answer than other intimate questions such as, "What does saliva taste like?" We take thinking, like saliva, so much for granted that it seems impossible to describe it.

The thinking question and the saliva question are, however, different in at least one important way: the question about how people think is an *interesting* one. We want to know how thinking takes place. We have been led to believe, for example, that women think differently from men, but is the *process* of women's thinking different, or is it merely the *content?* Or is the very notion of a sex difference in thinking a mistake? We are interested in what and how our husbands or wives or boyfriends or girlfriends think, but we are rarely successful in getting them to give adequate descriptions. We believe that language has an impact on how we think, but we don't have a clear idea of the extent of that impact. We believe that disorders of thinking are at the heart of problems as serious as schizophrenia, but we don't really know whether the schizophrenic's thought patterns are different from our own or whether the unusual speech patterns and behaviors we observe in schizophrenics occur without concomitant changes in the basic ways such persons think.

Are these issues without resolution both for the intelligent layman and the professional psychologist or psychiatrist? Surprisingly, yes. Learned individuals in our cultural heritage, from at least the time of Aristotle, have made repeated attempts to describe the thinking process. Yet despite these earnest efforts, the science of psychology has reached no general consensus about any of the previous paragraph's issues or many other questions central to the process of thinking. The historical reasons for this confusion are a subject for interesting studies in the sociology of science, but that is not our purpose here. We simply note that, for a variety of historical reasons, scientists in our tradition have theorized about the nature of thinking without having first gathered the basic data that should form the foundation for such theorizing. In fact, there has never been, as far as I am aware, a single careful description of any individual's everyday, ordinary thinking. You may find that surprising, and so do I. It is out of that surprise that the present project arose.

There have been, of course, data collected on thinking, including both naturalistic and experimental observations on particular aspects of thinking (problem solving, for example), and measurements on how thinking is affected by different environments (as in thinking-aloud studies in the laboratory). Furthermore, countless theories have been advanced purporting to explain how our thinking affects us (that self-deprecating thoughts make us depressed, for example). But these are all "upper-story" structures in a science whose foundation structures are missing; that is to say, they are hypotheses about factors that might influence thinking proposed in the absence of a basic understanding of thinking itself. In my opinion, this lack of foundation is a principle cause of the turmoil in modern psychology. For example, we are in the midst of a so-called cognitive revolution in which some psychologists believe that thinking is vitally important to behavior, while others ignore it entirely. People of good faith can hold such widely disparate views only in the absence of good basic data.

What we have been saying about thinking applies to all forms of inner experience: thinking, feeling, sensation, wondering, observing, etc. We must face the fact that we have very little data that would allow us to provide a general description of the kinds of inner experience people have as they go about their everyday activities.

Thus, we were led to attempt what we saw as a basic, yet nonexistent, activity of psychology: careful observation of the kind of normal everyday inner experience that occupies nearly all our waking life. But how should we proceed? Here again, strangely enough, mainstream modern psychology is silent. There is no generally accepted method for providing descriptions of any phenomenon, particularly not for describing the private events of inner experience. Again, it is beyond the scope of the present book to describe the sociological and historical reasons for this state of affairs. Suffice it to say, however, that modern psychology does not much trust descriptions of inner experience because such descriptions have often been inaccurate or contradictory, and it has not yet worked out ways of verifying whether descriptions are adequate.

While the historical research on thinking has not been successful in providing some essential basic data, it does provide guidance to our present study by illuminating several pitfalls that must be avoided in creating descriptions of inner experience. First, individuals cannot be asked to reflect on their thinking, to watch themselves think, so to speak, and then report their observations. Such a procedure does not examine normal thinking, but only a peculiar kind of thinking that is doubled back on itself reflectively. This reflective thinking may be substantially different from everyday thinking; for example, it is more likely to be verbal. To mistake the predominantly verbal reflective thinking for thinking in general may have been a major factor in leading the philosophers of the Western tradition, beginning with Aristotle, into the blind alley of seeking to explain thinking by some law of association that attempts to explain how one verbal thought triggers another.

Second, since people may not have a clear notion of what their inner experience is like, we will not arrive at an adequate understanding of it merely by asking people to describe their inner experience. This pitfall applies even if we ask many people to provide such descriptions and then we extract the characteristics they share in common. If the individual descriptions are themselves inadequate, any characterization of a collection of them is also likely to be inadequate. This mistake has plagued even recent phenomenologically oriented investigators, who elicit descriptions of a phenomenon from large numbers of subjects and then attempt to explicate the essential nature of the phenomenon by distilling the common features from the descriptions. The problem is even worse for experimentally oriented investigators who determine that one *group* is "significantly different" from another, and then conclude (possibly erroneously) that *individuals* (not groups) tend to differ because they are members of different groups.

Third, we must not assume that individuals will be aware of particular details of their inner experience, even very important details. This was the observation that led Freud to emphasize what he called the unconscious. However, the term "unconscious" may refer to two distinct processes: We may say that we have an unconscious idea if a concept has a significant effect on us, but the concept itself never reaches awareness; or we may say we have an unconscious idea if we have occasional (even frequent) occurrences of a concept in awareness, but in recollection systematically neglect to recall these occurrences. This distinction makes the unconscious either a characteristic of cognition or a defect in a memory process. We must avoid a method that fails to make this distinction or which cannot collect the relevant data to decide the issue.

Fourth, individuals cannot be given specialized training in observing certain aspects of inner experience and then be expected to report accurately on the presence or absence of these or other aspects, since their inner experiences may be shaped by the training procedure. This was essentially the problem that derailed the last major attempt to describe thinking, that of the introspectionists around the turn of this century. Different groups of introspectionists arrived at different conclusions about the existence of such characteristics as "imageless thought" because their subjects were highly trained and were expected either to find or not to find this phenomenon. At the same time, however, subjects must be prepared to look directly at their thinking. They must somehow acquire the skill of being ready to observe accurately without being unduly influenced by what they expect to see.

Fifth, both our subjects and we ourselves must avoid jumping to conclusions about their patterns of inner experience. It seems to be a characteristic of much of our science, as well as of most of our subjects, to get a glimpse of a phenomenon and then to generalize that glimpse immediately. This rushing to generalization often leads subjects to overlook important (perhaps the *most* important) features of the phenomenon under investigation, and leads investigators to fail to probe for possibly overlooked aspects. Furthermore, we must resist the temptation to quantify our data prematurely. Psychology can be legitimately criticized for its demand to quantify before it has thoroughly examined a problem area. We must recognize that quantification, while enabling the measurement of one aspect of a phenomenon, also serves to blind us to the remaining aspects of that phenomenon. This is the pitfall in questionnaire studies of thinking, since the construction of a questionnaire may prematurely fix the aspects of thinking being investigated. There is, of course, an appropriate time for quantification; but that is not until the phenomenon has been well understood.

Sixth, if we are interested in everyday inner experience, we must avoid as far as possible any way of biasing the situations where we observe it. We must not, for example, bring our subjects into a laboratory to observe their thinking. We must not assign them particular tasks to perform or problems to solve and then observe them while they are so performing. Rather, we must investigate inner experience, whatever its form, in its own natural habitat, the subjects' own everyday situations.

Seventh, we must avoid the trap of mistaking verbalizations that are said to be descriptions of inner experience for those that are not descriptions but instead are opinions, expectations, or preconceptions about inner experience. These can all masquerade as descriptions of inner experience itself.

Is there a well-established methodology that avoids these pitfalls? Not to my knowledge; so we will be forced to develop some new techniques to provide the observations we think are lacking. Our aim is simply to study inner experience as it naturally exists with as little distortion as possible. Our method will be one that seems to allow us to uncover inner experience while avoiding the mistakes that plagued earlier investigators. Our product will be written descriptions of a rather broad range of inner experience from which we may gain a new appreciation of the diversity of private events available to human beings.

We have shown that describing inner experience as it naturally occurs may be a profitable venture, and we have developed (and will describe in detail in Chapters 2 and 3) a method that might realize that goal. How can we show that our method does in fact reveal inner experience? Validation of a new method is a long, multifaceted procedure, but a first step is to show that individuals whose inner experiences are thought to be dramatically different from each other do in fact provide dramatically different results when our method is applied to them.

The distinction between schizophrenics and normals provides such an opportunity. Schizophrenia is generally held to be the most severe disorder of thinking, involving serious disturbances in perception, mood, and self-concept, as well as in the thought process itself. If our method is in fact sensitive to inner experience, then it should show how the inner experience of normal subjects is markedly different from that of schizophrenics. If our method does not show such big differences, then it cannot be adequate regardless of how well conceived it might have appeared to be. The fact is that the descriptions of schizophrenics (Chapters 11–14) *are* dramatically different from those of our normal subjects (Chapters 4–9), a result that provides some degree of confidence in the method as well as a compelling look at the world of schizophrenia.

Chapters 2 and 3 present and discuss the method that we used to generate these descriptions of inner experience. Readers not particularly concerned with details of the method may wish to skip ahead to Chapter 4 where the descriptions of the subjects themselves begin. The individuals described were chosen to be different from each other: male and female, university-educated and not, older and younger, artistically inclined and not, schizophrenic and normal, etc.

We must be clear, however, that our subjects were not randomly selected from the populations of males, educated persons, or schizophrenics, etc. You may, as you read these accounts, generate some hunches about how males differ from females, etc.; and I myself will discuss some general characteristics of normal inner experience in Chapter 10, and of schizophrenic experience in Chapter 15. But I would like us to keep clearly in mind that the main purpose of this project is to start at the beginning: to become familiar with single individuals' inner experience as it naturally occurs; any generalizations that we make will be only sketches of aspects that we take at the moment to be salient characteristics of inner experience.

We have been speaking as if this book has a single main goal—the description of the inner experience of ten individuals—and that, in fact, is true. But there is also a secondary opportunity for the reader of this book that requires some explanation.

I have expressed above my opinion that modern psychology does not have the data basic to an understanding of inner experience. In my judgment, a primary reason for this lack is what we referred to as a "rush to generalization": psychologists too frequently formulate hypotheses to explain an interesting phenomenon before they have an adequate understanding of the phenomenon under consideration. Furthermore, it is my observation that this rush to generalization is a pervasive tendency, not just of psychologists in their professional lives, but of many people much of the time. Because these are my opinions, they, of course, may or may not be true.

For you as an individual reader, however, it is probably less important to know whether or not these opinions are true in general than it is to know whether you *as an individual* rush to generalization, and I invite you to explore that inclination for yourself in the following manner. If you are similar to readers who have previewed this book, you may find yourself frequently distracted from the descriptive text by your own hypothesis-generating musings, giving your own private explanations for some characteristics of the individual being described.

For example, during your reading of the first descriptive chapter (Chapter 4), you may be intrigued by the fact that Jason occasionally saw images of himself viewed from an external perspective; for example, he saw himself as viewed from the other side of the room. You may find yourself advancing some theoretical explanation for this phenomenon, perhaps speculating that this external perspective signifies a lack of a clear sense of self. That is an example of premature generalization, if for no other reason than because you do not yet know whether external-perspective images occur in the inner experience of even the remaining nine individuals described in this book, let alone in the thinking of people in general. To attempt to explain a phenomenon without knowing whether it is the exception or the rule is undoubtedly to advance a bad explanation.

I believe this kind of premature generalization is a frequent occurrence, and you can explore for yourself the extent to which you yourself prematurely generalize. In the privacy of your own reading room, monitor yourself as you read the descriptive chapters. Keep track of how frequently you pause in reading the descriptions to generate explanations for the phenomena our subjects are describing, or to speculate about ways to test such hypotheses with other subjects. Then, at the moment when you are distracted from the description, ask yourself if your hypothesis, even if true, adds or detracts from your understanding of the single individual being described. If you have very many of these attempt-to-explain pauses before you have completed reading all of the ten descriptive chapters, or if they do distract you from experiencing a sense of understanding of the single individual being described, then you may have identified in yourself the same tendency to generalize prematurely that I believe exists in most of us, layman and professional psychologist alike.

The reason I emphasize this is that I believe that generalization always leads *away* from basic data, that is, away from the understanding of individuals; and that to the extent that we as individuals rush to generalize, we hurriedly blind ourselves to whatever fundamental observations that we, again as individuals, find the most exciting and compelling. Please notice that to test the global truth of this assertion would be itself an exercise in generalization, and would thus be contrary to the spirit of this book. Furthermore, in an important way, it would be pointless to attempt such a test. Even if we could demonstrate the tendency of our readership in general to "rush to generalization," you, the individual reader, would be no closer to identifying your own personal rush-to-generalize tendencies or to determining whether or not such tendencies draw you away from a full understanding of people. Thus, I hope to shape you temporarily away from an interest in "truths" about inner experience in general toward an understanding of each individual's characteristics, including your own. If you do find yourself rushing to generalize, then perhaps you will use this reading as an opportunity to practice suspending generalizations, at least until you get to Chapter 10.

In Chapters 10 and 15 we will ourselves generalize about the characteristics of normal and schizophrenic inner experience, based on all the data available. We will observe that the inner experience of our normal subjects was in fact strikingly different from that of our schizophrenics, and we will note that schizophrenic inner experience was strikingly different from that of depressed individuals we have sampled. Furthermore, the nature of these differences was a surprise to us. We will see in Chapter 15 that psychology and psychiatry's current understanding of schizophrenic experience does not prepare us to expect the distortions in inner images, the clear bodily representation of emotions, and the vivid seeing of words speeding toward, around, and through themselves that our schizophrenic subjects reported.

These observations may cause us to rethink schizophrenia; but before we can appreciate the schizophrenic characteristics, we must first understand normal individuals' inner experience and the method we used to explore it.

2

Method

We are interested in describing the inner experience of individuals: how people think and feel, what their bodily sensations, wonderings, and other characteristics of their inner world is like. We have seen that there are pitfalls to be avoided in describing inner experience, and that there is no generally accepted method for avoiding those pitfalls. Our position as explorers of inner experience is rather similar to geographic explorers. Geographic explorers typically have several more-or-less reliable reports of what they might expect to find in the region they seek to explore; but their method of exploration and description of findings would need to be shaped by the actual terrain they encountered. Furthermore, the descriptions they produce would not be intended as characterizations of the "essence" of the region, but instead as accurate descriptions of the major characteristics of the landscape as they saw it.

That is our goal also: to describe major *characteristics*, not *essences*, of inner experience. We will first give a general description of the method that we employed, and then describe each of its phases in detail.

We selected as the subjects to participate in this study a relatively diverse group. While no attempt was made to have the group of subjects be statistically representative of any larger population, an attempt *was* made to gather reports from a nonhomogeneous group of individuals. Thus, our subjects were both male and female; ranged in education from high school to the MD; were artistic and not artistically inclined; schizophrenic and normal, etc. Our aim was to provide a *description* of *some diverse* inner experiences, not to provide a complete *catalog* of the *range* of inner experience. We avoided talking with our subjects about their inner experiences in general; instead, we gave them a "beeper" which emitted an unmistakable tone at random intervals, and asked them to report about the particular moment of inner experience that was occurring at the moment of the beep. This report was amplified by in-depth interviewing, so that we obtained as detailed a description of that particular sampled inner experience as possible, all the while suspending our own preconceptions about what that person's experience might be like. We repeated this procedure for a series of randomly beeped moments. After we had thoroughly described a series of particular moments, we described the salient characteristics of each subject's series of experiences, preparing this description with the full collaboration of the subject him- or herself.

We may now turn to describe in more detail each of the characteristics of the method.

The subjects participated one at a time, each basically completing the entire procedure before the next subject began. The procedure was basically the same for all subjects with one important exception: the first two subjects to complete this study (Smith and Melancon, see Chapters 8 and 9) themselves identified the salient characteristics of their sampled experiences and wrote the description of those characteristics; while for all the other subjects, the authors performed the categorization and description tasks. This distinction is perhaps more formal than real, since in all cases the major descriptive categories and the words used to describe them had emerged and been used repeatedly during the detailed interviews with the subjects about their individual sampled experiences.

The description of the procedure that follows is written as it was embodied by Smith and Melancon, because this is the most complete realization of the method. Differences between the descriptions-written-by-subject and descriptions-written-by-author procedures will be noted in parentheses.

I discussed the goal of the research, providing a careful description of an individual's inner experiences, and the method as will be described below with each subject individually prior to agreeing to undertake the research project. We also discussed the time commitment: two to four weeks of daily meetings of one to two hours each, followed by several months of writing, reviewing, and rewriting descriptions of inner experience. We noted the possibility that the project could be personally intrusive: internal, inherently personal experiences were to be externalized, possibly for the first time; private events were to be rather intimately discussed, etc. Subjects were informed that they were free to tell me that something was none of my business; in fact, I encouraged them to do so. I told them that I would much prefer that they told me directly when they did not want to talk about some experience or some aspect of an experience, rather than simply gloss over or avoid discussing something about the experience. I recognized that all of us have aspects of experience that we do not, for whatever reason, wish to discuss, and I would not hold it against them if they so informed me. What was likely to be confusing to me, I said, was if they were reluctant to talk about something and simply led me away from it in our conversations rather than explicitly setting it off-limits.

Furthermore, I informed subjects that it was possible that the time commitments or personal commitments of either of us could become problematic enough that we might feel obliged to discontinue the project; if that happened, either of us should feel free to stop, and I would be entirely understanding if such a situation arose. With such an introductory discussion, we agreed to commence the procedure. The same instructions were reiterated repeatedly throughout the course of sampling in an attempt to communicate that I wanted an honest, open cooperation between the subject and myself.

The method itself consisted of six distinct and sequential phases. The individual subjects had a general understanding of the method from our initial conversations, but a more detailed understanding of each phase was attained by each subject only as that phase was encountered. Each subject was kept naive in the sense that he or she did not discuss the method or results with other participants in the present study, nor read descriptions of other subjects' thinking, until his or her own participation was concluded. Thus the subjects were encouraged to consider their own experiences as they apprehended them directly, not in comparison to someone else's. It is true, however, that I myself could not be kept naive regarding other subjects' participation, and one of the limitations of the present study is the possibility that I conveyed implicitly or explicitly to the subjects what I expected to find in their experiences.

Phase 1: *The Pre-Sampling Retrospective General Account of the Subject's Inner Experience* (omitted in author-written descriptions). The subject was asked before sampling began to reflect on her typical inner experience and to write a general description of it, not based on any particular methodology, but rather based on whatever natural reflection and retrospective generalization presented. The task was to respond to the question, "What do I think my inner experience is like?"

There are three distinct and important reasons for the presence of this phase in the method. First, it will be of interest to us at the conclusion of sampling to ask whether the subject had an accurate understanding of what her inner experience is like. If we are going to make such comparisons, we must ask subjects to commit themselves about what they think their experiential characteristics are, before we possibly alter that understanding by engaging in a protracted series of observations and descriptions of experience.

Second, in Phase 2 we will be asking each subject to describe straightforwardly his or her experiences as they actually occurred, not as they might have been *expected* to occur, according to some explicit or implicit understanding of inner experience. The phenomenologists refer to this as requesting that the subject suspend any preconceptions while engaging in the descriptive task. While it is easy to say that we should suspend preconceptions, it is far more difficult to do so, at least to do so adequately. The first phase of the method is an attempt to facilitate this suspension of preconceptions according to the following rationale advanced by the phenomenologists.

If we make our preconceptions explicit, in our case, if we write a description of what we *expect* the general characteristics of our inner experience to be, then it may be easier to take a dispassionate view of our expectations. We can say, as it were, "Now let us find out whether or not those descriptions are borne out by immediate experience." Making these expectations explicit may make it easier to suspend them, thus allowing the actual experience to be described as less biased by initial sub-rosa expectations. The third reason for this first phase is that when we make our preconceptions transparent to you, the reader, you can then decide for yourself whether the final descriptions based on the sampling merely slavishly support the original preconceptions.

Accordingly, the subject prepared the pre-sampling retrospective general account of what inner experience was thought to be like. I read it, asked questions, and made suggestions concerning the written description, and probed for whether the account seemed complete. The subject then rewrote it. The questioning and suggesting/rewriting continued until both the subject and I were satisfied that the pre-sampling retrospective general description adequately conveyed the sense of how her experience presented itself to her.

We performed this phase of the method for the first two subjects (Smith and Melancon, see Chapters 8 and 9) but omitted it for the remaining subjects for the following reason. The main purpose for writing the pre-sampling retrospective general account is to make preconceptions *explicit*, so that they *can* be suspended. After I had completed the entire pre-sampling/sampling/descriptive exercise twice (with Smith and Melancon) I had become convinced that I myself had enough experience in identifying and attempting to suspend my preconceptions about inner experience so that the preparation of more pre-sampling retrospective general accounts would no longer provide substantial additional safeguards for me. Since I would be a partner with all future subjects, I felt that I could communicate to them during the sampling itself the importance and the technique of holding in abeyance any conception they might have regarding their inner experience, without the necessity of the explicit pre-sampling exercise.

The reader can evaluate for him or herself whether that claim is justified; perhaps the best evidence is to examine the individual descriptions that form the body of this book. If they are quite distinctly different from each other, that is one piece of evidence that I was able to describe what *actually* occurred rather than what I *expected* to occur in inner experience. It is also the case that this study needs replication by others who may have different preconceptions, to see whether they obtain similar results.

Phase 2: *The Sampling Itself.* Instructions were given to each individual subject that might be paraphrased as follows: "I will provide you with a small (slightly larger than a cigarette package) device which emits a beep at random intervals through a small earphone similar to those used by inexpensive transistor radios. The earphone volume is adjustable so that you can select a level at which you can hear the beep distinctly but without being startled. How loud this beep must be depends on your current environment: in a quiet place, like a church or library, the tone can be soft, but while driving or in a crowd the volume must be loud.

"The apparatus was built for this series of studies. The beeps will occur at random intervals. Neither you nor I can predict when the next beep will occur; the device does that on its own. The longest interval between beeps will be approximately one hour, and the shortest interval will be a few seconds, with the average interval about a half hour. When the beep begins, it will continue until you respond to it by pressing a reset button.

"Your task when you hear a beep is to attempt to 'freeze' your current experience 'in mind,' and then to write a description of that experience in a 2-inch by 3-inch notebook which you will be carrying. The experience that you are to describe is the one that was occurring at the instant the beep began. Do *not* try to recall what might have been occurring a few seconds *before* the beep, even though it may be more interesting or more straightforward to report.

"Furthermore, do not, when beeped, report the next experience to emerge following the beep. Your task is to 'catch a thought in flight,' so to speak, and to report whatever was happening at the very instant you heard the beep. When you describe the experience, write only about the inner experience itself. Do not attempt to explain it or justify it or criticize it. Merely describe what was occurring in your inner experience at the moment the beep began. Write as much detail as possible so that you can accurately recreate the experience when we talk about it later.

"Use the apparatus from when you wake up until you go to bed at night. Wear it during all of your normal daily activities. You can expect to receive 20 or 30 beeps a day. [Subjects participating late in the study were asked to use the apparatus only about five hours per day, instead of from wake-up to bedtime, because as our interviewing techniques became more sophisticated, we found that we could discuss only ten beeps at most in a typical interview session.] Your task is the same for each beep: Freeze the ongoing experience and write about it in the notebook. If you receive a beep during an experience that for whatever reason you do not want to write down, write "private" in the notebook. I would much rather have you write "private" than simply omit a beep without my knowing it. If you receive a beep to which you cannot respond for some other reason, enter that reason in the notebook also. For example, if the volume was too low so that you weren't sure exactly when the beep started, write that the beep was weak.

"Each day during the sampling period, you and I will meet to discuss each of the experiences you have collected. We will focus on your experience-reports one at a time, and we will discuss each experience in detail and in sufficient depth so that either both you and I agree that I grasp the experience as you apprehended it, or until either of us believes that no more can be said, even though the experience is *not* completely understood. You can expect those meetings to last between one and two hours. We will continue this procedure of sampling for a day and meeting to discuss the sampled experiences until it seems as though we have collected enough thoughts to be representative of your everyday inner experience. You can expect this phase of the study to last two to four weeks."

Several comments on the rationale behind these instructions are in order. First, we developed a method for randomly sampling experiences. If we want our descriptions accurately to reflect everyday inner experience, we must randomly sample those experiences. It is not adequate to describe more easily available experiences, such as those attainable through reflection, or during problem solving or other laboratory tasks. If we randomly sample experiences throughout waking days, and we do so sufficiently often and over a sufficiently long period of time, then we are justified in claiming that the descriptions are quite likely to be of representative experiences.

Second, the tone used as the beep should have the following characteristics if it is to be effective in cueing sampling: It must be unmistakable and unambiguous. It must have a sudden onset, so that there is no mistaking exactly when the beep began. It must be loud enough, yet not so loud that it startles the subject.

Third, the subject's focus of description should be on the instant of interruption, not before or after. This is really a requirement of the randomness of the procedure. If we would allow the subject to choose an experience that is temporally close to the beep, then whatever biases or proclivities the subject carries with him or her may influence the selection of which thought to report. Therefore, we require the subject to report about what was happening *precisely* at the onset of the beep.

While the instructions were easily understood by the subjects, handling the details easily generally took some practice—typically, about a day of sampling. The first task was how to carry the random-interval-generating device: in a pocket, on a belt, etc. The next task was to become accustomed to setting the volume correctly and responding directly to the beep. The procedure was found by most subjects to be unobtrusive in the sense that most forgot very soon that they were carrying the device until it beeped, and very few subjects reported any significant number of sampled experiences related in any direct or indirect way to the device or procedure.

Each day during the sampling period the subject and I met to discuss the most recent set of sampled experiences. This discussion generally proceeded by our reading together the notebook account of the first sample, and then the subject describing in additional detail the particular beeped experience. In most cases the subject's opinion during this discussion was that it was possible for him or her to recreate the experience at the time of our conversation; that is, the written description in the notebook was enough to allow the subject to recall with what seemed to be clarity the original experience.

I continually reminded the subjects to try not to go beyond their direct recollections of the experiences and to guard against confabulated details. There is no conclusive objective evidence that this on-guardedness was successful; but in the few cases where it was possible to verify objectively the reported details (for example, if a thought were about some existing object that could subsequently be examined to verify those details), there was never a contradiction between what was reported and what was verified.

During these conversations, I encouraged the subjects to stay on the task of description and avoid straying to conclusions that may have come from some theoretical perspective. For example, if a subject said that she was probably unconsciously aware of another person's reaction, I would ask her whether there was anything in the experience being reported that could be described as "unconscious awareness," or was that a theory based on the present discussion? If her reply was that it was in the experience, I would press for exactly how that awareness made itself known to her. In other words, I might say, "How do you know that you were aware?" If, on the other hand, the unconscious experience was said to be the result of a present theoretical construction, I would remind the subject that we were attempting to exclude both preconceptual theoretical perspectives and also post hoc inferences, and that we would do better to stick to a purely descriptive account of what the experience was, *as* it was experienced at the moment of the beep.

During these discussions of the individual experiences, I repeatedly asked questions to clarify what exactly was meant by this description or that reference. For example, if the subject's report said, "I was thinking, 'I must choose a red one,'" I might first ask whether the words "I must choose a red one" were in fact a direct quote from the beeped experience, or did they merely represent the gist of the thought. If they were only the gist, I would ask the subject to save the use of quotation marks for direct quotes and to report gists in some other way. If the words were in fact a direct quotation, I would ask how the words presented themselves. "Were they perceived as written, or heard, or spoken, or understood directly, or what?"

If the response to this question was that they were spoken, I would ask whether they were spoken by the subject herself or by someone else, and if by her, how did she experience that speaking? Did she hear herself speak, or did she feel herself speaking, or was this speaking presented in some other way that I didn't know how to ask about? These questions and answers continued until such time as both of us felt that we had been describing the experience as it had actually occurred, and that the description was as accurate and complete as possible.

In some cases we were unable to arrive at such an understanding. That is to say, I either ran out of questions, or the subject's recalled experience seemed to fade under the scrutiny of my questioning, or the subject reported that she had simply not paid attention to the kind of details I was asking for. In those cases I repeatedly pointed out that there was no requirement that each and every sample should be explicated thoroughly; that while we were trying to obtain thorough descriptions, it was much more desirable to give up on the attempt to describe a particular beeped sample than to force the description beyond the clear recollection of the experience.

Furthermore, I reminded the subject, if a type of experience was indeed important, then we would be sampling additional similar experiences sooner or later in our sampling, and we could perhaps do a more complete job of description at the next occurrence. Thus it should be observed that the describing/questioning procedure served as training for the subject's future descriptive attempts. It was clearly the case that whenever the line of questioning ended with the conclusion, "I don't remember just how I experienced that," the subject would be more sensitive to that particular kind of detail in future experience reports.

As has been shown in some of the above examples, systematic attempts were made to exclude from our discussions preconceived notions about how thinking or experiencing takes place. It could be argued that each of my questions reflected some implicit understanding of the experiencing process; and that is no doubt true, at some level. However, I tried to keep each question open-ended, to state several possible alternatives when I asked a question to preclude leading the witness down my "favorite" path, and to include explicitly in my list of questioned alternatives a phrase such as, "or some other way which I don't know enough about to ask" so as to communicate as thoroughly as possible to the subject that I was trying not to operate from any set theory about thinking.

Our conversations were thus nearly always about particular individual moments of inner experience, and when subjects strayed to describe how they "usually" think, which happened frequently, I guided them back to the describe-the-particular-moment task. Generalizations about the *particular samples* we had been discussing did arise during the discussion sessions themselves, and I allowed these generalizations to be stated and subsequently reexamined and/or modified.

For example, one subject was repeatedly sampled during a kind of experience which she came to call "words still there," which connoted words with little or no meaning that seemed to be left over from a previous experience. Once these general characteristics of her particular samples became apparent, the phrase 'words still there' became part of our vocabulary during the discussion sessions. For example, the subject might say, "This is another example of 'words still there.'" Or, she might say, "This *seems* like 'words still there,' except that in this case I have no idea where the words came from or what they mean." This latter example shows how a generalization could be modified, even after it became a part of the discussion vocabulary. The rules that I applied governing the appearance of generalizations in the discussions were that we would be slow to identify any general characteristics of experience, and when we did identify a general characteristic, I would explicitly say again and again a phrase such as, "Well, for now we can call it 'words still there,' but we must keep that as a tentative title, and maybe something better will come along."

The sample-for-a-day and then discuss-each-experience-in-detail procedure continued essentially continuously throughout the subject's normal daily waking life. On weekends, when the discussion meetings typically did not occur, the subject either continued to sample as usual, or else discontinued sampling after about 15 samples had been collected, since it soon became apparent that 15 was about the maximum number of beeps (10 for later subjects) that could be dealt with in a single discussion period. This sample/discuss phase had no set endpoint; rather, the conclusion was mutually determined as being when it appeared that we had collected 'enough' samples. How many is enough is always a tricky question, but in the present study, enough was defined to be when (1) most new experience-samples were easily identified as belonging to one of the set of emerging categories described in the previous paragraph; (2) the emerging categories themselves were relatively stable in the sense that new experiences were no longer resulting in the modification of our understanding of the categories; and (3) the emerging categories seemed to be adequately defined.

What we mean in (3) is that, frequently as a category emerged, some aspect would not be initially clear—that is, the subject would not know how to respond to the question "How does that aspect present itself in your experience?" As has been described above, rather than force conclusions to such questions, we were content to wait until another exemplification or several more exemplifications of the characteristic occurred by chance in the sample, at which time we would continue the questioning about *that* aspect, until any ambiguity had been cleared. Thus, emerging categories were considered to be adequately defined when we were no longer waiting for further clarifying experiences to occur.

During each of the discussion sessions, I took notes about what was said, which were generally retained by the subject as an additional message that the subject had control over participation in the project. The purpose of the notes was to facilitate the writing task that would occur during later phases of the study. The notes themselves reflected the same kind of commitment to suspending preconceptions that we have been describing. For the most part, the notes reported some of what had been said, more or less verbatim, avoiding categorization or theory to the extent possible. The notes also recorded whenever the discussion reported that a particular experience was similar to or different from another experience, so that the boundaries of the particular characteristic under discussion could be exemplified when, in a later phase, the writing task took place. For some subjects, note taking seemed inadequate in that the richness of the verbalizations could not be captured in notes; in those cases, interviews were tape-recorded and transcribed verbatim.

Phase 3: *Writing the Descriptions.* This phase of the study began for each subject immediately upon the completion of the second phase. The task in this phase was to write a description of the samples: that is, to describe the experiences as they had actually occurred without embellishing them with theoretical conceptualizations or explanations. There was no expectation that the descriptions would provide a totally complete picture of the subject's experience; that would be impossible. Rather, the task was to describe what had emerged as the salient characteristics of the experiences.

The method was simple: the subject (or the author, in the case of author-written descriptions) took the notebook thought-descriptions and the notes that I had taken during our discussions of the experiences, and described what seemed to be the important characteristics. In most cases, the characteristics had been described in more or less detail during the discussions, so that the discussion notes contained some references to the obtained characteristics. That was not always the case, however, as some categories emerged for the first time during this third phase. The subject (or author) proceeded by reviewing each of the sampled experiences one at a time and then noting a characteristic that seemed salient.

A second pass through all of the samples identified which samples were relevant to the presently identified characteristic. Then the subject (or author) wrote a description of that salient characteristic and author and subject reviewed it together. This first review was usually aimed at eliminating instances where the written report strayed from the task of pure description into the realm of theory or opinion (some examples of this kind of error are given in the next chapter). The description was then revised.

After the first revision was complete, we reviewed it together again. Where necessary, I asked for clarification; for example, I asked repeatedly, "Is what you meant to convey here . . . ?" or, "This is how I understand this section. . . ." If the written description was discrepant with my recollection of either the particular experiences being described or the emergent category as we had discussed it over the sampling weeks, we would describe the apparent discrepancy, and discuss whether my memory was mistaken or whether the description was misleading, etc.

The report then was again revised by the subject (or author). This writing/discussing/rewriting continued until both of us were satisfied that the written description accurately conveyed the sense of the category or characteristic being described. Each salient characteristic description thus went through from two to seven or eight revisions. Typically, subjects required fewer revisions as they became more familiar with the study's requirements for pure description.

Once a salient characteristic was described satisfactorily, the procedure was repeated for another salient characteristic. That is, all of the notebook experiences and discussion notes were reviewed again to determine which was the next salient characteristic to be described; each of the experiences was then rechecked to identify those that were relevant to the present salient characteristic, and this set of experiences so identified was described in writing. This written report was reviewed and revised until it was found to be satisfactory. This procedure of review the experiences—identify a salient characteristic—identify those experiences that are relevant—describe the experiences—revise the descriptions—was recycled until no additional salient characteristics emerged. The result of this phase, then, was a series of written descriptions of what had emerged as salient characteristics of the sampled experiences.

Phase 4: *Reviewing Each Sampled Thought*. The fourth phase of the study constituted an integral check on the adequacy of the descriptions. After the written descriptions were complete, each sampled experience was reconsidered, one at a time, in light of the written reports of salient characteristics. Did that particular experience, when now reviewed, highlight any aspect of any of the written reports that needed to be modified? If so, the appropriate change was made. Were there any samples that were not adequately characterized by the salient characteristic descriptions and, if so, did additional salient characteristics need to be described? When this phase was completed, the written descriptions were considered preliminarily complete.

Phase 5: *Comparing Sampled Thought Descriptions to the Pre-Sampling Generalizations* (omitted in author-written descriptions). The fifth phase involved comparing the pre-sampling retrospective general account of what the subject had expected her experiences to be like with the newly prepared salient characteristic descriptions. The format of this discussion was not specified in advance, but the intention was to shed some light on whether inner experience was in fact the same as or different from what had been anticipated; and to give one final look into the question of whether preconceptions about inner experience had prevailed in the writing of the sampling-characteristic descriptions.

Phase 6: *The Follow-Up Sample* (omitted in author-written descriptions). The sixth phase was entered only after all the previous steps had been completed. That is, once the experiences had been sampled, written, reviewed, and compared, and the writing of each section had been completed, the subject began a new sampling period, the follow-up sample. The basic procedure during this phase was identical to that of Phase 2: the subject carried the beeper from morning to bedtime, responded to the beeps by writing descriptions of the individual experiences in a notebook, and met with me daily to discuss the samples.

There were two purposes of this follow-up sample. First, we used each of the samples collected in the follow-up sample to focus a reconsideration of the entire written description prepared during the first five phases. Thus, as each new experience was discussed in the daily meetings, we would attempt an understanding of that particular experience that was as thorough as had been required in Phase 2; and then explicitly ask the question, "Is there anything about this experience that leads us to question the adequacy of the previous descriptions?" In no case was it found necessary to change an original description. In a few cases it was found desirable to extend the initial descriptions somewhat, and these instances are clearly noted in the succeeding chapters. The second reason for the follow-up sample was to get a chance to see how stable were the characteristics we were describing: did the relative frequency of each of the characteristics stay the same or change?

Finishing the sixth phase completed a subject's participation in the study. Each of the above phases was designed to ensure that accurate descriptions of the actually sampled experiences were prepared. While we carefully attempted to prevent unwarranted preconceptions from influencing the data, there is no absolute guarantee that we were successful. Thus, replications by other investigators will be required to explore the adequacy of the present procedure and the representativeness of the present descriptions.

3

Method Considerations

The preceding chapter described the six rather complex phases of the method used in this study. The central or underlying goal of this complex method, however, is simple: to describe inner experiences without distortion. It is always a characteristic of such phenomenologically oriented attempts that the description of method is problematic in the sense that its most important feature is impossible to specify adequately. That central feature is the "without distortion" phrase in the above simple expression.

The method has nine characteristics which were designed to minimize possible distortions. First, the pre-sampling retrospective general account was prepared to make explicit any preconceptions that may unwittingly influence the perception of the data; once made explicit, it is easier to be on guard against that particular kind of bias. Second, the randomness of the sampling in Phase 2 assured that we would not be selecting experiences because of preordained interests. Third, the presence of two individuals (the subject and me) in the intensive discussions of each experience made it difficult for the subject to maintain any unwarranted assumption that his or her audience (first me and then the anticipated reader) 'of course' knew what was meant by any particular description. Such assumptions would now have to be shared by two individuals in order to be maintained. Fourth, the focus on the careful explicit descriptions of individual experiences, which was the essence of the daily discussions, made it less likely that any subsequent written generalization would gloss over the real data.

Fifth, the insistence that categories or characteristics identified during the intensive discussions would emerge tentatively and slowly served to remind us that the data was to shape our descriptions rather than vice versa. Sixth, the insistence in the early stages of preparing the written descriptions that every experience be reviewed as the descriptive category or characteristic emerged encouraged the author to be in close touch with the actual data at the time of beginning writing. Seventh, the write/review/rewrite collaboration between the subject and me, both of whom were present and involved in the original unfolding of the individual experience data, provided another check that the written descriptions conformed to the original data.

Eighth, the comparison between the pre-sampling retrospective general account and the written sampling descriptions served to bring into focus the preconceptions that had previously been identified and allow a reconsideration of whether those preconceptions had had an influence. And ninth, the follow-up sample was used to bring the entire sequence of events under scrutiny and to ensure that the already-prepared descriptions were applicable to new sampled experiences.

Careful and exhausting as these considerations are, they still fall short of constituting a complete set of rules for writing accurate descriptions of experiences. The crux of the matter, to write accurate descriptions without distortions, is still missing. We have a long series of phases aimed at accomplishing our goal, but no single phase or even all of them taken together guarantee that we will not distort.

It is possible to state the goal of this study another way: Don't write anything that leads the reader away from the original experiences. This also is a simple requirement to state but impossible to specify in practice, for there is an indeterminately large range of ways in which descriptions can mislead readers. What we *can* do is to give some common examples of the kinds of descriptions that are misleading. The set of examples should not be considered prescriptive or exhaustive, by any means; that is, someone attempting to replicate the present study should not merely seek to avoid these same mistakes, because in a description any single statement that fails to reflect accurately the experiences distracts from the overall intent. Nonetheless, the reader may find it useful to consider what kinds of statements we found to be frequent and misleading.

We will identify four classes of frequent errors; but first it might be noted that one characteristic pervaded, or perhaps was responsible for, many of the errors in all classes. That single characteristic is what we might call the 'rush to explanation.' In our experience in this and previous studies, we have found it a very rare individual who is content merely to describe an experience without seeming to flee from *contact with the raw experience* into what *seems the safer or more controllable terrain of explanation*. We have found that a report that has strayed from simple description to admit explanation tends to be flat, dull, and lifeless, in marked contrast to pure, explanation-free descriptions of particular experiences, which are full of sparks and vitality.

The reader may get a sense of what I am trying to describe by considering his or her own reaction to the present paragraph up to this point. Although I have been attempting to explain accurately a phenomenon I have repeatedly observed firsthand, my guess is that you will find the examples in the following paragraphs more compelling than the explanation in the present paragraph. This is not, I think, because the above explanation is badly written, but rather because it is a *generalization;* and generalizations, no matter how accurate, are dry and lifeless in contrast to lived experiences, no matter how mundane.

The examples that follow are all taken from the chapter by Susan Melancon (Chapter 9). This should in no way be construed to imply that Melancon's descriptions are less adequate than Smith's or my own, or that early drafts of her experiences were more fraught with errors. As a matter of fact, similar errors were found in all of our early attempts at descriptions; it was merely more convenient here to draw from a single chapter.

The first of the frequently occurring mistakes can be called the failure to focus directly on the particular experiences. Subjects often tended to "rush to a categorization," or meta-description, without providing any description of the individual particulars that provide instances of the category. Consider the following excerpt from an early draft:

> I'm also including in this category the mental repetition of a mantra, such as 'Jesus, mercy.' My mantra repetitions typically occurred when I was alone in quiet environments. At these times, my nonverbal focus of attention would concomitantly wander to awareness of various external sounds and stimuli (such as temperature or posture), physiological relaxation responses (breathing, heart rate), or nonverbal impressions, such as a sense of the passage of time. (Samples #4, 83, 128, 129)

There is nothing, as far as I know, inaccurate about this statement. However, it focuses on a class of thoughts (mantras) which includes not only the four sampled instances but hundreds of other unspecified (and unsampled as the word "typically" implies) occurrences of mantra-like experiences. Thus the description can give only a dry, vague account of an ill-defined category. The dryness is evidenced by the choice of the subjunctive mood ("my . . . focus . . . *would* . . . wander"); the subjunctive in a description usually indicates that something other than a particular experience is being described.

Consider now the final version of the same description, paying particular attention to your own reaction to the description, I believe you will find yourself more involved, caught up, interested in what it was actually like for Sue Melancon to experience meditation on a mantra:

> Both cases where I was repeating the phrase, 'Jesus, mercy,' occurred when I was sitting cross-legged with eyes closed, alone in a Catholic church, on my

> work lunch hour. Both times, while I was hearing the sound of my own mental voice silently speaking these words, I was not aware of hearing any other verbal thought. In one case, when the sampling buzzer sounded, I had just arrived at the church. I was mentally saying, 'Jesus, mercy,' but my nonverbal attention was focused on my physical repositioning of body weight and posture in the pew (Sample #128). In the other case, the buzzer went off towards the end of my lunch hour. Once again, my inner voice was repeating to myself, 'Jesus, mercy.' Here, however, I was aware of a nonverbal impression that it was time to go back to work (Sample #4). This impression or awareness of a sense of time was not accompanied by any recollected verbal dialogue; rather, I simply 'knew' it was time to leave.

In my opinion, the second description gives us a real glimpse into something that actually occurred, rather than a general talking-about something that may have occurred, as in the first description. The second description is thus sharp and informative while the first is dull and lifeless.

A related example of failure to focus directly on the experience follows:

> When writing, as I am writing now, I hear the words spoken concurrent with my putting them on paper.

As before, the description of the category is no doubt correct, but dull and uninformative. The problem again is that the description is not focusing with clarity on particular sampled experiences, but rather has allowed unspecified, unsampled experiences to slip into the description ("as I am writing now"). The final version makes the experience of writing much more vivid:

> When I was writing, I heard words mentally spoken concurrent with my putting them on paper. For example, I was writing down the following scripture quotation, "Pick up your stretcher and walk" (Sample #163). I heard each word inside my head at the same time as it was written.

This second description, even though it says almost identically the same thing as the first, is more penetrating and more believable because it focuses on something determinate, the particular scripture-writing thought, instead of something indeterminate, the vague semirecollection of writing experience in general.

The second category of errors involves failure to provide enough detail in a description so that what is being described is intelligible to the reader. Consider the following:

> Some remembered images included actual movement of the pictured figures and scene, although the movement was still viewed from a fixed perspective. For example, I was talking aloud to a friend at dinner, "I thought it was the greatest thing we had ever done" (Sample #188). As I was speaking, I was mentally picturing myself walking into my kitchen at home, and enthusi-

> astically talking to one of the women who lived there. The image did not include a memory of the words I had been saying; however, I could see where we were standing in the kitchen, the responding expressions on her face and the gestures I was using with my hands.

This description is precise as far as it goes, but it does not provide the detail necessary to let the description come alive. For example, it states that she could see "where we were standing" but does not say where, in fact, that was. Furthermore, while it states that she was "walking into my kitchen," it leaves unclear how much movement is actually seen. For example, a still photograph could be accurately described as showing a person walking into her kitchen, and a five-second videotape that showed the door opening and the actual path of her entrance could also be described the same way. Melancon's first description fails to discriminate between *implied* motion and *real* motion, thus making it difficult for the reader confidently to project him- or herself into the experience. Consider the rewrite of the present example:

> For example, I was talking aloud to a friend at dinner, "I thought it was the greatest thing we had ever done" (Sample #188). As I was speaking, I was mentally picturing myself walking a few steps across my kitchen at home, from the sink to the stove. In this case the perspective of the scene I was viewing was from over my left shoulder in the kitchen. As I walked in the image, I was enthusiastically talking to one of the women who lived there; I could see the responding expression on her face as she listened to me, and the gestures I was using with my hands. The image did not include the sound of my voice or a memory of the words I had been saying. Furthermore, the visual details that I recalled in the image included big items, such as the major appliances and a memory of the light shining from my stove, but I could not recall fine details, such as the clothes we were wearing or what was sitting on the kitchen counter tops. However, the focus of my attention in this thought was the words I was audibly saying in the dinner conversation to my friend, not the image being viewed. The remembered image, in this case, was more like a brief, background, visual display inside my head that exemplified the point I was verbalizing aloud.

The second version allows the reader to grasp what kind of movement and how much occurred in the thought itself, and also to see what the context of the image was.

The third type of failure to focus directly on the experience involves a depersonalizing, or being unclear about exactly who is doing the experiencing. For example, Melancon in an early draft described an image of a recent car accident. She concluded:

> The image, however, did have a strong sense of backward motion attached to it, although the picture was a static and unchanging one.

Upon closer examination, it was found to be more accurate to write:

> I did, however, have a strong sense of backward motion, although the picture itself was a static and unchanging one.

The first description had allowed the sense of motion to be erroneously attached to the image, when it was actually a direct experience of the subject. A second example:

> I was looking at a package of ground beef while preparing dinner and thinking, "This meat has discolored but should still be all right to cook" (Sample #19). I silently "heard" these words verbalized inside my head as I was thinking them.

This description is not clear about who is the source of these spoken words, and also is ambiguous about whether the words accompany the thought ("verbalized . . . as I was thinking them") or were actually the thought itself. The final description clears this up:

> For example, I was looking at a package of ground beef while preparing dinner and silently saying, "This meat has discolored but should be all right to cook" (Sample #19). I was speaking these words inside my head while deciding what to fix for dinner.

This simple expression makes it clearer what the direct experience was.

The last class of common errors involves allowing preconceptions about how thinking works to influence the descriptions. Descriptions, to the extent possible, should be conceptionless. A series of examples will delineate the problems:

> Occasionally, the emotional feeling triggered by the remembered mental image was very strong.

Closer examination revealed that the subject had no experiential awareness of any "triggering"; rather, it seemed more accurate to write that an emotional feeling "accompanied" her remembered mental image. It may or may not actually be the case that images trigger emotions; what is important is that in describing experiences we avoid *assuming* that such a triggering takes place—if we experience such a triggering directly, we will report it, and if not, not. Another example:

> Here again, I knew that I was questioning something when the buzzer went off, and I knew what I was wondering about, but I could not recall any associated verbal thoughts or images to describe by what process the wondering was taking place.

This description implies that verbal thoughts or images must be what carries meaning in experience, which may or may not be true. A good description should make it clear that what is being described here is just a *knowing*, not an absence of verbal thoughts or images. The final draft description is better:

> Here again, I knew that I was questioning whether the woman was in her office. However, there were not any words or images to convey that question; rather, the meaning and knowledge was simply experienced.

We should reiterate the reasons for displaying this series of blunders in the early stages of this work. Our attempt in the present chapter was to show that it is easier to say, "Describe the experiences themselves," than to do so without misleading. We have been trying to give a glimpse into our procedure which attempted to keep the descriptions accurate. As previously stated, the above was not an exhaustive list of the mistakes we made en route to presenting the chapters that follow, but was just a demonstrative sampling of some recurring types of errors. These examples lead to the following general observation which seems to me to be valid: Accurate descriptions of real categories or characteristics are bright and alive and gripping, while inaccurate descriptions or attempts at description of ill-defined categories or characteristics are dull and lifeless. The descriptive procedures used in the present study attempted, as much as possible, to provide the reader with an accurate and vivid glimpse into the everyday thoughts of a few individuals.

I

The Normal Subjects

The ten chapters that follow (the first six in this part, the first four in the next part) are the descriptions of inner experience toward which this study is aimed. All ten investigations had identical aims—to describe a subject's inner experience, based on careful sampling—but the method for each was slightly different in the several realizations, the biggest difference being between the two subject-written descriptions (Chapter 8 by Smith and Chapter 9 by Melancon) and the remaining eight author-written descriptions. The descriptions are also different from each other in writing style as well as in content. No attempt was made at uniformity in the descriptions, reflecting the freedom of each subject and author to characterize inner experience in whatever way seemed most adequate. The one exception was where several subjects seemed to be describing the same phenomenon but used different words; in those cases we tried to standardize usage. For example, we chose to use the term "Inner Speech" to signify the phenomenon our subjects variously called "subvocal speech," "silent speech," "myself talking to myself," etc.

You are reminded of the invitation that was extended at the end of Chapter 1 to monitor your own tendency to rush to generalization. These ten chapters provide that opportunity to practice suspending conceptualizations until all the data are at hand.

The first six chapters are descriptions of so-called normal individuals. These subjects were not selected to be perfect psychological specimens, by any means, but instead to comprise a relatively diverse group of people who do not have any particular psychiatric diagnosis. Our purpose here is not to define normalcy, but to give examples of the everyday experiences of people.

The method used to generate these descriptions was described in

Chapter 2 in detail: the subjects sampled for a day, then met with the author to discuss in detail the sampled experiences. This sample-and-discuss procedure continued day after day until no new characteristics seemed to be emerging. At the conclusion of the sampling period, the author categorized the experiences according to whatever characteristics seemed salient to him or her, and then wrote descriptions of the salient characteristics. These written descriptions were then taken back to the subject, and subject and author read them together.

This reading task was explained to the subject approximately as follows: "As we read this description of your experiences, we want you to point out any discrepancies between what is written and what you remember, or any word or phrase that does not seem accurate. Our goal here is to provide as accurate descriptions as we can, and your help is necessary to us. Don't hesitate to mention something just because it seems unimportant, but rather, whenever you have qualms about a wording or description, let us know, and we will discuss it with you. You should bear in mind that you still have total control over the course of this project: if any reason occurs to you that you do not wish this description to be made public, please let us know. Furthermore, if you wish your description to disguise your identity, also please let us know."

All of the subjects found the descriptions extremely accurate in detail, felt that their experiences were represented fairly in the overall descriptions, and elected to allow their descriptions to be presented, using their own names rather than pseudonyms. Each subject made some minor corrections and suggestions and, without exception, all suggestions and corrections were deemed improvements by the authors and were added to the manuscript. Thus the reader can be assured that the following accounts are judged by both subject and author to be accurate, careful descriptions of each subject's inner experiences. Perhaps because of this perceived accuracy of description, none of our normal subjects requested that we disguise their identities. We did so nevertheless, since this book is about describing inner experience, not directly about the particular people being described.

4

A College Freshman

with Susan M. Melancon

Jason Corvallis was, at the time of sampling, an 18-year-old freshman at the University of Nevada, Las Vegas. Jason had moved from his small hometown in northern Nevada a few months earlier, and volunteered to participate in the study after hearing it described in an introductory psychology class. We did not know Jason prior to beginning sampling, and so did not preselect him because of any foreknowledge either of his personal life or the salient characteristics of his thinking.

Jason participated in the study for a period of six days, collecting 53 samples which we characterized as follows: Images (22 samples), Verbal Thought (12), Wordless Speaking or Imageless Seeing (8), Paying Particular Attention (7), and Feelings (4).

IMAGES

Over one-third (22 of 53) of the inner experiences collected from Jason during the sampling period contained Images, that is, instances in which Jason had the experience of "seeing," even though the thing seen was not really present. Visual thought was thus one of the most salient characteristics of Jason's thinking: his Images varied greatly in their vividness, colorfulness, and complexity of detail, as well as being produced in a variety of environmental settings. For the present discussion, we have divided Jason's visual thoughts into four functional categories: Daydreaming, Problem-Solving Images, Comparison of Images with External Reality, and Revisualizations of External Details. The first category included the greatest number of Jason's Images. However, there was often overlap between these descriptive categories, and the aforementioned range of visual complexity was a factor in all of the category descriptions.

Daydreaming

We came to call 12 of Jason's 53 samples "daydreaming," all 12 of which contained Images as a salient feature. In these samples, Jason's attention at the moment he was signaled was focused on his internal "seeing," rather than his environmental surroundings, and the Images Jason was viewing were of people or places only remotely or tangentially related to his current activity.

For example, Jason was signaled during a hotel administration class. At the moment of the signal, he was imaginally seeing the Mt. Holly ski resort (Sample #53). The Image, which was experienced somewhere inside the center of Jason's head, was of a ski lodge, as if it were being viewed from the parking lot with the mountain slopes behind it. This mental picture was "framed" by darkness, that is, the edges of the "picture" ended abruptly. It was a color picture which Jason described as "vivid" and which gave an "impression of grandeur." However, Jason had never been to Mt. Holly, so the Image was not full of describable detail; for example, he was unable to say if the lodge was a one- or two-story building.

Jason described this visual experience as a freeze-frame, snapshot re-creation that was a conglomerate of pictures from a ski-area brochure he had been looking at on his way into the classroom a few minutes before, and memories of other ski resorts he had visited in the past. Even though he was unaware of particular details in the Image, the Image itself was experienced as crisp and clear. That is, Jason seemed to be taking in the picture as a whole and not noticing any particular details about it. In this sample, Jason's attention was not directed toward the professor who was lecturing to his class, although he was physically hearing him and, perhaps, was tracking along with the lecture at some other level of consciousness. Rather, at the moment of the tone, Jason's awareness was focused totally on his pictorial daydreaming, and he had temporarily ceased to be aware of the external voices and surroundings.

In another example, Jason was signaled during an English class while listening to the instructor lecture on syllogisms. At the moment he heard the tone, Jason had fallen "one step behind" the teacher and was focusing his attention on a mental Image of the Greek philosopher Socrates, who had been named in the instructor's "All philosophers are men; Socrates is a philosopher; therefore, Socrates is a man" example (Sample #25). Here again, the picture was situated by itself in some sort of space inside his head. He described the Image as being a black-and-white picture, something like a fuzzy composite of drawings he might have seen over the years in textbooks or encyclopedias. He was unable to recall specific details or features of the imagined philosopher, but "knew" that the Image he was viewing was of Socrates.

In the above examples, Jason's daydreams were visualized about some person or place he had never seen. At other times, the experiences we call daydreaming were recollections of remembered places or events. These memories were typically highly detailed and complex. For example, Jason was looking at the newspaper weather map and recreating in inner experience the weather in his northern Nevada hometown (Sample #28). He was imaginally seeing a colorful and accurately detailed view of his parents' house from the perspective of standing looking at it from the street. The Image included the neighboring houses on both sides, the brown grass and bare trees, and the "crisp blue sky."

Jason's experience was not merely visual, however, but also included hearing the sounds of wind rustling through the leafless trees, birds singing, and a clear whole-body sensation of coldness, as if standing in a wintry day. As in the above examples, the mental picture was experienced as situated somewhere within Jason's head. However, this Image had no sharp frame about it, but rather seemed to extend beyond the edges of his imaginal visual focus of attention; Jason described this sample as like "being there without being there," since it so strongly called all of his senses (visual, auditory, bodily) into play as a part of the total impression.

Another example of this type of vividly recalled experience occurred when Jason was speaking on the telephone to a friend about the student ambassador international travel program (Sample #26). When he heard the beep, Jason was experiencing a Swedish shopping market that he had once visited as a participant in this student program. He described the sample as capturing in one moment all of his Feelings and experiences of being in that country. As in the previous sample, it was, for Jason, "being there without being there."

The visual Image was in vivid detail: he saw the blue and gold banners hanging down between the buildings and the crowd milling around the square. Although the strongest experience of the sample was visual, it also contained other sensory experiences, such as the tastes of the food, the sounds and smells of the marketplace, and the sensation of Jason's moving through the crowd while shopping. These sensory details were not just metaphorical: Jason's experience of this sample was that it really was taste-full, full of sounds, etc., as well as being visually complex. For Jason, the impact of this sample, however, was in the overall experience; he stated that he could have focused on any single detail of the picture if he had chosen to do so. That is, at the moment of the signal, his attention was on the overall reliving of the trip which had been captured and experientially summarized in the Image he was viewing.

In one final example of Jason's vivid and complex memory experiences, he was sitting at his home, listening to a recording of *Olympic Fanfare* by John Williams, and picturing the opening ceremonies to the 1984 Olympics, which he had attended, and where this same music had been played (Sample #23). He described the visual experience at the moment of the signal as "grand" and "immensely detailed." This sample seemed to Jason to be almost a reliving of the past event, in a way that was predominantly visual. He was seeing the same colors, scale, and dimensionality that had been a part of the actual scene, as well as being aware of people sitting behind him. He described himself as emotionally "swelled up" with excitement, just as he had been while listening to the same climactic music at the Olympic ceremony.

However, there were some striking differences between the Image and the actual event: for example, the playing field in the Image was seen as an empty green expanse of grass, while in fact it had been crowded with participants during the real opening-day ceremony. The music he was externally listening to, and which had transported Jason back to this visual recollection, was also absent from the inner experience. His focus of attention was upon the crowd he was viewing, rather than the music or the stadium events below. The Image had a sense of general movement, a shifting of positions in the crowd, although no single individual was in actual motion in the picture.

In this sample, Jason also had a secondary sense of "seeing" himself and the crowd around him, as if he were observing the entire scene from above. This additional sense of viewing the overall scene, however, was a visual "knowing" what it looked like without seeing an actual picture (a phenomenon that will be discussed later in the Imageless Seeing category). Thus, in this sample, Jason's attention was primarily focused on a detailed, but selective, visual recollection of an event, the experience of which included emotional and Imageless Seeing qualities.

At other times, Jason's daydreaming was of specific future events in which he planned to participate. For example, he was talking on the telephone to a friend, making plans to play tennis later in the day (Sample #34). However, he was not paying attention to the words he was speaking (or hearing spoken) in the real telephone conversation, nor could he even recall them. Rather, at the sound of the signal, Jason's attention was focused on picturing himself as he was watching his friend and himself playing tennis on an outdoor asphalt tennis court.

Note that there are two imaginal Jasons in this experience: Jason the player, playing tennis with his friend, and Jason the observer, watching both of them play. The visual perspective of the Image of the players was that of looking over Jason the player's left back profile, with the court and other player in front of him. In other words, it was not seen from Jason the player's eyes, who was standing on the court with his friend, but rather from the perspective of a Jason who was standing beside and behind.

As in the previous Image, this mental picture seemed to have a sense of "general movement" associated with it, although Jason did not see any overt motion, such as a ball flying across the net or one of the players stepping forward. Unlike the last example, however, the color in this anticipatory Image was drab, washed out, almost approaching black-and-white; Jason compared it to a color television picture on which the color had been turned down low.

Furthermore, this Image included the experiential awareness of Jason the observer, who was known to be present watching the two play tennis. This additional Jason was not actually seen in the Image, but still was "visually" known to be present (an example of Imageless Seeing, to be described below). This Jason the observer was known to be standing watching the game from the perspective described above, and was being viewed as if from the back. Furthermore, Jason knew that the game itself was being viewed as if through Jason the observer's eyes.

Thus, in the experience of this sample there were three distinct Jasons: Jason the player, seen in the Image playing tennis with his friend; the non-Imaged Jason the observer, who was visually known to be watching the tennis game; and the real Jason, who was talking on the telephone when he heard the beeper, and was at that moment experiencing the first two Jasons. Jason was insistent that this additional component (Jason, watching "himself" watching himself and a friend play tennis) was distinctly different from, for example, the previous Olympics sample which Jason had described as being similar to an Imageless "seeing" of himself on television sitting amidst a crowd; that is, in the Olympics sample, there was no experience of a Jason the observer, but instead Jason in the crowd was viewed from a neutral external perspective. We may also note that this tennis Image was experienced by Jason as being more personal, being viewed through the more personal eyes of this "unseen" spectator—Jason.

Problem-Solving Images

Six of Jason's sampled thoughts contained Images that seemed to serve him in a problem-solving, utilitarian fashion. For example, Jason was shopping for clothes and was approaching the checkout counter with his four selections. At the same time, he was mentally adding the prices of the garments he wanted to buy (Sample #22). At the moment of the signal, he was seeing an Image of the four prices, lined up one above the other, with a line drawn beneath the bottom price as if a sum were to be computed. The numerals themselves were black numbers on a light or gray background, much like those that appear on an LCD calculator display, and the decimal points were aligned vertically. The far-right column had a "9" in place under the summation line, and at the moment of the "beep," Jason was "carrying the 1"; that is, a somewhat smaller "1" was just appearing at the top of the next column of numbers he was going to add.

The experience of "mentally adding" was nonverbal; he was not hearing or speaking any numbers. Instead, he was seeing on this visual screen the addition that was being done. However, this was not a passive viewing as if watching a slow calculator at work. Rather, the experience was of himself adding the column of numbers, with the "9" and "1" being displayed as a visual record of the addition he himself was carrying out. Yet, as previously stated, the experience of adding was strictly a visual one, with the numbers appearing to emerge almost automatically in response to his nonverbal addition.

In another example, Jason was playing tennis with a friend. At the moment he heard the signal, Jason's opponent had just hit the ball, and Jason was watching it come toward him (Sample #35). Simultaneously, Jason was seeing (in Image) a three-dimensional black line forming in an arc from where he was about to hit the ball to the part of his opponent's court where his own return shot would be aimed. This imaginary black line thus showed the route that Jason hoped his return would take.

The experience of this sample was that Jason was seeing the real world before him (including the ball coming toward him); but upon it was superimposed this black, animated, arching line. Jason saw the line constructing itself, growing from where he stood, crossing the net, and terminating where the anticipated shot would hit the ground in his partner's court. Jason metaphorically described the imaginary line's creation as being like observing a burning tennis ball which left a trail of smoke behind it as it crossed the court, or like watching a paintbrush leaving behind a trail of paint (although he saw neither a burning ball or paintbrush in the Image). The speed of the animated, growing line seemed comparable to, or perhaps a little faster than, the speed the actual ball would travel after it was hit. The superimposed line was not a lasting phenomenon; that is, it did not hold its appearance for any length of time, but instead formed itself and then disappeared.

Once again, the experience of this sample for Jason was that of actually seeing the line form itself across the net in anticipation of the return shot he hoped to make; the experience was definitely not that he was idly observing a separate Image to the exclusion of reality, as had been the case in the above daydreaming examples.

The next sample (Sample #36) also occurred while Jason was playing tennis, and included a similar "seeing" of a black line crossing the court, only this time, Jason had already hit the ball and was watching it travel along the line toward his opponent's side of the court.

We might note in passing that Jason was a beginning tennis player, and had not realized that such visual phenomena were a part of his playing tennis. Once he had made the observation in these two samples, he reported that he tried to concentrate on these Images as a means of improving his tennis game.

In other Images, Jason's daydreaming and problem-solving types of Images seemed to overlap; that is, they were functionally less distinct from one another. For example, Jason was once again in his psychology class, where the instructor was lecturing on fish eyes (Sample #52). When he heard the signal, Jason had fallen "one step behind" the lecture and was seeing (in imagination) his apartment, picturing it in a rather idle, daydreaming fashion. The Image he was viewing was seen as if through his own eyes, looking into his apartment from the front doorway, seeing the apartment as a whole. In the Image, the apartment was lit and he was aware that it was night outside. The Image was a motionless, freeze-frame picture that ended with the edges of the room and was surrounded by nothingness. Jason himself did not appear in the Image. In the visualized room, three identical fish tanks were sitting at three different locations: one tank was to his left, sitting on a coffee table in front of the couch; one was sitting on a black metal stand to his right, near the refrigerator and wall at the entryway of the kitchen; and the third was straight before him in the dinette area. In his real apartment, this latter perspective would have been an impossible one because of a wall that blocked the view.

Jason's actual apartment did not have any fish tanks in it: he was picturing his apartment with tanks sitting at these three different locations as a means of considering where would be the best place eventually to put a tank. This evaluation process was not experienced by Jason as being a sequential, consider-them-one-at-a-time process, nor was it a verbal asking of himself where the best placement site would be. Rather, he was visually taking in the entire apartment as a whole, and simultaneously seeing all three tanks at their separate locations. Thus, in this sample, Jason's visual thought was serving him in a problem-solving way, helping him to evaluate a decision, but was experienced in an undirected, mind-wandering fashion.

Comparison of Images with External Reality

Jason was sampled seven times when he was making a visual comparison between an Image and some particular characteristic of the external scene he was viewing. For example, Jason was sitting in a McDonald's restaurant having dinner and visually comparing its decor with that of an Image of other McDonald's he had seen (Sample #39). At the moment of the beep, Jason was looking at some plants in the McDonald's where he was sitting, and at the same time seeing a mental picture of a "generic" McDonald's, without such plants. In other words, he was not remembering a specific time and place in his imagination, but picturing a composite type of place he had been many times before. This Image was a color, snapshot-type Image which seemed to be placed slightly to the right side of his field of vision.

In the comparison, Jason alternately focused his attention, one moment on the external scene he was viewing the next moment on the internal Image that was his own creation. However, this internal picture did not cease to exist when he was focused on external reality, but rather it "stayed there," outside the center of attention, so that Jason was aware of its presence concurrent with his looking at the physical scene around him.

His experience of this comparison was that the McDonald's where he was sitting was more nicely decorated than others he had visited, but there were no words expressing this opinion. The comparison was strictly a visual one. Jason also noted about this Image that, although he compared it to a photograph in its vivid reality, the picture had no edges nor could he sense any peripheral vision beyond it. The Image simply filled his mental view, and he was looking back and forth at the external world and the simultaneously present mental picture, evaluating or contrasting the differences between them.

In another example, Jason was watching television and had noted a bright yellow necklace that a woman on the screen was wearing (Sample #30). At the moment that he heard the signal, Jason had turned his attention to a picture, inside his head, of a yellow spectrum; that is, a series of 10 to 15 different shades of yellow were displayed like a row of dominoes, as sequential yellow rectangles against a white background. This spectrum included only distinct shades of yellow; that is, there were no oranges or greens, nor did Jason have the impression that the spectrum continued to other colors beyond his field of vision. The white background Jason described as "framed" because it seemed to end sharply, to have edges, although there was nothing beyond these edges that he could perceive. Beneath this series of rectangles was another rectangular swatch of yellow that corresponded to the color of the necklace he had been viewing, and was positioned beneath its exact matching shade on the spectrum.

Jason's experience was that a distinct comparison was being made between the yellow he had externally seen and the shades of yellow that were displayed in this Image. He described the visual comparison as being not so much just an idle, mind-wandering experience, but rather an activity that produced in him a Feeling of "Oh! That's where it goes. . ."

Another example of this kind of visual comparison was one of the most complex visual thoughts Jason reported during the sampling period. In this sample, Jason was watching the opening credits of a television mini-series (Sample #49). When he heard the signal, the screen before him was showing an etched-glass profile or silhouette of one of the show's actors, with the actor's name printed beside it. At the same time that Jason was looking at the television screen, he was imaging a color picture of this same actor's face, full-face instead of profile, but matching the etched silhouette in size and scale.

Jason described the mental Image as being on a mauve background (which matched the background on the screen before him), and resembling a photograph that one might see in a "glossy model magazine"; the Image was not, however, an actual picture from a magazine that he was remembering. In the sample, Jason was mentally "holding up" this color picture side by side with the silhouetted profile he was viewing on the screen ("real world" picture to the left, mental Image to the right), and comparing them.

However, in this sample there was also a third visualization occurring; namely, he was imaging talking to this author (S.M.) in their meeting the previous day. This additional Image was in color and included details of the office where he had met her and how she had been dressed; the perspective was as if the office were viewed by someone standing slightly behind Jason, so that his own back was included in the picture. The memory Image did not include any verbal or auditory components. All three visualizations—the television picture being externally viewed, the Image being compared with the television picture, and the memory Image—had equal potency for Jason, and he was looking at them all with equal attention.

In trying to explain this sampled experience, Jason stated that the memory Image almost seemed to overlie the other visual pictures, but was also not like an overlay in that the Images were not blurred nor did the details of one interfere with his perception of the other. He simply was looking at all three at the same moment when he heard the signaling tone.

Revisualizations of External Details

There were two samples collected during the study period where Jason seemed to be revisualizing external details. In other words, Jason's attention at the moment of the signal was focused (to a greater or lesser extent) on a visual creation of his own that in some way mirrored what he was externally viewing in reality.

For example, Jason was in a psychology lecture where the instructor had just drawn a schematic neuron horizontally on the blackboard, and now was describing the myelin sheath and its function (Sample #19). When he heard the signal, Jason was visualizing a neuron that was not simply an imaginal repetition of the instructor's drawing on the board, but was of a segment of a single horizontal axon, white or illuminated against a surrounding dark background which seemed to be empty space. Jason "knew" the neuron he was imaging was wrapped in the myelin sheath, and that this sheath would be slippery if he felt it (which reflected what the lecturer had said). The Image was not sharply cut off at the edges of the segment, but rather it seemed to Jason that his attention was only focused on the portion of the neuron he was seeing, and that the remainder of the neuron could have been seen if he had chosen to look at it.

This Image, then, was a revisualizing type of experience, in that although he was still physically looking at the blackboard in front of him and hearing the instructor's lecture, at the moment of the signal, Jason's attention was totally focused on the internal picture he was viewing. In other words, his own created Image took precedence in awareness over what he was seeing or hearing externally (although the Image was quite closely tied to external reality). We might note that the Image also seemed to serve a "problem-solving" function for Jason, in that he seemed to be using it to understand or assimilate the material being presented in the lecture he was attending.

In another example, Jason was sitting in a classroom, waiting for class to begin, idly looking at the people in the room. He stated that he was just taking in the whole scene, not looking at anyone in particular (Sample #51). Simultaneously, he was seeing an Image of the same classroom which he perceived to be identical to the scene that he was externally viewing. That is, Jason was seeing both reality and an Image that exactly paralleled reality, and seeing both at the same time. The mental picture seemed in his "mind's eye" to be positioned in front of him, almost superimposed over the visual reality.

It was almost as if the Image and the external visual perception were one and the same; yet Jason was very clear in his description that the two visualizations were experientially distinct from one another. He described the Image as almost "bigger than life," in front of him, but not so far in front so as to be on top of the actual people sitting in the classroom. His thought experience was not that he was actively comparing the external scene with the mental Image; he was merely "killing time," and watching both reality and the Image of it with equal emphasis.

This was a difficult visual experience for Jason to describe, and was an isolated event during the sampling period. He stressed that it was not the same experience as either simply seeing a mental Image on a mental screen, nor as simply gazing at a room full of people. Both—the Image and the external view—were experientially real and distinct from one another; both were the same in detail, depth perspective, dimension, and color; and both equally were occupying Jason's attention at the moment he was signaled.

VERBAL THOUGHT

Of the 53 samples collected from Jason during the study period, 12 fell into a category we will call Verbal Thought. Jason experienced verbal thought in two ways: (1) the Inner Hearing of two distinct voices, the "auditorium voice" and the "teacher"; and (2) Inner Speech in his own voice. Each of these three voices was experienced as being separate and distinctly different from one another. Jason never reported experiencing more than one of them in any given example. Interestingly, Jason also reported no occasion during the sampling period in which visual Images appeared concurrently with his experiences of Inner Hearing or Inner Speech.

Inner Hearing

The "auditorium voice" was the first to emerge. Jason experienced the Inner Hearing of this disembodied male voice as booming, resonant, and clear, as if the voice were making an authoritarian announcement. The voice seemed "alone" or surrounded by empty space, thus giving it the quality of a voice speaking in an auditorium. Jason experienced the voice as independent of himself; that is, the words were "heard" rather than spoken by him. The voice had an impersonal quality, as if the words were addressed to people in general rather than anyone in particular; Jason compared it to an announcement coming across a PA system that is meant to be heard by everyone in a crowded arena. (Jason of course knew that, while the voice seemed to be speaking to everyone or anyone, he alone was the only person who could hear it.) The voice was not that of any person Jason knew in his external life, such as a friend or family member, and was perceived by Jason to be located inside the center of his head.

This auditorium voice could be forceful and full of inflection; for example, Jason was gazing at a newspaper comic page and heard the voice exclaim, "What a stupid comic!" with an inflection full of disdain (Sample #2). At other times the voice was flat, and speaking matter-of-factly, as when it was asking, "What is on television at 6 PM?" (Sample #5). In another example, this auditorium voice was speaking with a tone of irritation, "Gosh, this peanut butter is too thick to spread" (Sample #8), although Jason stated that he himself was not "Feeling" irritated at the time he heard the words. Finally, on one occasion, Jason heard the auditorium voice state, "Gosh, I'm sleepy" (Sample #31). Even though the words were spoken in the first person, they were not experienced by Jason as being directly solely at him. Rather, the words carried the same forceful, authoritarian, impersonal characteristics as a PA announcer speaking to an arena of people. Thus, in all of these examples, despite the fact that the message being spoken might be relevant only for Jason, the voice was heard as impersonal, directed to everyone and anyone who might be listening.

There was also one sample in which Jason heard the auditorium voice, but the quality of impersonalness characteristic of this voice was not present. In this sample, Jason was watching television and heard the voice emphatically ask about the scene he was viewing, "Is Peter going to get shot?" (Sample #14). Jason reported that this questioning was asked in the auditorium voice, but, in this case, the question was directed only to him, to Jason, not to some unspecified "everyone." This was an important distinction for Jason, and although he could not explain exactly what vocal characteristics constituted this difference, the distinction was as experientially distinct as listening to a general announcement or listening to a personal conversation.

The second Inner Hearing "voice" that Jason experienced emerged at the end of the sampling period, and was only captured in a single sample. At the moment he heard the tone, Jason was working on an English homework assignment, and was Inner-Hearing the words, "A teacher is like a gardener" (Sample #46). Jason was hearing the voice, and did not have the sense of creating it that we associate with the phenomenon of Inner Speech. The voice was male and pleasant and was speaking words Jason had read earlier. The male voice was not one Jason identified with any known individual, nor was it either his own voice or that which he had previously identified as the "auditorium voice." Jason described this voice as one that seemed directed to a group of people, but that also was directed personally, one on one, to each individual in that group. Jason compared hearing this "teacher voice" to the experience of being in a classroom, listening to a teacher who was speaking to the whole class but who also was communicating to each student personally. Thus, this teacher voice was different from the auditorium voice in two important ways: first, Jason experienced the tone and quality of the voice itself as being distinctly different, and second, the "teacher voice" communicated a sense of speaking personally to Jason, and also to Jason as a member of a somehow related group.

Inner Speech

A second form of verbal thought that Jason described was that of himself "speaking inside his head," without making any external sounds or movements—the phenomenon we call Inner Speech. In these examples, Jason was both "speaking" and hearing the sound of his own inner voice, although the focus of the experience was on the active speaking, rather than the hearing. The characteristics of his Inner Speaking were experienced as identical to his real aloud speech; that is, the Inner Speech had the same rhythm, tempo, and inflections as his external speech. Thus, this type of verbal thought was experienced primarily actively by Jason, as opposed to the "auditorium voice" and "teacher voice" thoughts in which Jason perceived himself as primarily a passive listener. Furthermore, the "Jason speaking" experience seemed to be more diffusely centered somewhere within his head; that is, Jason did not experience these thoughts as isolated or closed in the center of an empty surrounding space, as was the quality of the "auditorium voice" described above.

Inner Speech was spoken and heard by Jason with a wide range of tonal inflection. For example, one day in a store, the beep captured Jason animatedly speaking to himself with a tone of admiration, "That is one real good-looking girl!" (Sample #3); another time, hurried and impatiently stopped in traffic, he was thinking, *"I hate traffic lights!"* (Sample #40) with a definite tone (and Feeling) of irritation. At other times, the signal caught Jason talking to himself more matter-of-factly, for example, saying about his apartment, "It is too cold in here" (Sample #27). In these examples, Jason's experience was that he was just generally speaking to himself; there was never any sense of the words being directed to anyone in particular.

In considering Jason's verbal thought experiences, we never became aware of any relationship between the content of a given thought, and the "voice" in which the thought was silently verbalized. For example, Jason was watching a commercial on TV and was saying to himself in Inner Speech, "That is one of the most absurd things I have ever seen" (Sample #50). The words were experienced as spoken in his own voice with a strong inflection of disbelief, as if he were mentally acknowledging a personal opinion to himself. The content of this thought was similar to one previously described, where Jason was Inner Hearing the words, "What a stupid comic" (Sample #2), in the "auditorium voice." Thus, two messages that seemed quite similar in content were voiced and experienced quite differently. Perhaps if we had sampled for a longer time we would have begun to see some selective pattern underlying Jason's varied experiences of verbal thought. At the present time, however, we can only note that Jason experienced a variety of "voices" in the expression of his verbal thinking that were not obviously related to the subject matter of the thought itself.

WORDLESS SPEECH AND IMAGELESS SEEING

We have seen that Jason was capable of experiencing verbal and pictorial thought in ways that were vivid, clear, and filled with specific detail. However, Jason also had samples that he reported were definitely experienced as being verbal, but in which no explicit words were mentally spoken or heard. Similarly, there were samples in which Jason had a distinct, visual impression of "seeing"; but where there were no accompanying mental Images. These experiences seemed to be different from the nonverbal/nonvisual experiences of "paying attention" or holding a thought in memory (see below), in that, when concentrating, Jason's attention was focused on a particular task that had an intensity or an engrossing quality about it. The Wordless Speech and Imageless Seeing experiences to be discussed, on the other hand, seemed more similar to Jason's overtly verbal and imaginal thinking, except that they lay at the least vivid or clearly describable end of his continuum of inner experiences.

Wordless Speech

There were five samples reported by Jason in which his experience was that he "knew" he was internally speaking words (as in the Inner Speech section above), and he understood the words' meaning; but there were no specific words experienced. That is, Jason had a distinct impression that he was speaking to himself but without using words. We must be clear in distinguishing this Wordless Speaking from a mere nonverbal knowing or comprehending the meaning of the thoughts. The experience of these samples was that of *speaking*, not of merely knowing what was meant. In other words, Jason had an experience that was quite similar to what we have described as Inner Speech, and he knew precisely what his speaking meant, but no words were present to him.

For example, at the moment he heard one beep, Jason was thinking a thought which, if it were expressed in words, might be something like, "I despise my French class. It is really too difficult. My other classes are suffering" (Sample #7), accompanied by a Feeling of despair. However, Jason reported that these words were not actually experienced; he did not hear them spoken, either in his own voice or in the other voices that we have seen characterized his verbal thought. Nevertheless, he had a distinct impression of speaking this meaning, even though no particular words were spoken.

This Wordless Speaking was a very difficult experience for Jason to describe, although he was clear that it was different from his other verbal and nonverbal samples. In another example, he was watching television and was thinking a thought which, if expressed verbally, might be something like, "Why does everyone think the Russians are so evil?—they are people too" (Sample #4). At the same time, he was also experiencing a sense of visually "seeing" something related to the question, although there was no imaginal picture accompanying the thought. Thus this sample had both Wordless Speaking and Imageless Seeing components to it. In this sample, Jason's attention was not on the TV program he was externally viewing but rather was on his own thoughts about it. However, there were no explicit words heard or spoken to express the above question. Jason's experience was that this thought contained an underlying verbal question, and that he "knew" the meaning of the question; furthermore, he was aware of Feeling bewildered in response to it. Nevertheless, there were no verbal words heard or spoken in the thought.

At other times, Jason's Wordless Speech was related to the experience of trying to figure out or remember something. In these instances, it was as if Jason were aware of waiting for words that did exist somewhere to pop up or come forward. For example, he had been called upon in class to describe how to say "12 noon" in French (Sample #15). As he was trying to think of the correct response, Jason was aware that internal words were somehow being formulated and put together in different trial combinations, but he did not actually picture or hear them spoken.

Imageless Seeing

There were also samples in which Jason reported that he knew he was internally seeing, but there was no particular Image being seen.

Thus, this Imageless Seeing experience was just like what we have referred to above as seeing an Image, and Jason was cognizant of what was being seen, yet the Image itself was absent. For example, he was in a hotel management class listening to a discussion on commissaries (Sample #21). At the moment of the signaling beep, he had turned his attention away from the instructor's words and was "seeing" a commissary, visualizing it, but without any actual Image. As with the Wordless Speaking, this kind of experience was difficult for Jason to describe: he knew the thought was visual, i.e., he experienced himself as looking at a commissary and he knew what the commissary looked like, but there was no actual picture or Image in the experience. Yet this particular non-Imaged seeing was very clear for Jason; he emphasized that this non-visual picturing experience was very vivid, despite his inability to see it or express or describe it in words.

The other example of this Imageless Seeing occurred in the sample described above under Wordless Speaking, in which Jason was watching television and thinking: "Why does everyone think the Russians are so evil—they are people too" (Sample #4). In this case, Jason knew that the thought was not only verbal-without-words, but also was perceived by him as being distinctly visual but without any mental pictures. In other words, Jason's experience was that the thought had a definite visual component—he was experiencing "seeing" something—but there was nothing that he could describe that was being seen. Here again, Jason seemed quite clear that what he was attempting to describe was a visual phenomenon experienced in a nonvisual way; he was just unable to put the experience into words except to say that he knew this was the case.

PAYING PARTICULAR ATTENTION

There were six occasions when sampling captured Jason more or less intensely concentrating on something that he was seeing or hearing, or trying to "hold" some thought in memory in a concentrated fashion. In all of these thoughts, the experience of being engrossed in what he was doing was not accompanied by any explicitly verbal or visual thought, although it did seem to Jason that he had a clear sensation of understanding or comprehending something. In other words, Jason was not thinking about something; he was simply paying attention.

For example, at Sample #9, Jason was concentrating on how to conjugate a phrase in French. He was physically looking at a page in his French textbook; this looking was not an idle gazing, nor was it a reading line by line or one word at a time, but was a concentrating on an entire part of the page. Simultaneously, he was writing down words on a piece of paper; however, his attention was not directed at what he was writing. Rather, the focus of the thought was his concentrating on the page in the book, comprehending the meaning of what he was seeing, and somehow trying to apply it to the conjugation task. There were no additional mental Images or words associated with the thought.

In a similar example, Jason was studying an English assignment, reading a story about clichés (Sample #41). The only way he could describe this sample was to say that he was concentrating on the page in front of him. He was not creating an Image of the page in his mind, nor reading it silently to himself in one of his mental voices, although he did recognize the meaning of the words printed before him. He was simply "concentrating," with no other associated thoughts. One other time, Jason was with a friend watching a horror movie on television (Sample #37). At the moment he heard the signal, Jason was seeing the film's action on the screen and was "engrossed" in the movie. He could not recall any particular conversations in the movie, nor any associated verbal or imaginal thoughts he had been having about what he was seeing. However, the experience was also different from having no thought at all. Jason was "paying attention," and this concentration was the whole substance of his thought experience at the moment.

In two cases, Jason was concentrating in an attempt to "hold" in his mind some specific thought. His experience was similar to that of the other paying-attention samples in that he knew he was thinking, but could not describe *how* he was doing it or what exactly he was doing. In these cases, it was not that Jason felt the thoughts were distinctly verbal or visual, but just too deep to reach; neither was it that he was experiencing an absence of thought. Furthermore, he could not say how or where this "holding" or concentrating thought activity was localized or taking place. He simply knew it was there. For example, the sampling device signaled only a minute after the previous tone had been emitted (Sample #10). When he heard the second tone, Jason was concentrating on remembering and writing down the experience from the previous signal. He was not repeating the previous thought verbally inside his head, nor was he picturing it in any way. Yet he knew he was "holding" it there, although he could not describe the way he was doing it.

In a more complex example, Jason had been comparing advertisements for toaster ovens in the newspaper, and was holding the prices of the three ovens he was considering "inside his mind" (Sample #47). This comparison was different from the visual thought comparisons previously described in that there was no mental image of the ovens, nor pictures of the three prices or numbers, nor was he verbally repeating them in his mind. He just "knew" they were somewhere "up there." This being "up there" was also not experienced as their being stored in any localized place inside his head. Jason didn't know in what order the numbers were stored, nor exactly what he was doing with them in the comparison. He only knew that the numbers were being actively held and considered in some way that he was unable fully to describe.

FEELINGS

There were four samples in which Jason described some sort of emotion or "Feeling" as being his primary experience at the moment of the tone. There were many cases in which Jason's more complex experiences (described above) included some sort of Feeling or emotion. For example, the "Why does everyone think the Russians are so evil?" experience (Sample #4), included a Feeling of bewilderment or puzzlement; the *"I hate traffic lights!"* experience (Sample #40) included impatience; and the 1984 Olympics experience (Sample #23) included Feeling "swelled up" with excitement in response to the music he was hearing. In other words, Jason was capable of a wide range of emotions, and often reported these emotions as an aspect of the experiences he was describing.

The samples described in the present category, however, seemed to be unique in Jason's experiences, in that, in these cases, his attention was focused entirely on the Feeling or emotional experience he was reporting. For example, Jason was watching a morning news program and was experiencing how pleasant the show hosts were (Sample #44). He described the sample as being purely an emotional experience, e.g., that these were the type of people he would like to know. The words he later used to describe the Feeling experience were "nice, pleasant, happy, homey"; but at the time of the signal he was not thinking these actual words, nor was his attention on what the hosts were saying on the television screen. Rather, the focus of this sample was on his emotional reaction to what he was viewing. In another example, Jason was in his apartment, hearing someone jangling keys outside the door, and was wondering who it was (Sample #11). Once again, he was experiencing no mental words or Images at the time of the signal, but was aware of a sense of curiosity or "wonderment" about who was outside.

This type of emotional experience at times was quite strong for Jason. For example, he was in an English class and had just realized he had done the wrong homework assignment (Sample #45). At the moment of the signal, Jason reported he was Feeling "mad at himself, stupid, really dumb." He was not aware of any mental words being said nor of any Images. He described the Feeling of being mad at himself as also having the flavor that he should somehow punish himself for the mistake; however, this sense of needing punishment was less strong in the emotional experience than was the Feeling of simple self-anger. In another example, when he heard the signal, Jason's whole attention was focused on the experience of Feeling hungry, of his body needing something to eat (Sample #6). He was not mentally picturing any food at the time, nor was he verbally commenting on the hunger. Rather, the whole of the experience was in his Feeling aware that he wanted or needed to eat dinner.

DISCUSSION

One of the most striking characteristics of Jason's inner experiences during the sampling period was the frequent occurrence of visual Images, which appeared in 22 of his 53 samples. Jason's Imagery was highly complex; it was full of colorful detail and at times accompanied by other sensory experiences, such as the feel of cold, wintry air on his skin and the sound of wind rustling through trees while he was seeing an Image of his parents' home in northern Nevada. Many of Jason's Images (12 of 53 samples) were of an idle, daydreaming nature that held his attention to the temporary exclusion of his awareness of external voices and surroundings. At other times, the Images were revisualizations of external details (2 of 53 samples). In these samples, Jason's attention at the moment of the signal was focused on a visual creation of his own which mirrored, more or less accurately, what he was externally viewing in reality.

At still other times (6 of 53 samples), Jason seemed to use his imaginal thought in a problem-solving capacity (such as to help him mentally add a column of numbers or to improve his tennis game), or to visually "compare" particular characteristics of his surrounding environment with the Image he was seeing (7 of 53 samples). Thus, during this 6-day period, over one-third of Jason's sampled experiences included a "seeing" of Images that often held his attention more strongly than did the external world around him.

Another noteworthy characteristic of Jason's samples during this period was his use of verbal thought (12 of 53 samples). Jason experienced verbal thought in two distinctly different ways: (1) Inner Hearing words spoken by two different voices: an authoritarian, announcer-type male voice whose words seemed directly to anyone or everyone, not only to Jason, and the teacher voice which was a male voice that had a quality that seemed more personal and directed to Jason than did the announcer; and (2) Inner Speech, Jason speaking to himself in his own voice.

We asked Jason, after sampling was completed, whether he had known of the existence of these different voices prior to sampling. His reply was that the announcer voice and the experience of Jason speaking to himself had "always been the same," that is, he had always been aware of these forms of verbal thought. The teacher voice, however, Jason seemed less sure of, saying that it seemed that there had always been a "third voice," but that the qualities of the particular voice perhaps changed over time.

A third aspect of Jason's samples that seemed particularly striking was his experience of Wordless Speaking or Imageless Seeing. In these samples, Jason was insistent that the experience he was describing went beyond a mere nonverbal or nonvisual "knowing" of the verbal or pictorial content of a sample (although he always did know what was being said or seen). Rather, Jason's experience in these samples was distinctly that of speaking or seeing, but without any actual words or Images.

5

A Professional Potter

Jim Lincoln, the subject of this description, was 35 years old at the time of sampling. He was an acquaintance of the author, and was recruited as a participant in the sampling exercise primarily because of his vocation: He is a professional potter, thought by many to be one of the most creative ceramicists in the Las Vegas, Nevada area. He is a graduate of a university biology department, having switched majors from chemistry, although art was a major emphasis during his senior year.

He was intrigued, yet apprehensive, about being involved in the project from my first mentioning the possibility to him. The interest seemed to stem from his rather introspective nature, and in fact he characterized his interest in how he himself "worked" as one of the main motivators behind his creative drive. The apprehension seemed to stem from three concerns: first, whether the project would interfere with the energy he had available for his work and so put him behind his artistic schedule; second, whether I would subtly pressure him to be someone he wasn't, in particular to be somehow representative of artists in general; and third, whether his experiences would be at all interesting to me.

Following reassurances, particularly with emphasis that participation in the project was entirely voluntary and could be discontinued at any time, Jim agreed to give it a try on the condition that we sample just during the "work portion" of his day. That compromise was agreeable, not because I was particularly interested in his experiences while at work, but because that was the amount of energy he had available for this project at that time. The sampling proceeded for 6 sampling days and produced 43 samples.

The 43 samples revealed six rather striking characteristics: Feelings (18 of 43); Images (15); Noticing Characteristics (14); Just Doing (6); Body Sense (3); and Verbal Thought (3). Jim was asked to participate in this study because his vocation is primarily nonverbal and because his visual/spatial aesthetic sense is well developed. His inner experiences reflected this artistic nature: His visual sense predominated, both in inner Images and in Noticing the Characteristics of the external environment, and he was clearly aware of the physical and emotion aspects of his body. It is quite tempting to speculate that these are characteristics of artists in general, and that in fact may be so; however, confirmation of that hypothesis must await further research.

FEELINGS

About a third (18 of 43) of Jim's inner experience had as an important component some emotional or organismically gripping aspect. This impact could be more or less intense, and more or less pleasant, as we will see, but the general characteristic is that these samples were experienced as having an emotional quality that extended beyond what might be called matter-of-factness.

Some of these experiences were pleasant. For example, Sample #25 involved Jim's experience of Feeling his whole body tighten as he forced clay down on his wheel while centering it. As this moment, his attention was focused in his body; not some particular part of it, but the body as a whole. The Feeling was warm and good—a full Feeling like being wrapped tightly in a blanket. A similar Feeling occurred at Sample #30, while Jim was ribbing up the wall of a pot. Although his eyes were focused on the pot, his attention was directed toward an Image of himself throwing a pot at ISOMATA, a summer workshop where he would teach ceramics the following summer. The Image was of himself at the potter's wheel, with three or four people standing nearby watching. There was also a warm and pleasant Feeling associated with impressing or being valued by the onlookers. The Feeling seemed to be located in his body, but at no particular place in the body.

Some of the emotional tones experienced during sampling were unpleasant. For example, at Sample #43 Jim was rushing to unload bisqued pots from a plywood lid during a raku firing. The newspaper fire that was part of the raku process needed to be quickly covered so that the glaze reduction would be adequate, and there was a clear bodily sense of rushing before the fire got too big. This rushing sense was paralleled by a twinge or squeeze in the gut that was recognized to be a sense of worry.

In Sample #44, he was moving a pot and simultaneously noticing another greenware pot that was lying on its side to facilitate the drying of its bottom. While thus noticing the pot, and in particular noticing the black opening that was facing him, his attention was on an Image of the form of the lower part of the pot with the side flattened, as might happen if it were set on its side before the side had thoroughly dried. Accompanying this Image was an unpleasant Feeling associated with having ruined the pot. This Feeling could not be traced to any particular part of the body—just an unpleasant sensation.

In Sample #11, Jim had just completed a telephone conversation with a person who was asking him to participate in an art show. In the conversation, Jim had agreed to participate, but now he was having second thoughts. His attention was focused on an Image of the telephone caller's face. The Image itself occupied the center of his "mind's eye," but was blurry or uncrisp, rather as if it were out of focus. At the same time he was angry with himself for not being able to make a decision, or not being clear about his intent. He was mulling over his decision or lack of it, but there were no words associated with this mulling.

We have seen that the emotional quality of his experience could range from pleasant to unpleasant. We now provide examples to illustrate that either pleasant or unpleasant experiences could range in intensity. First we will take two similar examples, both of which are pleasant emotional experiences, but the first of which is quite powerful while the second is rather mild. Sample #28 took place while Jim was in the middle of a "pull," that is, the shaping of a vase at the wheel. His eyes were on the vase, and he was aware that the song *You Turn Me On* was playing on the radio. The center of his awareness was the emotional Feeling that this particular clay had the capacity to swell into a full, wide (desirable) shape. This Feeling was best described as a body consciousness, like expanding the chest to take a full breath, in bodily analogy to the clay's expanding to fill out the wide form. The whole sensation was an extremely pleasurable experience, in that the clay was working well, Jim was working well, and the music was complementing both. It was as if the clay were "turned on" or Jim were turned on. While the body consciousness was centered in Jim's body, his real body was not, in fact, expanding at the chest or taking a full breath; on the contrary, the technique of the pull required that the body be held quite rigid, stable, and tight. For the present section, the aspect of this experience that is relevant is that the emotional impact on Jim was very strong, a powerful sense of things going well.

By contrast, Sample #22 is a much milder, and yet similar emotional experience. Jim was "opening" the clay at the wheel (that is, beginning to shape the rotating clay). He was attending to the clay that was just beyond his fingertips. This is perhaps best described as an almost visual experience. The Feeling of the clay led to the realization that there was a rock, or perhaps an air bubble, in the clay, and this realization was almost visual, as if he were looking imaginally at a lump of the proper size and shape in the matrix; but the Image itself was not clear. Of interest in the present paragraph is the concomitant mildly pleasurable realization that the clay was plastic, that is, it was working well. However, this realization was much less powerful than the body-expanding awareness of the previous sample, that is, it is closer to a matter-of-fact imagining of the characteristic of the clay than it was to the powerful "turned on" experience of Sample #28.

We will provide a few additional examples to give an idea of the range of experiences that were experienced as emotionally impactful. Sample #10 occurred when Jim was attempting to repair a radio. He had taken the radio apart, and was looking at the word "CAUTION" that was printed in red letters on a label inside the case. The focus of attention was more on the color than the word, and in particular the attention included an awareness that it was a "nice" red color. Thus, this emotional impact stemmed from the color of the letters rather than the semantic meaning of the letters.

Sample #9 also occurred when Jim was taking the radio apart. He was looking at a screw in the case, and had just realized that this particular screw was the one that remained holding the case together. The experience was something of an "aha" reaction, like seeing that screw for the very first time (which was not so in reality). There were no words associated with the experience, but it was as if he were saying *"That's what's holding it together!"*

In Sample #39, Jim was talking to his wife Julie about whether a bus tour was coming to visit his studio. As Julie was speaking, Jim was experiencing an Image of people's heads milling around, and this Image was superimposed around the real perception of Julie's face. At the same time, Jim was experiencing a Feeling of acceptance that seemed to emanate from the gut. The Feeling of acceptance reflected the facts that the tour would provide a welcome source of income, but was not considered pleasant.

In Sample #34, Jim was pouring Diet Coke into a Styrofoam cup, and was watching the foam rise up to rim faster than the liquid was pouring into the cup. There was a sense of disbelief or curiosity—as if this increase in the foam's volume defied some physical law (which he knew full well was not in fact true). Nonetheless, this comparing of the two volumes was accompanied by a moderately strong sense of curiosity.

In Sample #19, he was scoring the clay on a pot in preparation to attaching a handle-like construction. The handle would fit into two notches, one on either side of the opening of the pot, and he was scratching the surfaces of the notches to strengthen the joint on assembly. While thus scratching the surface of the clay, he was associating the two cut-out shapes, noticing their alignment and the similarity of their shapes. Simultaneously, there was a mild emotional impact associated with this visual alignment, which, although nonverbal, could be expressed with the words "That's interesting," or "That's neat."

IMAGES

Images were frequent characteristics of Jim's inner experience (15 out of 43 samples). In general, these Images were experienced just like physical seeings, except that the thing seen was not physically present. That is, the Images were in appropriate color, were viewed from a particular perspective, did not have a border or frame around them, and were experienced as being in motion, although the particular movement was frequently difficult to describe, perhaps because the Images themselves were fleeting.

Most of the Images took place while Jim was engaging in some activity, and his eyes were open and watching whatever real object was engaging him. However, his attention was experienced as being focused on the Image, and the real existing scene was not experienced as being seen at the moment.

One example occurred in Sample #24, where Jim was at the wheel centering clay. At the moment of the beep, while physically watching the clay on the wheel, his attention was focused on an Image of half an orange peel. The Image had relevance in that Jim was considering using an orange peel as part of the organic material in an upcoming salt bisque firing. The Image itself was experienced exactly as looking at a real orange peel: it was a bright, fresh orange color, as if it had just been removed intact from a juicy orange. There was a direct knowledge that the orange had been peeled for the sake of the bisque process, not for eating. The peel itself was seen as if suspended in space, in that there was no visual background. Furthermore, there was no visual detail or characteristic that identified the peel as existing only in Image, that is, there was no border or frame or other visual cues to unreality. Nonetheless, Jim "knew" that this was an Image only, and that the orange peel was being considered for part of the bisque process rather than for eating. At that moment, there was no awareness of the real visual world, even though Jim was actively responding to it.

While that Image superseded a physical visualization entirely, there was one example in Jim's sample where both Image and external visualization were experienced superimposed (Sample #39). This is an example cited above in the Feelings section, where the physical view of Jim's wife Julie's face occurred simultaneously with an Image of prospective bus tour visitors. In this particular dual visualization, Julie was rather far away as the conversation took place, so her face occupied a rather small portion of Jim's visual field. The Image surrounded her face, and was of strangers' heads as if milling around. The imaginal faces themselves were not clearly defined. Thus we see that there were, in Jim's samples, a range of visual experiences, from pure seeing of external reality (e.g., the "CAUTION" thought #10 above), to pure visual imaginings (e.g., the orange peel Image #24 above), with superimposed awareness in between.

Some of Jim's Images could be described to be part of a planful consideration, or problem-solving or mulling-over process; that is, they seemed to be phases of a course of events designed to evaluate or form Jim's interactions with the real world. These problem-solving Images could be part of a short-term direct assessment, or of a long-term, diffuse, general nature, with the orange-peel example cited above (Sample #24) somewhere in the middle of this range.

An example of a short-term, direct, planful-consideration Image is Sample #17, which occurred in the glaze room. Jim had just picked up a glaze squirter, and was in midswing, turning from picking up the squirter to the plate he was about to glaze. His attention was on a superimposed visual experience, a seeing of the real plate on which was superimposed a visualization of the glaze splash that he was about to effect. The visualizations were in realistic color, and the color of the glaze itself was its current tan rather than the blue color to which it would be transformed during firing. The experience was not that subsequently Jim would try to "fill in" the Imaged shape with actual glaze, as if painting by number, but rather that the Image previsualized what the desired shape might be.

Another Image that seemed to involve a direct, planful consideration of Jim's interaction with the real world occurred at Sample #32. Jim was at the wheel trimming a large pot, with his left arm up to his elbow inside the pot, his left hand against the inside wall of the pot a few inches from the bottom. His right hand was at the same location outside the rotating pot, holding a trimming tool, and he was peeling off excess clay to obtain the desired thickness. His eyes were watching the pot and the clay being removed, but his attention was focused on an Image of a small slab of clay, as if a small square of the pot wall had been cut and removed from the pot, rotated so that the thickness of the section could be seen directly, and now was being held between the thumb and forefinger of his left hand. The focus of his attention was on the clay cross-section, and the fingers that held it were comparatively in the background. The Image was clearly available to Jim as a way of directly seeing the thickness of the pot's wall in a way that was physically impossible, and yet was the main consideration in the task Jim was performing.

An example of a more diffuse problem-solving Image occurred at Sample #35. Jim was in his studio putting his arm in a cylindrical form of clay. While his eyes were focused on the cylinder, his attention was fixed on an Image of a judge who is an acquaintance of his. The Image was a seeing of the judge in black robe seated on the courtroom dais, with the focus of attention the judge's face. At the same time, Jim had a sense of trying to figure out whether the judge was just. This "figuring out" was not verbal, nor was it contained as an aspect of the Image (for example, it was not a part of the judge's expression). Nonetheless, it was clear to Jim that this Image was part of a process of considering whether the judge was fair. A few moments after the interruption, Jim became aware that the radio was playing the song *Innocent Man* by Billy Joel. Whether this song motivated the Image and train of thought or whether it was coincidence is not possible to determine. For the present, however, this sample provides an example of an Image that seemed to be not directly tied to any particular current concern, but instead is part of a long-range, diffuse, general problem-solving strategy.

By contrast, some Images did not seem to be tied to anything that might remotely be called problem solving. For example, Sample #16 occurred while Jim was loading the kiln. He heard the distant roar of an automobile engine which he recognized as a Volkswagen dune buggy. An Image of a yellow dune buggy appeared, bright yellow with a chrome exhaust pipe angled out the back. This Imaged dune buggy was not associable to real existing dune buggy, but seemed rather a simple visual display in some way paralleling the real physical sound. While the Image occurred, Jim was busy comparing pot sizes in the kiln, but the attention was more on the Image.

Two of the Images were of Jim himself. The first was Sample #1, where Jim had an Image of himself in an elm tree in his father's back yard, pruning the tree as he had in reality done the previous weekend. The image was from the perspective of standing on the ground, looking up at Jim, who was perhaps 10 feet up in the tree sawing a branch. Jim was seen from the front and below, and the experience was just like looking at the real Jim, although it would be, of course, in reality impossible to maintain that perspective on oneself. Jim experienced himself in this Image as being accurately portrayed, wearing recognizably colored clothes, etc. The Image was in color, but the colors present were rather dull—it was a gray day and the bark was brown with no leaves present in the wintry scene.

The other Image of Jim himself occurred at Sample #30, which is the Image of himself seated at the wheel, throwing a pot at an upcoming summer school described above in the Feelings section. In this particular Image, the perspective was of Jim from the front and 45 degrees to the right, with the viewers standing in back of Jim and the wheel. These two Images are somewhat similar in that both may involve some sense of imagining what others think of Jim. This was immediately apparent in #30, where the emotional impact was a pleasant Feeling of impressing onlookers. It also may be a part, not quite so clear, of the elm-tree-pruning Image (#1), which Jim associated with some kind of consideration of how his father views him—the perspective was as if his father were standing on the ground looking up at him. (This sample occurred during Jim's first sampling day, and the skill of freezing the particular experience is one that takes practice. It is quite possible that, had he been more skillful at the time of Sample #1, he would have been able to be clearer about the presence or absence of a sense of his father's point of view.)

Some of the Images were not visually clear; that is, they were experienced as blurry or not crisp or out of focus. For example, Sample #29 occurred while Jim was working at the wheel doing a pull. He noticed a pain in his finger, the result of developing a new (to him) pulling technique to which his fingers were not yet accustomed. The pain was simply experienced, not particularly meaningfully except in the sense that there was at some level of awareness the knowledge that he wasn't going to do anything about it until the procedure was completed. At the same time, his attention was focused on an Image of Julie's teacher (whom he had never met) at the front of a large lecture hall. The perspective was from the back of the hall, looking over the lecture hall as it descended towards the podium. The teacher himself was wearing beige pants and possibly a beige jacket, but the Image was not clear in the region of the teacher's face. Accompanying this Image was a nonverbal desire to listen to him, but how that desire was communicated was not clear. Here, the lack of focus of the teacher's face seemed to reflect the fact that Jim did not know this individual.

Sample #11, however, was of a familiar individual, but the face was still blurry. Sample #1 was described above in the Feelings section, and took place just after Jim had finished a telephone conversation with a man who asked him to do a show. The man's face was blurry or out of focus, even though Jim knew him well. Here, the lack of focus seemed to reflect Jim's lack of clarity about the decision the man was asking him to make.

The third Image, which was to some degree blurry, occurred at Sample #14. At this moment, Jim's attention was focused on an Image of the interior of a particular art gallery. The Image had all the characteristics of actually seeing the gallery, viewed from the perspective of standing next to the main office looking down the ramp into the secondary gallery. Parts of this Image were in crisp focus, such as the shelves where the art objects would be displayed and the step down into the gallery. However, the particular art objects on the shelves were themselves indistinct. Here again, as in #11, the blurriness seemed to carry a particular meaning for Jim, as the lack of focus on the particular art seems to have lent a particular sense of "gallery-ness" to the Image.

The last characteristic of the Images to be noted is relevant to our later discussion of the role of words in Jim's thoughts. In one sample (#37), Jim was eating lunch, and simultaneously focusing on an Image of the word "bereavement." This word had been used by a salesman who had telephoned selling burial plots a few minutes earlier. At the present moment, however, the word "bereavement" itself was seen imaginally, as if printed in a familiar handwritten style, possibly Jim's own. The experience was of looking at the letters that make up the word, and in particular at their spatial relationships: that is, the way the shape of the "b" fit with the shape of the "e" was the focus of Jim's attention. Thus, this example is similar to the real visualization of the "CAUTION" sign, in that visual characteristics, not semantic meanings, were the focus of attention.

NOTICING CHARACTERISTICS

The next characteristic, which we will call Noticing Characteristics, occurred 14 times in the 43 samples. In each of these examples, Jim was focused on some particular aspect of a visual scene. In Sample #41, he was putting kiln wash on the kiln prior to firing. He was observing a particular brick in the kiln wall, where the soft brick had been eaten away by fire. There was nothing that could be said to be thematic about this observation. That is, he was not considering whether to replace that brick, or thinking about how hot that spot must have been, etc. Rather, he was simply noticing that particular brick and its erosion.

In Sample #8, he was walking toward the garbage can with some trash, and was taking in the characteristics of the cardboard box that was sticking out of the can. Although he recognized the box as being one he had put into the can earlier, at the time of the beep he was not recognizing or recollecting, but merely noticing the particular cardboard emerging from the can.

In Sample #40, he was in the glaze area, and was turning around to view three bisqued pots. He was at that moment observing the roundness of the forms, that is, the shape of the pots. Here again, there was no additional meaning, merely an observing of the forms.

In Sample #45, he was reading the word "Interest" on his bank statement, and was focused on the visual effect (not the meaning) of the word. In this example, he was not focused on or comparing individual letters, but rather taking in the effect of the whole word.

Some of these Noticings were comparisons of two or more objects. In Sample #42, Jim was loading the kiln and visually comparing the size of the setting bricks and a vase that he was about to put in place. Both objects were in sight, with the focus being more on the vase than the bricks. There was a direct recognition that the vace was too tall, although there were no words used in that comparison.

We have described Sample #19 and #34 above in the Feelings section. Sample #19 was the observing of the two cut-out spaces in a pot that was notched for a handle-like construction. The focus of that observation was on the alignment or relationship of the two negative spaces. Sample #34 was the pouring of Coke into a Styrofoam cup, and noticing the relative volume of the poured liquid and the rising foam. Sample #37, where Jim was noticing the relationship of the letters in the word "bereavement" printed in imagination, was described in the Image section, and illustrates that this kind of comparative noticing need not be limited to actual visualizations, but may take place in imagination also.

The above examples of Noticings have all involved the visual shapes of the objects noticed. There were two examples where the noticing was a direct apprehension of color. Here again, as in the previous paragraph, one was a simple noticing of color, while the other was a comparative noticing. The simple noticing of color involved focusing on the particular shade of red in which the word "CAUTION" was printed (described above in the Feelings section, Sample #10). The center of this experience was the noticing of the redness.

The comparative example is Sample #33, where Jim was in the process of attaching a handle to a pot. He had filled in the surfaces where the handle attached with slip, a diluted form of clay, and was noticing the different colors: the reddish-brown color of the slip and the greenish color of the clay form. While this difference in color had artistic significance in that the fired slip would be a somewhat different color from the rest of the pot (which would affect the glazing), and therefore

Jim knew he would eventually have to be careful to remove any traces of the slip, at the moment of the beep neither of these meanings was evident. Jim was merely noticing the two colors.

JUST DOING

There were five samples which we will call Just Doing, where Jim was performing some action without the accompaniment of any Image or particular Noticing, etc. Sample #12 occurred while Jim was trying to fix the radio. He was using a screwdriver to short possible connections together as a way of discovering which part of the circuit might have a problem. The experience was of being "sort of on automatic," manipulating the radio, touching first one connection and then the next. There were no associated Images or verbalizations, and no particular Noticings of any visual aspect of the radio at that time. Sample #38 occurred while Jim was walking through his living room, and he had just heard a "boom." Somewhat startled, he looked around to his left. There was no detectable Image or meaningful attention; for example, he was not wondering what had fallen. At that moment, he was merely reacting.

Sample #43 had been described in the Feelings section, and occurred while Jim was rushing to unload bisque from a plywood lid during a newspaper fire. Here again, the meaning of the moment was apparently carried entirely by the action, in that there was no Image or verbal or nonverbal consideration of, for example, the possible outcome of moving two slowly. Sample #31 occurred when Jim was turning a large bucket of clay that had a greenware pot on top of it. He was intent on the turning, being careful not to knock over the pot. His concentration was merely on the turning.

The Just Doing category seems to merge into the category we have called Noticing. For example, Sample #15 occurred while Jim was closing the door. At that moment, he was humming *Yellow Submarine* and looking at the door handle, and the experience seemed tightly tied in with the moment. This sample was seen as rather similar to #8, described in the Noticing section, where Jim was walking toward the garbage can Noticing the cardboard box sticking out of it.

The two experiences are similar in that there seems to be nothing in the experience that extends beyond the immediate moment. However, the two are slightly different in that, while the door handle is merely being seen, the cardboard box seems to be the target of a slightly more active seeing which we have called Noticing. The same kind of comment could be made regarding Sample #42, also described above in the Noticing section. The comparing of size of brick and pot while loading the kiln seemed to be just slightly more active or thematic than merely seeing; so the experience was considered to be an example of a Noticing rather than merely of Doing.

BODY SENSE

The next characteristic we call a focus on Body Sense, and it occurred three times in the sample. The first example was Sample #25, described above in the Feelings section, where Jim was at the wheel forcing clay down on the wheel. His attention was focused on the sense of his whole body tightening as he gripped the clay. In a sense, he was "reading" his body. The next example is Sample #29, where he experienced a pain in his finger as he was doing a pull, and simultaneously focusing on the Image of Julie's teacher (described in the section on Images). The pain was clearly available to experience.

The third example is #28, described in the Emotional Impact section, where Jim was in the middle of a pull and was experiencing his body expanding in the same way that the clay was expanding, even though his body in reality was being held rigid and tight. This last example of Body Sense is different from the first two in that the body awareness is imaginal, rather than existing in reality. Nonetheless, these experiences share in common the meaningful understanding of bodily sensations (real or imagined).

VERBAL THOUGHT

Semantically meaningful verbalizations were present in Jim's experience at three samples. The first verbal sample occurred at #3. Jim was at his work table wedging clay, a process of working the raw clay to remove air bubbles, etc. He was looking at a piece of paper lying on the table on which was written the words "All it's cracked up to be," which he had previously jotted down as a possible punned title for a ceramic piece. While thus engaged, he was aware of the words "Is life honest?" being "spoken" in imagination. The experience was of himself speaking the words, although no real sound was present; that is, the words were more created as in speaking than heard as in listening. The words themselves were experienced as being in Jim's own voice, naturally inflected as if said out loud, and we will therefore refer to them as being in Inner Speech. The overall experience seemed to be part of a process of mulling over whether life is full. He was at that moment Feeling slightly depressed or low.

Sample #20 occurred while Jim was snacking. At the same time, he was saying the words to a song "in his mind." The radio was playing that particular song, and Jim's experience was as if reading the words off an album cover in time with the music. Exactly how the words were experienced was difficult to describe: they seemed to be "sort of independent of my control," and "almost like seeing the words," rather than speaking them. The experience was more like talking than singing, in that the words appeared like the screened words during a sing-along. That is, the words were just "marching along," rather than being melodic.

The last example where words are used with their semantic meanings intact occurred at experience #4. The Beatles song *P.S. I Love You* was on the radio. Jim was thinking of the letters "PO" as in "pissed off," and wondering about how people use initials for the words or things they are thinking about. The experience was somewhat like an "aha" reaction, a sort of "explosion" with the quality of enlightenment, as if a particular concept were coming together for the first time. The words, the meaning, and their significance all seemed present at that moment.

Words also occurred in three samples which have been described in the section on Noticing, and are mentioned here in the Verbal Thought section because they involve words, even though the meanings of those words is not important to the experience. Sample #10 was an observation of the red color of the word "CAUTION," Sample #37 was the noticing of the interrelationship of the shapes of the letters in the word "bereavement," and Sample #45 was noticing the visual effect of the word "Interest" printed on a bank statement. We must emphasize the *lack* of semantic meaning in these experiences. Even though words themselves were present and being looked at (actually or in imagination), the meaning of the words was not the focus of attention.

DISCUSSION

Perhaps most remarkable in Jim's sample is the role (or lack of role) of verbal meaning in his experiences. As we shall see, meaningful verbal thought occupies more than half of most of our normal subjects' inner experiences, while for Jim, the percentage was much, much lower. Furthermore, even when Jim did have a verbal experience, it was as if some or all of the semantic meaning of the experience had been eliminated.

Thus he could appreciate the redness of the letters in the word "CAUTION" without attending to the meaning of the word, or experience the words of a song as "just marching along" without their being experienced particularly meaningfully.

There are many ways to explain this nonverbal characteristic of Jim's thinking: Jim's artistic profession is by nature nonverbal, so that he had selectively eliminated verbalizations from his experiences as he practiced his art; or the nonverbal nature of Jim's thinking is what led him to the artistic endeavor in the first place; or Jim's thoughts during the sampling period really did include verbalizations, but the beeper happened to miss sampling them; or Jim's sampled experiences were in fact verbal, but the beeper technique somehow disturbed his way of apprehending the verbalness of his thoughts; or our other subjects exaggerated the verbalness of their experience because verbal thoughts are easier to report; and so on.

For the present, these possibilities must stand as rival hypotheses to be tested. The most likely explanation seems to me to be some kind of feedback between his artistic endeavor and his inner experience: His nonverbal nature may have led him to pursue artistic activities in the first place, and the predominance of nonverbal activity diminishes the frequency of verbal thinking. While that hypothesis is attractive, it remains to be tested with other subjects.

By comparison to our other subjects, Jim seemed more focused on the emotional or bodily aspect of experience, as when his body seemed to swell with the pot he was building, or when he was experiencing an unpleasant sensation associated with possibly having ruined a pot. Here again, there are many possible explanations: This clear access is the cause of (or the result of) his artistic temperament; or other subjects also experienced the same kind of emotional impact but failed to report it for whatever reason, etc. For now, we must be content merely to notice that this seems to be an interesting characteristic which further study may clarify.

A third characteristic which seems somewhat remarkable is the way Jim used Images in his samples. Some of his Images were quite clearly related to his task as a ceramicist, for example, visualizing the cross-sectional thickness of a pot as if held between his fingers, or visualizing glaze as if already splashed onto a plate, or visualizing the rock or air bubble in the clay he was squeezing at the wheel. The other characteristic of the Images that seemed unusual was the appearance of blurriness of meaningful portions of his Images, as when he imaginally viewed a gallery but the particular art objects on display were out of focus.

A fourth characteristic which distinguishes Jim's sample is the frequency of what we have called Noticing Characteristics of the environment. Most of our other subjects are focused most of the time on creations of their own experience: on Images, on Inner Speech, on Feelings, etc., and spend relatively little time directly focused on aspects of the external environment. Jim, by contrast, had frequent moments in which he was simply absorbed in some visual aspect of the environment, taking it in directly without at the same time mediating it through his own creations.

6

A Record Store Manager

with Susan M. Melancon

Benjamin Way was 20 years old at the time of sampling, and worked as a store manager at a record store. Ben, a native Las Vegan, had recently returned from Los Angeles, where he had lived with friends and worked in a record store for a year following his graduation from a Las Vegas high school. He was an acquaintance of the author, and had expressed an interest in participating in the sampling study after hearing it described one night at a social gathering. Ben provided us with a glimpse into the inner experiences of an individual whose life-style was somewhat different from that of other persons we had sampled. Ben, unlike our other subjects, had not attended college; while intelligent enough to be successful in college, he had thus far avoided that environment in favor of working. He was an avid musician; he loved modern popular music and it followed him everywhere. He was a single, socially active young man who dated and partied regularly and lived with three friends in a shared apartment. He was also a frequent user of recreational drugs and alcohol.

The 47 samples that Ben collected were relatively complex, and therefore almost all of Ben's sampled experiences reflected multiple salient characteristics. These categories, with their relative frequencies of appearance, were: Unsymbolized Thinking (25 of 47 samples), Feelings (21), Verbal Thought (22), Altered States (11), Visual Thought (5), and No Thought (1).

UNSYMBOLIZED THINKING

The most salient characteristic of Ben's thinking during the sampling period was what Ben came to call "implied or assumed experience," phenomena which we will refer to in this book as Unsymbolized Thinking. Over half of Ben's samples included some experience of comprehending or "knowing" that was not itself experienced in a concrete verbal or visual way. That is, the experience of the moment included some particular thinking or awareness of wondering which was somehow directly known to be ongoing even though no words, images, or any other kind of symbol was present in awareness. These implied or assumed experiences seemed to supplement or shape whatever physical action Ben was performing, or words he was speaking to himself or aloud, or visualizations he was seeing, or emotions he was Feeling. In other words, many of his sampled experiences had attached knowledge or information of which Ben was aware, and which he insisted was a real part of the experience being sampled at the moment of the beep, but which was Unsymbolized, rather than being a specifically noticeable part of his experience.

In some samples, the Unsymbolized component of Ben's experience was fairly straightforward and simple. For example, he was at work, scanning down two columns of numbers on a computerized inventory of cassette tapes (Sample #3). At the moment of the signal, he was seeing, side by side, the numbers 37 (the quantity of a particular kind of tape in stock the previous week) and 33 (the quantity in stock this week). Simultaneously, he was experiencing a "knowing" that he didn't have to order any of this brand of tape. He was not thinking in words, "I don't need to order," nor was he experiencing an Image of some kind which carried that message. Instead, the don't-need-to-order knowledge was implied or directly apprehended in the looking at the numbers. Ben's experience in this example of looking at the numbers was shaped by this don't-need-to-order knowledge in that the sweep of his attention down the columns of numbers was not interrupted or suspended (whereas if the numbers had been greatly different from one another, his Unsymbolized knowledge would have prompted him to stop and consider whether or how many additional tapes to order). This knowledge did not seem to emerge as a result of the looking, after the fact, but instead seemed to be a particular way of looking *during* the sampled moment.

The point we are underscoring is that Ben's knowledge that no tapes needed to be ordered was a characteristic of the experience of looking itself; this knowledge was not apprehended separately as a fact, verbal, visual, or otherwise (i.e., there was no thought such as "I don't have to order"); but rather was an indissoluble constituent of the immediate experience.

Another time, Ben was standing next to Chris, a friend and employee, at the front cash register, holding a compact disc "hit list" in his hand. At the moment of the beep, he was experiencing a nonverbal thought that, were he to have put it into words, would have been something like, "I have to teach Chris how to do this" (Sample #10). Ben was seeing the hit list he was holding in his hands; he was also aware of a customer in front of the counter, and of Chris standing at the register behind him, ringing up a sale. The experience of wanting to teach this employee something, and an associated Feeling of familiarity since he frequently taught his employees new tasks, was the center of his experience at the moment, but was recognized as being Unsymbolized, present in immediate experience, rather than explicitly stated or sequentially figured out.

In a third example, Ben was at home, talking out loud to a roommate about the contents of a rock magazine he had been leafing through, saying, "Just a general year in review" (Sample #17). At the moment of the signal, he was speaking the word "general" and had just turned to see that his roommate had fallen asleep, and was no longer listening. Ben's experience was an instantaneous "knowing" that his friend was asleep (which caused him to stop in midsentence) and that what he had been talking about didn't matter very much, anyway. If Ben were to have expressed this Implied or Assumed knowing in a verbal way, he might have said to himself, "Chris doesn't want to hear about this magazine; he's asleep!" However, at the moment of the beep, Ben was not thinking these words, nor did the experience have a sequential, one-thought-at-a-time quality about it. All of the dimensions described above were simultaneously present: Ben turned and stopped talking, immediately recognizing that his friend was asleep so was no longer listening to the conversation that was not very important anyway. While none of these dimensions was explicitly expressed in the sample experience, all were important Unsymbolized aspects of the experience itself.

Many of Ben's Unsymbolized Thinkings were linked to emotional events. For example, he had picked up a memorandum from the store management announcing a stock item price increase (Sample #20). At the moment of the beep, Ben's attention was not focused on reading the words printed in front of him; rather, he was Feeling angry and frustrated at the requested change, while at the same time seeing the paper he held in his hand. This experience was not verbal; he was not saying to himself in words, "I hate this," or, "This is dumb," although words such as those would express his reaction. He immediately recognized his Feelings, and, furthermore, recognized that the Feelings were not directed at the paper itself, but rather at the whole process that the paper represented: upper-level out-of-town management dictating decisions that would make it difficult for Ben to run the store as he would like and to stay competitive with other stores in the area. The Feeling he was experiencing, then, implied or assumed the significance of all the elements involved with the paper in his hand, as well as the memory of all the other times he had been given such a memo and felt the same anger or disgust or helpless frustration at what he was reading.

Another time, Ben was at work, rewinding a Chuck Berry tape he was about to play, and singing aloud *Maybelline,* the title and first word of a song on the tape he was about to play (Sample #25). At the moment of the beep, he was listening to or monitoring the sounds of the goings-on in the store, not attending to any one sound in particular, but rather keeping track of all the store's activity. At the same time, he was experiencing a strong sense of happy anticipation, of knowing the music would be playing soon. This emotional anticipation was directed at the song, *Maybelline,* but also was colored by a nonverbal Implied Feeling of familiarity with and appreciation of Chuck Berry's music, and also a direct Unsymbolized recognition that the "old music is best." This high-energy familiarity and appreciation was experienced by Ben as "security"; that is, Ben's anticipation was that in a few moments he would be transported by the music into the carefree familiar friendliness of Chuck Berry's music. *Maybelline* was experienced as part of himself; he later stated, "You take away my money, you take away my job, you take away my house: Chuck Berry in my head forever." None of the above verbal descriptions, however, were explicitly part of Ben's sampled experience at the moment of the beep. Rather, they were all implied or assumed, giving flavor or character to the sense of positive anticipation that he was experiencing when he heard the signal that day.

At other times, Ben's Unsymbolized Thinking was an unstated knowledge about an action he was about to take, or about the outcome of some event he was experiencing. For example, a customer had just returned a rental videotape and handed Ben two dollar bills to cover the cost of the rental (Sample #31). At the moment of the beep, Ben's attention was directed at the feeling of the paper money between his fingers and a nonverbal sense that it felt like more than two bills. This feeling was not exclusively focused on the bills themselves; that is, he was not particularly focused on the wrinkles or folds of the paper against his fingers. Neither was he thinking in words, "This is more than two dollars." Rather, the sense that occupied his attention at that moment was an awareness that it "felt" like more than two bills, and that it seemed that the customer had overpaid him. Furthermore, this sense or awareness carried the Implied significance of the consequences of overpayment: Ben would have to give the extra money back to the customer, it would throw his register off balance if it went uncorrected, etc. Thus, the attention was less on a sensory, tactile Feeling of the paper than it was directed at the Implied meaning of this Feeling and the Assumed consequences that would follow if his perception were correct.

The above examples illustrate, then, the range of complexity that characterized Ben's Unsymbolized Thinking. These experiences could be as simple as knowing that his friend was asleep or that the numbers he was seeing before him meant that he didn't have to reorder tapes this week. On the other hand, they could be as complex as an elaborate emotional reflection on the personal significance of hearing some Fifties rock-and-roll music, or the steps that he would have to take to correct a potential overpayment by a customer.

FEELINGS

Almost half of Ben's sampled experiences contained awareness of emotions as one of their salient characteristics. These emotional experiences ran the gamut from mild to intense, and were often associated with other experiences described in this chapter, such as Imaginal visualizations, verbal thought, or Unsymbolized Thinking. However, these Feelings, when they were present, were typically an important part of Ben's total inner experience.

For example, in a sample described above in the Unsymbolized Thinking section, Ben was reading a memo he had received regarding a store item price change, and was Feeling angry and frustrated at the required change (Sample #20). He was not speaking to himself any words, nor could he identify where the Feeling was experienced, that is, whether it was a bodily experience or one centered somewhere in his head. Furthermore, he was unable to describe how he knew his Feelings were a mixture of anger, frustration, and helplessness (as opposed to some other emotional or physical sensation). In other words, Ben was clear about the experience at the moment, and clear about what he was Feeling, but not clear *how* the Feeling communicated itself to him. He was simply looking at the paper and Feeling angry.

In another example, Ben was at work where a clerk had just asked him what he would say if she requested a certain two days off (Sample #36). At the moment of the beep, Ben was saying aloud, "I would say no," and was turning away from the clerk, waiting for her response. When he heard the signal, Ben was Feeling a sense of expectancy and mischievousness since he knew he ultimately would grant her request, but that his initial refusal would provoke her to complain and ask him to change his mind. In other words, Ben's verbal response was intended to tease the employee, to elicit a particular reaction from her, and the mischievous, humorous Feelings he was simultaneously experiencing characterized his true intention. Thus, although this Feeling experience was milder than the one described above, it was intrinsic to the meaning of the experience, and was more the focus of Ben's attention at the moment than were the words he was saying aloud.

At times, Ben's Feelings could be clearly defined as being physical or bodily centered. For example, he was in a bar with a girl on a date (Sample #4). At the moment of the signal, he and the girl were embracing and his total attention was focused on a bodily Feeling of arousal. The experience contained no words or visualizations. He was not hearing the noise of the crowded bar, nor the music that was playing. Instead, he was totally focused on the physical contact of their bodies, and on the accompanying emotions and rushing Feelings of arousal. It was an overwhelming, lusty, physical Feeling that contained no organized thought. His descriptions of the experience were almost entirely metaphorical: he called it "an incredibly hot Feeling inside," but not heat in a physical sense. There were "fireworks" without actually seeing inside his head any Image of fireworks. He was "thinking 'I love her' in colors, kind of like a red," with no words or colors actually present in experience.

We might note that this sample was collected early in the study period; perhaps if it had come later, he would have been better able to describe his experience in nonmetaphorical terms. At the moment, however, he could only say he was totally immersed in the intense emotional arousal of the experience that was centered somewhere in his body as he embraced the girl.

In another sample, Ben was at work, ordering compact discs (Sample #12). At the moment of the signal, he was physically looking at the numbers on an order sheet in front of him, but his attention was focused on a Feeling of guilt and uneasiness or fear that his girlfriend (who was not the girl with him in the bar [Sample #4] the previous night) would walk into the store. This Feeling of uncertainty was physically centered in his stomach. However, it also altered his experience of the store around him, as the door had become something of a place of dreaded expectancy, a place where his girlfriend might appear. Ben was not able to describe the Feeling more clearly; for example, he could not explain how he knew the Feeling was guilt or fear, rather than indigestion or contentment. Furthermore, he was not thinking anything in words, nor visualizing any Image of the girlfriend. His experience was not a cognitive wondering if she was going to come. Rather, it was a nonverbal guilty expecting to see her walk in the door that was centered in his stomach, and that fully commanded his attention at the moment.

At other times, Ben's experience was nonbodily emotional, that is, he was Feeling something, but the Feeling seemed to be centered inside his head rather than elsewhere in his body. For example, he was at work, singing aloud, "Na na na na na," using those syllables to vocalize a guitar solo from the introduction to the REM song *The Passion*, which he knew was about to play over the stereo (Sample #41). When he heard the beep, Ben was squatting behind the front register counter, singing and "playing an air guitar" (that is, pretending to play an imaginary guitar), and looking for a pen. The center of his experience was a Feeling of mild frustration because he could not find a pen. This frustration was not expressed in words, although if it had been, Ben might have been saying, "A pen should be here; why is it taking me so long to find a pen?" Thus, the frustration was associated with a sense of impatience at his unnecessarily wasting time. The frustration, however, was not felt bodily, as in his stomach or through the tensing of his muscles, at least not insofar as Ben was aware. He said that, instead, the frustration was all "mental," in his head. It affected his attitude but did not seem to be physically expressed.

In another example at work, Ben was listening to a recording of a woman vocalist over the stereo at the same time he was scanning an in-store transfer form he had just completed filling out (Sample #35). At the moment of the signal, Ben was noticing the way the woman was singing; she was just singing the word "never" with a nasal expressive pronunciation that made the word sound like "nevah." Ben's attention was focused on a negative Feeling or reaction to the way the word sounded; he thought her singing was terrible. This negative Feeling, however, was not experienced bodily. Neither was he speaking any words to himself about what he was hearing. Rather, the Feeling was a negative judgment or opinion inside his head that he knew meant he didn't want to hear that record ever again, although he could not say exactly how he knew the meaning of the Feeling.

Finally, there were a few cases in which Ben was visualizing an Image inside his head, with, attached to the Image, a remembered-Feeling experience. In these cases, Ben recognized and identified the Feeling, but the experience was not like Feeling an emotional experience in the present. For example, he was at work, describing to coworkers an incident that had happened to him when he had been on the telephone earlier in the week (Sample #1). At the moment of the signal, Ben was saying aloud, "Excuse me—I'm talking on the phone!" and simultaneously was picturing an in-color Image inside his head of store customers turning to look at him in surprise, as they had done when he had loudly spoken these same words a few days before. Part of the experience of this Image was, for Ben, his remembering the Feeling of fear he had experienced when the remembered event had actually occurred. At the moment of the beep, Ben was Feeling this kind of fear again (the fear being that someone in the crowd would complain about Ben to his superiors), but the Feeling was less strong than it had been that actual day. The fear seemed to be a part of the Image, in particular, a part of the expressions he was seeing on the faces in the crowd. He was Feeling fear from looking at the faces, but this Feeling seemed more to be tied to the Image itself than an emotional experience of the present. In other words, it was as if the fear were a descriptive element attached to the Image, in the same sense as the color or facial expressions were attached, rather than an emotion he was personally Feeling at the moment.

In another example, Ben was standing in his bathroom at home, looking at himself in the mirror, rubbing a hickey on his neck with a spoon to try to make it disappear (Sample #15). At the moment of the beep, he was seeing an Image of himself and his first girlfriend when they were both 12 years old; the two were sitting on the pool deck in her backyard at night, rubbing a hickey on her neck with a spoon in the same way Ben was doing now. The Image was dark, seen as if he were viewing the young Ben and his girlfriend from in front and slightly above. The faces of the people were not clear, nor did he see all the detail of the surrounding pool and yard. However, Ben's focus of attention in this sample was not on the pictorial detail of the Image, but on the remembered fear the two had felt that night as they tried to remove the unsightly mark from the girl's neck before their parents came home.

Ben's experience at this moment, then, was that he was seeing an inner visualization that carried for him a memory of his youthful urgency and despair, and he was reexperiencing that fear, but in a much milder way. Ben was definite that this experience was different from Feeling emotionally afraid or desperate as an adult, standing looking at himself in a bathroom mirror. Rather, it was that he was Feeling-in-recollection the emotions he remembered experiencing that night eight years before.

VERBAL THOUGHT

Inner Speech

Ten of Ben's sampled thoughts included experiences of silently speaking or singing inside his head. In most of these samples, Ben was silently speaking to himself. For example, he was filling out a deposit slip at work to deposit checks the store had received that day from customer purchases (Sample #32). At the moment he heard the beep, Ben was silently saying to himself, "Ninety-four seventy-two," which was the bank number of a check he was about to enter on the deposit slip. His experience was of speaking the numbers somewhere inside his head, hearing the words as said in his own voice. His attention was totally focused on the bank number he was repeating; he was not paying attention to the people in the store, or to the music that was playing, etc. He was simply repeating the number to himself to ensure that he would enter it correctly on the deposit slip.

In another example, Ben was walking through his store, saying to himself silently in Inner Speech, "I have to make this appointment" (Sample #8). Once again, Ben perceived these internal words as spoken in his own voice, somewhere inside his head. At the moment of the beep, he was seeing the store around him and was also Feeling a sense of guilt at having missed an earlier appointment that had now been rescheduled. His primary focus of attention, however, was on the words he was internally speaking.

In the above examples, Ben seemed to use his Inner Speech as a tool for remembering or concentrating. At other times, his Inner Speech was less directed or purposeful. For example, he was lying on his living room floor at home, watching television. At the moment of the beep, Ben was gazing at the random-tone-generator device he was holding in his left hand, and silently speaking to himself, "Twenty-six East Charleston" (Sample #18). These words were part of an address that he had heard a few moments before on a TV commercial, which had said "Nineteen-twenty-six East Charleston." Ben's experience was that he was idly repeating the fragment of the address to himself inside his head. He was not paying attention to the meaning of the words or trying to remember them; in fact, he was only saying the last two digits of the four-digit address he had heard. The silent words in this case were just a meaningless internal repetition of something he had externally heard that had no personal significance or value for him.

Inner Hearing

There were also samples in which Ben was listening to a song being silently sung at the moment he was signaled. In the first of these, Ben was just leaving his apartment, and Hearing inside his head a recording of a song by a friend of his in Los Angeles (Sample #19). Ben reported that the song he was Inner-Hearing at the moment of the beep was an exact replica of the actual recording; he could hear his friend's voice singing the melody and lyrics (". . . All the animals in the trees, from the graveyard I can see . . ."), and the accompanying instruments (piano, guitars, drums). He said it was like hearing a good-quality reproduction that seemed to be located somewhere inside and near the top of his head. In this sample, Ben's experience was totally a passive listening to the song. At the moment of the beep, he was also seeing, in reality, his roommate putting soup away in the cabinets, and reported that she was speaking to him but he wasn't listening to her words. Rather, his attention was focused on the song he was Inner-Hearing.

In the other example Ben was at home, stoned on marijuana, watching the late night news on television. At the moment of the beep, however, he was not listening to the news he was viewing. Rather, he was hearing a song by the group XTC inside his head. In this sample, he was hearing the lead singer, Andy Partridge, singing the words "*blue over all*"; at the same time, he was hearing himself, Ben, singing along with Andy (Sample #47). The experience of the sample was that the two voices were so much in unison that only one voice (a composite of the two) was actually heard. However, Ben knew that this single voice being heard was made up to the two voices, his own and Andy's.

Ben was insistent that the experience was not that of hearing his own voice merely doing an imitation of Andy Partridge, nor was it the same as only hearing the recording. Furthermore, the experience of his own voice was that of hearing it singing along, not of actively singing it himself. The choppy drum and guitar background music that underlies the actual recording, on the other hand, was not so clearly heard. Rather, it seemed to be more implied, but in a hearing sense. Ben described it as being just "bits and pieces," an echo or shadow of music beneath the definite vocals he was hearing.

Speaking Aloud

Twelve of Ben's sampled experiences captured him speaking or singing aloud. In some cases, his words accompanied the performance of a routine manual task. For example, he was at work singing aloud, "*Hey, hey, we're the Monkees . . .*" while reaching to pull a Memorex head cleaner box off the shelf for a customer (Sample #9). At the moment of the beep he was aware of the woman customer standing behind him, but was not thinking anything specifically about her; similarly, he recognized the brand of the head cleaner he was reaching for but was not reading the name on the box or remarking to himself about it. He was simply singing out loud while pulling the box down from the shelf.

In another example, Ben was at work, describing to a friend an earlier scene when he had "chewed out" an employee over a scheduling problem. At the moment of the beep, Ben was saying, "And he just jumped back . . . ," describing the employee's reaction to his scolding (Sample #13). However, Ben's attention was not directed at the story he was relating, but rather at his mechanical folding of a piece of aluminum foil that had been wrapped around a grilled cheese sandwich he had just finished eating. His words, although full of meaning and inflection, were merely part of an idle conversation to pass time. Ben's main attention was focused on carefully folding the greasy foil into a "perfect" square that would match several others that had already been folded by his lunch companion.

Some of Ben's Speaking Aloud samples were straightforward, declarative statements in which the semantic content of what he was saying occupied the center of his attention. In one such example, Ben was doing an audit with an employee at work, who had just come up one dollar short after counting the contents of her register (Sample #38). When he heard the signal, Ben was saying "Where'd we lose a buck?" with the word "buck" being spoken at the exact moment of the beep. He was simply speaking aloud and gazing at the cash drawer before him, without seeing any additional Images or speaking any additional words to himself. His tone of voice carried a matter-of-fact or mild, friendly inflection that was intended to communicate to the clerk that this was not a big problem, although he knew the missing dollar meant they would have to count again. However, at the moment of the signal, Ben's attention was not on a nonverbal thinking about counting again (such as was the case in other Unsymbolized Thinking samples), nor on any Feelings of irritation at the time delay; he was simply speaking the friendly words out loud.

At other times, Ben's externally spoken verbal thought was specifically intended to elicit a particular response from the listener. For example, Ben was standing in line at a grocery store checkout counter, singing aloud, *"Oh, to live on Sugar Mountain . . ."* a line from Neil Young's song, *Sugar Mountain* (Sample #14). When he heard the signal, Ben was gazing at a package of M&M's in the candy rack near the checkout counter, and simultaneously seeing a picture inside his head of the girl he had been with the night before. The Image he was seeing was of the girl's face, and was seen just for a second. The fleeting Image was accompanied by a positive Feeling towards the girl, and a sense of wanting to see her again. At the same time, he was aware of how the people standing around in line—an old woman behind him and a young boy in front—where reacting to his boisterous singing. However, in this sample, the focus of Ben's attention was on the Image he was viewing, rather than either the words he was singing or his perception of the people around him.

VISUAL THOUGHT

Images

Of Ben's 47 sampled experiences, 5 included some sort of picture or Image that was viewed inside his head. These Images were experienced as having a range of colorfulness, detail, and associated emotional or Unsymbolized content. For example, Ben was at work, fading up the volume control for a tape he had just put on to play (Sample #28). At the moment of the beep, Ben was mechanically adjusting the tape volume, listening to how the fade sounded and Feeling mildly satisfied with the result.

His attention, however, was focused on an Image inside his head of a woman who was presently elsewhere in the store, and who he suspected was a shoplifter. This Image was of the woman viewed from the side, just as he had been seeing her at a distance down the aisle a few moments previously. In the Image, he saw the tan trenchcoat the woman was wearing, her big purse, and her black hair, all silhouetted against a tan or colorless light background. The Image had no borders or sharp edges around it. It did not include any details of the store, nor was the woman's face clearly in focus. The center of Ben's attention was the trenchcoat and large purse.

Accompanying the Image for Ben was a Feeling of hurry, of his wanting to get back to watching her, and also a sense of Unsymbolized knowledge about shoplifters in general: how to handle them, what signs to look for, the significance of the trenchcoat and large purse, etc. None of this knowledge about shoplifters, however, was being considered in a verbal or sequential way. Rather, Ben just "knew" all these things, as if they provided the context or foundation of the picture he was internally viewing. At the moment of the signal, Ben was also physically looking at his surroundings in the store, near where he was adjusting the tape volume. However, he was not paying attention to the scene he was physically seeing; his experience of the moment was directed at his internal Image of the woman in his store, and his concern that she was a shoplifter.

In another example, Ben again was at work. A woman coworker had just asked him how many copies of the new Judas Priest album they should order, and he was looking at an inventory sheet in front of him where the numbers 0 (this week's inventory) and 4 (last week's inventory) were written (Sample #11). At the moment of the beep, Ben was seeing inside his head an Image of the picture from the cover for the album they were discussing. The Image was in color, showing a neon hand with long fingernails wrapped around a gearshift on a colorless background. The Image was not seen as the entire album cover; that is, it was not a 12 × 12 inch square that sat apart from the rest of the background, nor was the album title visible in the Image. The Image had no border around it, but was just a colorful picture of the hand seen in the middle of an edgeless space somewhere inside Ben's head. He was not thinking any words at the moment, although he was aware that he was simultaneously seeing the numbers 0 and 4 on the inventory sheet. However, his main attention was directed at the colorful album cover Image that he was visualizing.

Ben's Imaged visualizations were at times very fleeting and difficult to describe. He could understand the content and meaning of the Image, but in explaining it would use phrases like, "it was almost an outline," or, "it wasn't a complete picture." For example, in a thought described above in the Speaking Aloud section, Ben was standing in a grocery store checkout line, singing loudly, *"Oh, to live on Sugar Mountain . . ."* (Sample #14). At the moment of the beep, Ben was aware of the surrounding shoppers' reactions to his singing, but was primarily focused on a fleeting Image of the face of a girl he had been with the night before. He was uncertain as to whether the picture he was seeing was in color or black-and-white; it did not even seem to be a complete picture of her face (with details of her hair or features), but rather was just like a passing glimpse or outline that carried enough detail for Ben to recognize her identity. However, this visualization was also unique for Ben in that Ben's experience of the Image was not that it was located somewhere inside his head, as was the case with his other Images. When he heard the signal, Ben was staring at a brown package of M&M's in the candy rack near the counter where he was standing. The brief Image of the girlfriend's face which was the focus of Ben's attention was perceived by Ben as being forward in placement, somewhere "out with the M&M's," or in his eyes, rather than back inside his head. This Image was more as if the girl had, for an instant, actually been present, although the Image did not block out or overlie the external brown package of candy he was physically seeing. (Ben, of course, knew that the girl's face had not been there, and that he was internally imagining her face in some way.) Nevertheless, his experience was distinctly different from that of his other daydreaming-type visualizations, both in its fleeting, incomplete structure, and in Ben's perception of where he experienced it to be located.

ALTERED STATES

There were 11 samples collected from Ben during the study period in which he had been either drinking alcohol or smoking marijuana. His subsequent descriptions of these experiences were in many respects similar to his descriptions of samples that had been collected when he was not under the influence; that is, he was typically responding to external events in his environment, his samples often contained Unsymbolized Thinking, etc. There were also differences, however. At times, Ben's Altered States experiences were characterized by a greater sense of confusion than he normally reported during sampling. Contradictorily, at other times he felt a sense of greater-than-usual clarity and insight into his immediate experience (although when we discussed those experiences the next day, that clarity was usually less evident than it had seemed to him at the moment). The one common characteristic in all these samples was Ben's highly focused attention. Whether he was focused on an emotional Feeling, or a tactile sensation, or an inner experience of words or Images, at these Altered State moments, Ben's attention was highly directed, almost to the total exclusion of his immediate surroundings.

For example, he was at a party, and he had been drinking alcohol. At the moment of the beep, a woman holding her baby had just sat down in her husband's lap across the dining room table from Ben. When he heard the signal, Ben was experiencing a strong sense of appreciation for their happiness as a family and their obvious love for one another (Sample #30). Ben was primarily focused on the expressions on the couple's faces; he could see their happiness and love in these expressions. His appreciation of what he was seeing was not verbally stated, but had an unspoken meaning, as if he had said to himself, "How beautiful."

His center of attention, however, was not on his own Feelings, but rather was directed at the couple, at the apprehending of their happiness and situation that somehow he was able to share or vicariously experience. He later described the sample as "kind of eavesdropping," not on what they were saying but on the Feelings they had for each other. This sense of appreciation was not experienced as a physical feeling for Ben; that is, he was not feeling any bodily tingling or physical warmth. However, he was totally involved in the experience. He was not aware of the crowd of people who were walking around and sitting at the table beside him, nor of the loud live music being played in the next room. Rather, his attention was completely focused on the facial expressions of the couple he was looking at, and on his vicarious nonverbal appreciation of the affectionate scene.

There were cases in which Ben's Altered States samples were focused on his own bodily experiences. For example, he had been smoking marijuana, and now was eating some coleslaw that had been sitting out and was getting warm (Sample #27). At the moment of the beep, Ben's attention was directed to a sensory awareness of the slaw inside his mouth; he was particularly aware that the slaw was warm and not very tasty. At the same time that he had this sensory focus on the feeling and taste of slaw in his mouth, he had an Unsymbolized awareness that he was tired of talking about the thought-sampling device and procedure, and that he hoped his companions would not ask him any more questions about it. He was not paying attention to these companions at the moment, however, nor visualizing them inside his head, nor was he saying to himself in words, "Please don't ask me about it again." He was simply focusing on the nonverbal awareness that he was tired of talking about the thought-sampling study, and simultaneously experiencing the feeling of warm coleslaw in his mouth.

As mentioned earlier, Ben's sampled experiences when he was drinking alcohol or smoking marijuana were at times seemingly clear and fluid, that is, they seemed easy for him to grasp, but at other times were highly abstruse. For example, he was sitting at home, smoking pot, and listening to an Eric Clapton record on the stereo. At the moment of the beep he was holding a stack of 45 rpm records in his hands, and was idly leafing through them (Sample #21). While in the process of leafing, he was Feeling a fondness or appreciation for the records themselves. That is, he was appreciating the vinyl discs, not thinking about the artists who had recorded them, nor about the titles he was seeing. This positive appreciation was not expressed verbally, yet he recognized it as appreciation, and also implicitly knew that the Feeling included an awareness that he needed to store the records in a safer place than where he had found them. He was hearing Clapton through the speakers sitting beside him; however, his attention was directed at this Feeling of appreciation for the records he held in his hand. Thus, this inner experience was fairly simple for Ben to describe.

In comparison, another sample collected while Ben was stoned was one of his most confusing and difficult to describe. He was leaning against a wall at home, coughing, his back turned to three friends seated at a table. At the moment of the beep, his eyes were closed and he was seeing an Image inside his head of the three friends who were behind him (Sample #26). The Image was fleeting; he saw a glimpse of his friends' faces, but they were unclear and incomplete. He perceived them as almost overlaid on one another, like a flashing collage. This transient, fragmented Image was accompanied by a mildly unpleasant sensation of his friends' presence being "inside his head," somehow too close, pressuring him, and it was this sensation that was the focus of Ben's sampled experience. Their presence seemed like an energy or closeness projected into his awareness that was more personal and intrusive than normal thinking about them would have been.

When we discussed this experience the next day, Ben stated that it was hard for him to organize his experience at the moment, probably because he was stoned, and his thinking seemed even more Unsymbolized or automatic than was usually the case. The slightly disagreeable sense of his friends' presence inside his head, and the abstract, fleeting glimpse of their faces that was only just enough for him to recognize, was very difficult for Ben to describe.

This confusion was in striking contrast to a later sample also collected from Ben when he was stoned. He was watching television at home, and at the moment of the beep, was saying to himself, "Eighteen or nineteen," which was an idle guess at the age of an actor he had just seen on a commercial (Sample #44). When he heard the signal, Ben's experience was that his thinking was unusually fluid and clear. He felt he could exactly pinpoint the words he was saying to himself at that instant. At the same time, Ben was also manipulating a bag of peanuts in his hands, trying to get a peanut out to eat. He knew clearly that he was looking at the bag, and that he was feeling the bag, but that his attention was more on his silent speaking to himself the words, "eighteen or nineteen." Earlier in the study, Ben had noted that his sampled experiences were usually hard to grasp and describe, that there seemed to be more to the experiences than he was able to express. At the moment of this particular sample, however, it seemed to Ben that he was totally apprehending his inner experience. He reported the sample in almost exultant terms: it was easy to know what his experience was, it was easy to write it down (that is, the physical task of writing was easy), and it was easy to express himself exactly. Furthermore, he knew at the moment of the signal that the entire sampling process was easy. For the time, there was nothing confusing and vague about thinking for Ben; rather, the whole process seemed illuminatingly clear.

However, it should be noted that when we discussed this experience the next day, Ben's recollections about the sample were less clear than the experience had seemed when it occurred. He was slow to decide whether his feelings of fluidity and ease were related to the experience of thinking, or of writing, or of expressing himself clearly; all seemed to be somewhat true. In other words, it was much more difficult to explain the experience clearly in retrospect than it had seemed to be when Ben was experiencing it at the moment.

NO THOUGHT

There was one sample collected from Ben in which his experience of the moment was that he was not thinking about anything (Sample #42). In the sample, Ben was at work, walking through the store to a storage area in a back room where defective tapes were kept. He knew that when he got to the defective tape, he would be looking for a specific U2 tape he wanted to hear. However, at the moment of the signal, Ben was not saying to himself, "I wonder if the U2 tape is there?" nor was he visualizing the tape he hoped to find or the area in the back room where he was heading. He was eating a cold mushroom as he walked, but at that moment, he was not Noticing how the mushroom felt or tasted in his mouth. He had just finished talking to a fellow employee about scheduling; but at the moment of the beep he was not thinking about or remembering the conversation in any way. At the moment of the signal, Ben was just walking without thought, an experience he described as being like having a "void within."

DISCUSSION

In summary, we will highlight four characteristics of Ben's inner experience. The first characteristic is the complex nature of his inner experience. Almost all of Ben's samples contained some sort of implied information or emotional experience associated with his more direct verbal or imaginal thought. The Unsymbolized nature of his experiences made the sample-and-discuss procedure of this study at times a frustrating one for Ben, since he often had to struggle to describe his Unsymbolized experiences in an explicit way. Nevertheless, it is clear that in most of his samples, Ben was simultaneously aware of his actions and surroundings and Feelings and verbal or pictorial thought as well as many of the implications underlying these experiences.

The second striking characteristic of Ben's samples was the small role that verbal thought played in his inner experience. Although words spoken aloud were found in almost one-quarter of his samples, there were no examples in which the semantic content of the words he was speaking solely occupied his attention. This is distinctly different from other individuals who have been sampled while speaking aloud. Most individuals, when sampled while speaking aloud, report the words that they were saying and that nothing else simultaneously occupied their awareness. For Ben, by contrast, rarely were the words or their meaning at center-stage in his experience, and never in these samples did the words capture his entire attention.

For example, Ben might sing to entertain himself while he was focused on performing some routine task, or say something aloud while focused on the reaction from the listener that his words had been intended to elicit. Similarly, many of his internal verbal samples were replays of songs he enjoyed, or idle repetitions of words related or unrelated to his activity. However, much of his task-directed thought, such as completing an inventory form at work, or ringing up a sale at the cash register, was nonverbally experienced. He simply "knew" what to do, and recognized the meaning of the situation at hand, without having to verbally express it.

The third characteristic of Ben's experiences relates to those samples in which he had been either drinking alcohol or smoking marijuana. Although Ben's samples at these times contained the same complex mixture of inner experiences as when he was not "stoned," he here showed an unusual intensity of concentration. Whether he was focused on a Feeling, or a tactile sensation, or an internal verbalization or Image or awareness, Ben's attention was highly focused, and his immediate surroundings were temporarily ignored. Interestingly, at times this concentrated intoxicated state made the sampling process seemingly easier for Ben; his inner experiences became for him "crystal-clear."

On the other hand, sometimes his Altered States inner experiences seemed more difficult than usual to grasp or describe. Furthermore, the experiences that seemed so clear and fluid at the moment of sampling were typically less clear when Ben tried to describe them to us the next day. Thus, although drugs and alcohol seemed at times to heighten his perception and awareness, the clarity was temporary and difficult to recapture in subsequent conversations.

The fourth discussion that Ben's samples inspire is related to, or contained in, each of the first three aspects previously discussed; namely, that Ben's inner experience seemed to be an organic, unitary process, not easily broken down into separate units such as Inner Speech, Images, or Feelings. This organic, unitary quality lies at the heart of the complexity of Ben's samples. He did experience Images, Inner Speech, and Feelings, but not as distinctly separate entities, as has seemed to be the case with other samplers. Rather, Ben's Feelings and words and Images seemed to become separate experiences only in his subsequent efforts to describe them to us. He used words, but paid more attention to their Feeling-effect than to their semantic meaning (as in Sample #36, where he was mischievously responding to a clerk). He experienced Feelings as qualified by rather cognitive "knowings" (such as in Sample #20, where he was angry while reading a memo at work), and saw Images as inextricably conveying Feelings (as in Sample #26, when an Image of his friends conveyed an unpleasant sense of being "too close," somehow "inside his head").

Thus, for Ben, inner experience seemed to be something like a compost heap, where individual aspects of experience altered, and were altered by, each other in an organic whole. This is in contrast to other samplers, where Inner Speaking, Imaging, and Feelings more often seemed to be separate, but parallel and related, processes.

7

A Medical Doctor

Helen Jansen was a 25-year-old medical doctor working in a research department of a Dutch medical school. She was born in the Limburg district of southern Holland, and thus the dialect unique to that region was her native tongue. She also spoke fluent Dutch, English, and German. Our sampling conversations were conducted entirely in English. The sampling experience was part of her familiarization with the sampling procedure, as she would serve as translator for later sampling with Dutch- or dialect-speaking individuals.

Sampling took place over a four-week period, with a ten-day break in the middle for illness and vacation. It was possible to discuss between 6 and 9 experiences in a 60- to 90-minute session, and a total of 50 experiences were described.

Helen's inner experiences were predominantly verbal, with the most frequent characteristic being the presence of subvocally spoken sentences. These Inner Speech samples were apprehended as being in her own voice and localized in the front-center of her head. They were distinguishable from external speech in that they frequently were experienced as occurring at a faster-than-externally-possible rate of speed. She also had verbal experiences that were more like inner hearing than speaking. There was a range of completeness in the wording of both her Inner Speech and Inner Hearing expressions, ranging from complete and accurate expression in words to being verbal even though no words at all were present in experience. When she was speaking out loud, her inner experience was absent as if absorbed completely in the speaking

This work took place while the author was a visiting professor at Rijksuniversiteit Limburg, Maastricht, The Netherlands.

task. She also had inner experiences that were nonverbal, including feelings and images. Feelings were experienced as particular, meaningful, bodily sensations that could be localized in discrete bodily regions but whose further physical characteristics could not be described. Cognitive aspects such as meanings were frequently experienced as particular feelings. There were a few images present to her experience, one clear and distinct, another less distinct, and a third experience which seemed clearly visual but which did not include an image at all. Many of her experiences include several or many of these aspects simultaneously or cycling repetitively in quick succession.

VERBAL INNER EXPERIENCE

Most (at least 32 of 50 samples) of Helen's experiences included some verbal aspect. These verbalizations ranged from straightforward examples of Inner Speech, where her experience was just as if she were actually speaking out loud, except that there was no sound, to Inner Hearing, where she heard her own voice speaking words subvocally; to experiencing words that were Just There as if frozen in time in her experience, to Wordless Verbalizations, where she had the experience of speaking or hearing and the understanding of what she was saying but there were no words present in experience to represent that meaning. We will describe each characteristic in turn.

Inner Speech

The most frequent characteristic of Helen's experience (17 of 50 samples) was samples that occurred while she was speaking subvocally. These Inner Speakings were experienced very much as speaking out loud, in that her experience included an awareness of the activity of creating or originating the words being spoken. That is, Helen clearly apprehended herself as being the agent who authored the words being said. The experience was felt to be located inside Helen's head, not in her chest or throat, for example, and, in particular, in the *center* of her head just forward of the midline, approximately between the temples. The words were spoken and heard to be in her own voice, with the same inflection as if she had spoken them aloud, and the particular words being said were easily available to her.

While the characteristics of these Inner Speakings were quite similar to outer speech, there was one dimension that differentiated Inner from outer speech, namely that Inner Speech was apprehended to occur at a variety of speeds, ranging from the same rate as outer speech to considerably faster. For example (Sample #18), she was cleaning her cat's litter box, and while doing so was speaking subvocally to herself—"Just a quick cleaning up." These words, which were in Dutch, were present very clearly in the front center of her head, and had the clear characteristic of being spoken rather than of being heard, and seemed to be the only characteristic present to experience at the moment (she was, of course, meaningfully observing her environment and acting on the litter box at the moment). However, the words occurred at a faster rate than would be spoken aloud, in fact, at a rate faster than could possibly be spoken aloud.

In another example (Sample #21), she had just finished reading a short story and had caught a glimpse of the title of the next story, which was (in English) *Big Two-Hearted River: I.* At the moment of the beep she was thinking (in Dutch), "So there will be a number II." These words again were experienced as being spoken in her own voice subvocally, in the front-center space inside her head. Here again, the rate of speaking was faster than the normal out-loud rate, but not as fast as the "quick cleaning up" example. At the same moment, she was slightly aware of the radio playing in the background. It was not a clear awareness; that is, she was not paying attention to the song by Prince that was playing, and yet she was aware that the song was playing.

In other samples, the rate of Inner Speech was experienced by Helen as the same as that of her outer speech. For example, in Sample #12 she was on the flat roof outside her apartment looking at the violas that grew in pots there. She was focused on the seeds of the flowers, and the words "still too green" (in Dutch) were being said in Inner Speech, as if talking to herself inside the front center of her head, in her own voice, and at the normal exterior speech rate. At the same time that these words were being spoken, she had an inner visualization of the viola seed pods (this aspect of this sample will be discussed below in the section titled Visual Experience).

Helen's Inner Speech was experienced as directed at a variety of targets. Sometimes the words were directed at nobody or nothing in particular, and were merely said seemingly as an accompaniment to the ongoing activity. Examples are the "quick cleaning up" sample (#18) and the "still too green" sample (#12) above. Sometimes the words were directed toward some particular individual. For example, in Sample #39, Helen was in the kitchen putting away dishes she had washed. At the moment of the beep, she was subvocally speaking the words (in English), ". . . medically or psychologically disabled . . ." and this sentence was directed toward an imagined presence of the present author as part of an imagined explanation of the Dutch Army draft. The words themselves had the same characteristics as other Inner Speech: her own voice in natural inflection in the front-center of her head, this time at the natural out-loud rate. The inflection of her words in this imagined conversation included the slight halting difficulty of choosing the proper English expression, just as she would experience it in spoken English. The words were clearly directed to me as if I were there in her experience, but also had the characteristics of a monologue, as if I were not expected to respond. There was no inner representation of me in her experience; that is, there was no image of me. She just knew that her explanation was directed to me.

At other times, the target of her inner verbalizations was only partially specified. For example, in Sample #29 she was in the process of rather idly thinking about going to her parents' home wearing the beeper from this sampling study. At the moment of the beep, the words "Maybe I'm too much on my own," were being spoken in front-center, normal-speed Inner (English) Speech. In this case, the target of this sentence was partially identified: she knew it was a man, English or American, and that she liked him, but he was not any specific individual. In particular, he was not a member of her family, even though her family was the center focus of the overall train of thought, and despite the fact that only one of her family members could have understood a description in English. As in the "psychologically disabled" experience where she was subvocally talking to me, the English or American man in the present sample also was not expected to respond. In her experience, she knew he was "there" and "listening" and that was sufficient.

In one sample (#27b) the target of the verbalizations responded, so that the experience was more a conversation than a monolog. In this example, Helen was reading the debriefing questionnaire of an experiment she was conducting and thinking about the word "relationship" as it was used there. At the moment of the beep, she was saying in Inner Speech, "You're asking me how that relationship was," as if directed to a neutral, unspecified coworker. This phrase had the front-center, own-voice, normal-rate characteristics we have been describing. However, this example also included the experience of the Inner Hearing of a reply. This reply was more heard than said (see the description of Inner Hearing below), and even though there was a listener present to her experience, it was not the listener who was replying—it was Helen herself. The reply was heard in Helen's own voice, and this hearing experience was not in her ears, any more than the speaking experience we have been describing was in her throat. Instead, the voice seemed to come from a location somewhere rather distant behind her. The exact distance was impossible to describe (that is, it did not seem to be measurable in meters, for example), but it did, nonetheless, for some reason seem distant. This inner dialogue was actually experienced as being of lesser importance than a more central feature of this experience, which was a comment to herself that the meaning of the word "relationship" was closer to "emotional contact" than "efficiency," as the debriefing instructions seemed to imply. This inner comment was experienced as verbal, and the meaning was quite clearly "It means emotional contact not efficiency," but the actual words themselves were not present. This last characteristic we will describe below in the section called Wordless Speech.

Inner Hearing

In the Inner Speech examples we have considered so far, the central experience of the verbalization was that Helen was creating the words; that is, that it felt as if she were speaking, except that there were no actual sounds being created. There were three examples, however, where the experience of verbalization was more like listening to herself speak than of actively speaking, the phenomenon we call Inner Hearing. In Sample #15, for example, she was standing at the kitchen table picking up her cat. The cat had just put her paws on Helen's face, and at the moment of the beep the words, "How cold your paws are," were present, in dialect, to Helen's awareness. She had been talking aloud to the cat a few moments before, but at this moment, the words were heard, almost as if hearing actual words being spoken, in that they were in her own voice with her own natural rate, inflection, and intonation. The experience seemed to be localized in her ears, rather than in the front-center of her head in the Inner Speech examples above. However, the localization of Inner Hearing experiences was not always in her ears. For example, the "relationship" example described above in the section on Inner Speech (Sample 27b) included a hearing response that was localized rather distantly behind Helen.

The Use of a Foreign Language

As we have noted, Helen was multilingual. Her native tongue was the dialect unique to the Limburg region of southern Holland (and adjacent areas of Belgium and Germany). Most of her daily conversations, however, were in Dutch. English, while primarily a reading language for her, was, however, being used daily in the present research and our interactions surrounding it. She was also fluent in German. Of interest in the present context is whether Helen experienced those different languages differently, and the general answer to that question is no. Twelve of her Inner Speech experiences were in Dutch, while two were in dialect and three were in English. Except for the language difference, there was nothing to distinguish the three groups of experiences. Inner Speech was experienced in her own voice, front-center, at varying rates, whether in Dutch, dialect, or English, and the front-center location was indistinguishable for each. The same can be said for the Inner Hearing experiences. Helen expected, before sampling began, that certain kinds of thoughts would be in particular languages, for example, that thoughts about home and family would be in dialect. This was only partially true: the "How cold your paws are" example was in dialect as expected (Sample #15), but the talking to her family/Englishman (Sample #29) was in English. The general conclusion was that the three languages were more or less interchangeable in Helen's inner experience, and that the inner characteristics of them were indistinguishable.

Partially Wordless Speech

In each of the verbal examples described above, the verbalization itself, whether spoken or heard, was a complete sentence. In this section and the one following, we observe that her verbalizations were by no means always complete. In one example (Sample #6), Inner Speech was present but in a compressed or telegraphic style. In this sample, there were three verbal meanings occurring simultaneously and sequentially, interleaved and overlapped with each other and cyclically repeating one after the other and then the first again, etc., with a full cycle being repeated every second or two.

She was at home clearing away the dishes. At the moment of the beep there were present to her experience three verbalizations that had to do with eating. Each of the three verbalizations was in words in dialect, and each of the three had the characteristics of Inner Speech that we have been describing: spoken rather than heard, in her own voice in the front-center of her head, this time spoken quite rapidly. But the three verbalizations also shared the characteristic of being *incompletely* worded: some of the words in each sentence were present to experience, but not *all* the words. The whole experience alternated so rapidly that it was impossible to specify exactly which of the phrases or what parts of them were present or absent, but the overall experience was clearly of three incomplete verbalizations.

The three meanings, if they were completely expressed, would be (1) "I have to put these things in the refrigerator and rearrange" (because the item being put in was too big to fit as the refrigerator was currently organized); (2) "Will I have another piece of pie—it's late to eat"; and (3) "I have to put this plate back in the cupboard." The first of these three thoughts was experienced as the most important, and was the most completely expressed, while the meanings of the latter two were more telegraphic. The three sentence fragments alternated in experience, with the previous phrase apparently still there, while the succeeding phrase was vocalized over it, and the succession of experiences felt rushed or pressured. The whole experience was seen as a choice-point, as if the three verbalizations were competing with each other for priority in the sequence of actions which were to follow.

Wordless Verbalization

We have seen in the previous section that Helen had one verbal experience in which a verbal thought was incompletely represented in words. She also had 8 samples (out of 50) in which an experience seemed to be clearly verbal, and the meaning was clearly present, and yet there were no actual words present at the moment of the beep. It was as if Helen were Inner-Speaking, but with no specific words being formed. We have encountered one such example in the "relationship" experience (Sample #27b) described above in the Inner Speech section. In a simpler example (Sample #45), Helen was reading a newspaper article about an auction where Napoleon's hat was sold. The article was a correction to the previous day's newspaper where a story about the same auction had appeared, accompanied mistakenly by a picture not of Napoleon's hat but of the hat of a common soldier. The common soldier's hat was in fact fancier than Napoleon's. The present newspaper article pictured both hats side by side, and at the moment of the beep, Helen was looking at the picture of Napoleon's hat and speaking to herself a sentence the meaning of which might be carried by the words "What's so special about it?" However, there were no words present to carry the meaning. Despite the lack of words, the experience was verbal, and could even be confidently said to be in Dutch, even though no Dutch words were present and no further explanation of how she knew it was in Dutch could be given. The experience seemed to be located in the front of her head, but not in the same front-center place as other experiences we have described. This time the location was more towards both sides of her head, behind her eyes.

Wordless Verbalizations could also occur simultaneously, both with other Inner Speech examples and with other Wordless Verbalizations. In Sample #47, for example, Helen was typing her notes about a patient, and reading in Inner Speech her handwritten notes which said (in Dutch), "Continual back pain." At the moment of the beep, there were also two simultaneous experiences which, if they were expressed in words, might be, "I should go to lunch," and, "I do not have enough beeps yet," referring to the data collection of the present study. However, there were not any words present in either experience. The meanings were clear, simultaneous, verbal, and in Dutch (although they did not include words), and were experienced as being localized inside the back of her head, in the middle.

The Wordless Verbalizations we have described so far were of Helen's Inner Speech, but there was also an example of her Inner *Hearing* without particular words being present to experience. In Sample #35, she was at work coding a research notebook, on which the subject had written the note "Funny situation." At the moment of the beep, Helen was saying the words "Funny situation" in Inner Speech as she read them, and simultaneously Inner-Hearing the woman's voice as it had sounded during the debriefing interview several days before. This Inner Hearing was rather hazy and unclear, but nonetheless could be adequately described as a recollected hearing of the woman's voice that did not include words but that did convey her vocal characteristics, and that also included the situation in which she had explained her remark.

We might note in passing that the Wordless Speech type of experience was not easily apprehended at first. In early samples of this type, Helen used such words as "like a feeling," or "rather strange," or "vague," or "rather far away," to express her difficulty in recognizing that it was quite possible for her to have experiences that were definitely verbal, and even definitely in a particular language, but that did not include words. Similarly, we will further note when we discuss Helen's inner images below, Helen was also capable of having visual experiences without corresponding images. We should also note that Helen's Wordless Verbalizations are to be distinguished from Helen's and other subjects' Unsymbolized Thinking, since Helen confidently apprehended her Wordless experiences as verbal. Furthermore, she could distinguish between Wordless hearing and speaking and identify whether it was in English or Dutch, etc. These characteristics are not typical of Unsymbolized Thinking.

Reading

Helen frequently was beeped while reading either the newspaper or short stories, or more technical information. Most of these experiences included at least some experience of what we have called Inner Speech above. That is, Helen was speaking subvocally the words she was reading, in the front-center of her head, in her own voice, and usually at a rate somewhat faster than out loud. In four samples, however, Helen experienced a powerful feeling of comprehension or meaning which was nonverbal and which seemed to rise up from her body accompanying (after a slight delay) the verbal aspects of her reading. These examples are described below in the sections called Feeling and Images.

Word Repetitions

On two occasions, words appeared in Helen's inner experience that were neither Inner Speech nor Inner Hearing, but that just seemed to still be there, left over from some earlier experience. In the first example (Sample #38), she was reading the paper while eating dinner. She had read the first part of a sentence, and then paused in the reading to cut a piece of the meat she was eating. The words "must in the week of" then remained present in her inner experience, as if time had stopped so the words did not disappear as usual. The words had originally been said in Inner Speech while reading, but now they remained, not being spoken over and over, and not being heard again and again, but just frozen in experience.

The second example also occurred while Helen was reading the newspaper (Sample #28). She had just turned the page, and the words "STREET FAIR," which had been part of a headline on the previous page, were still present in her experience. She had said the words in Inner Speech a moment before, but had not read the story because the topic did not interest her. Now the words were still there in her inner experience, again not being repeated subvocally, but as if time had stopped. This time the experience was also visual, as if she were also seeing the words "STREET FAIR," although no image of that word was present.

Absorbed in Speaking

On two occasions the beep occurred while Helen was talking out loud. In both cases, what she was saying occupied her entire inner experience, as if her thoughts and her speech were one and the same thing. For example, she was talking to a friend about a schizophrenic patient, and was saying the words "deeply unhappy" (in Dutch) at the moment of the beep (Sample #26). There was no other inner experience: no images, no words said or heard inwardly to prepare for the external speaking, no emotional or feeling response. She was simply absorbed in speaking. In the other example, she was looking up the telephone number of a colleague, trying to find the right page in the telephone book, and whispering aloud, "Alfons, Alfons, Alfons." Again, there were no other characteristics of her inner experience.

Paying Attention

On six occasions, Helen was beeped while she was listening or paying attention to something or someone. These experiences ranged from just barely paying attention to being completely absorbed in listening. An example at the more absorbed end of this continuum was Sample #25, where she was listening to a friend talk about a professor the friend didn't like. As in the Absorbed in Speaking examples above, there was nothing else present in her experience—she was simply absorbed in listening to what her friend was saying. In another example, she was listening to the radio on which was an announcement about a particular pop group (Sample #19). She was actively paying attention to the message, oriented to the radio as if she had "pricked up her ears" and was expecting to learn something new. At the same time, she was adding up numbers on her pocket calculator, looking at the column of numbers and entering them in the keyboard. However, even though she was actively engaging in this task, she was not paying attention to it, and instead was entirely oriented to the radio. At the barely-paying-attention end of this continuum is the *Big Two-Hearted River: I* sample (#21) described above in the Inner Speech section. In that example, Helen was also listening to the radio while engaged in another task, in this case, reading. But here, the attention was just barely present, unclear, just a step above not paying attention at all.

Paying attention was more than a mere orienting response, but instead was sometimes rather a meaningful expectation than just a heightened state of alertness. We have seen one example in the previous paragraph, where Helen was paying attention to the announcement about a pop group on the radio (Sample #19). Here, the attentiveness was with the particular expectation of learning something. In another example, she was watching a TV episode of *Lou Grant,* about a supposed psychopath who had been accused of murder. Before the beep, she had taken the position that the character had been wrongly accused. At the moment of the beep, she was absorbed in watching the show, but with a particular expectation which, if expressed in words, might be, "What's the outcome going to be?" However, there were no words, but rather just a feeling of bodily orientation or suspense directed toward the television show's outcome.

NONVERBAL INNER EXPERIENCE

Feelings

In the sections above, we saw that Helen frequently apprehended meaning in a verbal way, either through the use of words or when words themselves were not present in experience. Here, we see that Helen also occasionally apprehended meaning without experiencing any verbal aspect at all. In those cases that we call Feelings, meaning was clearly present to Helen in a bodily manner. For example, in Sample #7, Helen was tired and was watching TV to relax. At the moment of the beep, she was experiencing a Feeling, which seemed mostly in her chest, of uneasiness or dissatisfaction, as if she should have been doing something else or that she had to excuse herself for watching TV. This Feeling was not like a real, clear physical presence (such as a pressure or pain, etc.), but nonetheless could be localized in a physical part of her body (namely, her chest).

Feeling was an important aspect of her Reading experience (4 out of 10 Reading experiences), both as a way that comprehension was expressed and as a way of taking a personal stance towards what she was reading. For example, in Sample #10, she was reading a newspaper article about recent escapes from jail. Previous articles on the same topic had laid the blame for the escapes on the jail staff, an attribution which Helen had thought was unfair. The present article was putting the responsibility more where Helen thought it belonged, on the understaffing caused by tight finances. At the moment of the beep, she was experiencing a Feeling of satisfaction, as if she were saying "Ha! At last!" although no words were present. This Feeling seemed to be localized in her chest just above her heart, although no additional physical details could be supplied. At the same time, she was Feeling a little hungry, and this Feeling was also expressed bodily, this time in the region of her stomach. The two Feelings were not simultaneous, but alternated back and forth at perhaps half-second intervals. These alternating feelings were not experienced as entirely distinct, but seemed to flow or dissolve into one another, interleaved, much as the Partially Wordless Verbalizations example (#6) about the refrigerator had, although in the present example there was no Feeling of rushing or decision.

Meaning while reading was also represented by feelings. In Sample #27a, Helen was reading an article, the particular sentence of which was "Everyone is a social scientist, and to ignore it is bad social science." The beep occurred during the phrase "bad social science," which was being spoken in Inner Speech. At the same time, the phrase "everyone is a social scientist" was experienced, not in words, but as a Feeling located in the region of her head, although the exact location was difficult to describe since her head at that moment felt bigger than it actually was. The experience was that her head was bigger and less dense than usual, and the meaning was felt like a cloudy presence inside that expanded head. There were no words associated with that cloudy presence, but it nonetheless was clear that it meant the "everyone is a social scientist" idea which gave the context for the phrase currently being read.

Another example (#14) illustrates this Feeling of meaning and its comprehension. She was reading a Dutch newspaper article describing the conflict between a neo-Nazi group called the "*Nordische Ring*" and a group of anti-Nazi protesters. At the moment of the beep, she had interrupted her reading to return her focus to the words "*Nordische Ring*," and this refocusing inherently expressed the observation that the word "*Nordische*" was incorrectly spelled in German, as if she were saying, "They didn't spell it right!" although there were no words to convey that expression. Simultaneously, there was a slow, gradually increasing Feeling of comprehension about which of the two groups was being described. The article had at one point been describing a "group," and it was somewhat unclear whether that reference was to the *Nordische Ring* or the protester group, and she had jut reread the previous paragraph in an attempt to clarify the membership for herself. The Feeling of gradual comprehension came from the body, like a wave of expansion that began in the chest and rose slowly towards eye level. The Feeling was similar to that experienced when riding an "up" elevator when it slows down to stop—as if the body is slightly uplifted. When that Feeling reached eye level, there was a sense of comprehension, a mild "Aha!" experience.

Before leaving the discussion of Feelings, we note that, for Helen, Feelings were always clearly associated with some particular more cognitive component, rather than being experienced on their own or free-floating. We will cite in the Multiple Experiences section below an example that amplifies this observation.

Unsymbolized Thinking

In one sample (#20), Helen had an experience of meaning that was carried neither by words or Images or Feelings, and yet she was quite clear what the experience meant, namely, that she was wondering about some particular thing. A moment before the beep, she had heard on the radio the words "brothers in arms." The radio had been on in the background while she was drawing a picture of her room in preparation for redecorating, but she had not been paying attention to it. However, the words "brothers in arms" had penetrated her awareness. At the moment of the beep, she was wondering why she had heard those particular words and not others that had been on the radio. This wondering was not verbal nor visual, nor did it involve bodily Feeling, although it could be said that it came from the back of her head. Thus, this experience of wondering is an example of what we have been calling Unsymbolized Thinking, and was the lone such occurrence in Helen's sample. At the same time, she was looking at the sketch of her room and realizing that it was not right—that the room was too big and the furniture too small. This realization was experienced as if it were being said, even though the words themselves were not present to experience, and is thus an example of Wordless Speech; this aspect of Helen's experience was in the front-center of her head, going too fast to be said, but definitely verbal.

VISUAL EXPERIENCE

Images

Three (of 50) samples involved some form of inner visual experience. These three experiences varied as to the level of clarity of the images present, ranging from very clear Images, to moderately clear Images, to Images not present, even though the experience was visual, paralleling the clearly present, Partially Wordless, and Wordless Verbal experiences which we have described above. The clearest of the three visual experiences was partially described above in the Inner Speech section, where Helen was standing on her roof observing the violas growing there and subvocally speaking the words "Still too green" (Sample #12), referring to the seed pods that she was observing. At the same time, she was simultaneously seeing in inner experience an Image that was clear and present simultaneously with the real seeing of the seed pods. The Image was of a dry, ripe seed pod, so ripe that it would soon pop open. The pod was seen below eye level as if held between the thumb and forefinger of her right hand, and included the feeling of pressure in her fingers against the pod, but the Image itself did not include her fingers. The Image was in natural color and natural size, just as if she were in fact looking at a real pod held between her fingers, and did not appear framed or in some other context, but instead was as if suspended in empty space.

The next example (Sample #9) was somewhat less distinct. She was reading a newspaper, and experienced herself as concentrated and clearly focused on the words she was reading, this time not repeating them in Inner Speech. The words themselves seemed to enter awareness directly, unspoken, and the meaning of the words followed just a moment later, conveyed as a quick bodily Feeling of expansion. Simultaneous with this Feeling was an Image of the *Hoofdgebouw* (main university building) entry hall as seen from near the ceiling with one's back to the front wall. There were no people present in the room, but other visual details of the room, for example, the stairs and openings into other rooms, were part of the Image. But all these visual details were visually indistinct, present only in shades of brown, as if Helen were there seeing and feeling the space around her, and knew the details were there but was not focusing on any particular detail. The experience was thus halfway between seeing and feeling.

Imageless Seeing

The last example of inner visual experience was the "STREET FAIR" sample (#28) that we described above in the Word Repetitions section. Of particular interest here is that while in this example Helen was clearly experiencing an inner seeing of the word "STREET FAIR," there was no Image of that word being visualized. She experienced herself as seeing, even though the thing being looked at was not actually seen in inner experience. This seems entirely analogous to the Wordless Verbalization experiences, where the experience was verbal but there were no words being formed.

OTHER CHARACTERISTICS OF HELEN'S INNER EXPERIENCE

Multiple Experiences

We have seen that many (10 of 50 samples) of Helen's inner experiences involved more than one rather separate experience at a time. These multiple experiences included interleaved alternations (the refrigerator Sample #6; the feeling hungry/feeling-meaning-while-reading Sample #10); simultaneous words and Image (the viola seed pods #12); simultaneous reading and experience of meaning (the *Nordische Ring* Sample #14); etc. The most complex sample in this regard involved six separable aspects of inner experience occurring simultaneously (Sample #41). In this example, Helen was reading a technical paper written by a coworker, and at the moment of the beep, the following six characteristics of her experience could be identified: (1) Wordless Speech, seemingly located in the back of her head, where she was asking herself (with no particular words) whether a group leader had had a hand in the writing of this article; (2) The visual and verbal recollection of a moment that had occurred a year ago when the group leader had, in a group meeting, commented on an earlier draft of the article. This recollection recurred as if in one piece, not particularly clearly, but included all the visual and verbal details of that interaction in its entirety. She was not seeing or hearing each individual detail, yet she knew that all the details were there; (3) Reading, in Inner Speech, front-center, faster than normal, the words "traditional medical skills need"; (4) The word "traditional" was a Word Repetition, experienced as being heard, overlapping the rest of the sentence as it had unfolded in Inner Speech; (5) A bodily Feeling of pleasure which was associated with the memory of the group meeting being remembered, pleasure in that she liked the people involved in the meeting and liked being a part of that group; and (6) A separate Feeling of ambivalence connected with the group leader's having had a hand in altering the paper—ambivalence because, on the one hand, the paper was the better for his intervention, but on the other hand, what right did he have to influence it?

All six aspects were experienced as simultaneous. Furthermore, the two Feeling aspects were experienced as being directly linked to their respective cognitive aspect. That is, the Feeling of pleasure was definitely linked to the memory of the group meeting, and the Feeling of ambivalence was directly linked to the question of whether the group leader had had a hand in the paper rewrite. How this linking took place could not be described, but that it *took* place was clear.

8

A Graduate Student

Sonja Smith

Sonja Smith (not her real name) was a 35-year-old graduate student in psychology; at the time of the sampling, she was married, with a small child. Sonja was born and lived in Austria until late adolescence, at which time she lived in London for several years, moving to the United States about seven years before the present study. Thus, her native language is German and American English is the second English dialect she acquired. Nonetheless, she was an extremely fluent American English speaker. The words quoted from the thoughts described in this chapter were originally in English; that is, they are not translated.

She sampled for nine days, collecting 296 samples, which had the following characteristics: Word Repetition, Self-Aware Thoughts, Images, Reverie, Taking in the Quality of Objects, and Actions.

WORD REPETITION

Sonja frequently experienced a type of thinking that included a mindless inner repeating of words, sentence fragments, or even whole sentences (32 of 296 samples). These words had lost their original mean-

This chapter, written by the subject herself in collaboration with the author, is a condensation of part of her master's thesis in psychology. This study was the first of this series of descriptions of random samples of inner experience. This chapter differs from the others in that (1) it was written by the subject herself (the chapter by Sue Melancon was also subject-written in collaboration with the author); (2) we used a different (mutually exclusive) system for counting the frequencies of occurrence of each category, so frequencies are not reported here; and (3) we were not as precise in making some distinctions (as for example between Inner Hearing and Inner Speech).

ing, and sometimes the words themselves had become altered; but she was nonetheless repeating them silently; furthermore, she was unaware of this repetition characteristic of her thinking until she participated in this study and examined experiences that were signaled by the beeper. At the same time that she was mindlessly repeating such words, she was also usually both concentrating on a manual task, such as driving, buttering toast, etc., and engaging in some unknown daydream or Reverie (for descriptions of Reverie, see the later section in this chapter), which may or may not have been related to the sampled words.

One morning she was standing in the kitchen buttering toast for breakfast when the beeper signaled her, and she realized that she was still thinking, "I am surprisingly nervous," a thought which she had consciously entertained just before she began buttering the toast. Sonja was confident that had the beeper not interrupted her, she would not have known that the "I am surprisingly nervous" words remained; but they were still there, "floating around" aimlessly, easily apprehended, but also surprisingly empty of meaning. At the same time she was also concentrating on the movements involved in buttering the toast, but without conscious step-by-step attention to the task. She automatically executed all the necessary movements. Also at approximately the same time (it was difficult to say exactly if it was in rapid succession or simultaneously) she was engaged in a deep Reverie, the content of which eluded her promptly as the signal sounded.

At another time, she was driving and listening to the radio and realized when beeped that she was still silently repeating the words "farm basket." These words had been spoken in a radio advertisement. She was also at the same time looking into the rearview mirror, and there was some Reverie that she could not put into words but that had to do with restlessness.

The words Sonja was so mindlessly repeating were quite varied, ranging from single words such as "help," to sentence fragments such as "I have never wanted" and "feeling frustrated," to whole sentences, such as, "I am too heavy," "I think so," "goodnight, my love." If sentences were whole, they were usually fairly short. The word content covered a great variety of themes and seemed unrelated to the reason that the words had become repetitive and mindless. However, length seemed to be a consideration in the Word Repetitions since most of them were relatively short, even when they were complete sentences.

Some of the Word Repetitions had experienced an alteration or distortion of their original form, which occurred outside Sonja's conscious control. Sometimes this alteration was slight, so that the words could be traced back to their original form. For example, the Word Repetition "eighty-eight" occurred when she had just finished reading about the famous photographer, Ansel Adams, turning eighty; "eighty-eight" was a corruption or alteration of the original "eighty." Another time she was repeating "3:41"; the original thought had been "12:31," the time of the last beep that she had just reviewed. Another Word Repetition was "lunch bag," which apparently was a corruption of bringing *tea* bags to a friend's office. Another sample found "I missed Thursday, Friday, Saturday" being repeated; the original thought had been about Thursday and Friday, with the word "Saturday" being added to the words as they became mindless.

In all of the above examples, the words had assumed a life of their own with her concentration or Reverie being otherwise engaged. Assuming a life of their own without her conscious control, the Word Repetitions seemed to undergo changes and deviations that were not directed by her but just "happened." The Word Repetitions always occurred while Sonja was executing a manual task that involved some attention but that did not require a precise attention to detail. Furthermore, the Word Repetitions also frequently (but not always) occurred simultaneously with the type of thinking called Reverie which we will describe below.

SELF-AWARE THOUGHTS

A second characteristic of Sonja's thinking was that she was a close observer of herself, her actions, and her interactions with others (62 of 296). She was not only a participant but also an observer of her participation. This self-aware stance ranged from mere self-observational awareness, which largely precluded judgment and was mainly restricted to neutral, emotion-free observations; to self-conscious awareness, which was colored by feelings of awkwardness and discomfort based on self-evaluation; to self-critical awareness, which was dominated by negative feelings due to a highly critical, negative judgment of herself.

Self-observational awareness represented the neutral aspect of Sonja's self-aware, self-evaluating thinking. During this self-observational awareness she was simply noting and recording herself, her words, her feelings, and her interactions without passing particular judgment or experiencing strong emotional attitude.

For example, during a shopping expedition, she was repeating to herself "granola bars, Twinkies" (a Word Repetition), and she was also aware that she was moving very fast. This awareness was separate from the fast-moving itself; that is, she was moving fast *and* she was *aware* that she was moving fast. There may have been a very slight judgment included in this awareness in that she may have judged herself as moving *too* fast; but if that judgment was present, it was so slight as to be difficult to determine. Another time she was observing herself in the process of forming an opinion of what was being said to her by a friend. She was listening to her friend and also simultaneously observing herself, her listening, her forming of an opinion.

Frequently Sonja's awareness was focused on herself in interactions with others. For example, listening to a friend saying, "I haven't in years," in response to Sonja's question, she was aware of their interaction in detail, of the expression on her friend's face and how it affected her, of the tone in her voice, and of Sonja's own response, which was that of feeling hurt. She was aware that she was not including a judgment in that awareness, merely observing. As another example, she was beeped in the middle of a conversation with a friend. She had become aware how serious they must seem and this seriousness struck her as slightly ridiculous and inappropriate. This self-observational awareness interrupted her participation in the conversation and turned her into an observer of it. The judgment of ridiculousness, however, was not *part* of the self-observation, but followed it.

In another example, Sonja was talking to her family; she was aware of their interaction and that she was feeling good about having a pleasant, happy, kidding exchange. In response to her son's repeated questions, she said impatiently, "They are on the table," and was aware and observant of the impatience in her voice. She was simply aware of this impatience, not self-consciously or self-critically. In other examples she was looking at a friend's smiling face, and she was aware of how pleasing her friend's expression was to her. Sonja was not only enjoying the smile; she was aware of enjoying the smile. Saying to her son impatiently, "Get your shoes on—let's go," she was not only saying these words, she was aware that she was saying them. Smiling a polite, social smile at a fellow exerciser, she was at the same time aware of the quality of her own smile as well as how she imagined it would be received by the other person. Talking to a friend, gesturing, she became aware of her own gestures. In all these samples, Sonja was not only acting or feeling or speaking, but was actually paying attention herself as the actor, feeler, or speaker.

The examples we have described so far in this section are simple observations of self. We turn now to describe self-conscious awarenesses, which included the presence of feelings of awkwardness and/or embarrassment. When self-consciously aware, Sonja focused her awareness on herself in such a way that it highlighted an already-present sense of feeling ill at ease. In other words, she became *uncomfortably* aware of herself, her words, her actions, and her interactions.

For example, driving with her son, she said aloud, "I should have asked her to have lunch with us—oh well, I forgot." She was looking at her son in the rearview mirror and exaggerating the last syllables as she finished the sentence. She was also uncomfortably aware of the exaggerated manner of speaking, which she judged to be contrived, unnatural, and a poor attempt at creating an ease that she did not feel. In another example, she was in the middle of talking to a friend, using hand gestures to emphasize her words. She became self-consciously aware of her hands and their movements. They assumed a larger-than-life quality in her field of vision. What began as a spontaneous gesture ended as an uncomfortable, self-conscious one.

Lack of spontaneity seemed to be involved in other self-conscious occasions. For example, smiling at her stepdaughter who had turned around in the airplane seat to look at her, Sonja was aware that her own smile was somewhat forced, not spontaneous and real. She had intended it to be a real smile, but for some reason when she became aware of herself smiling, the smile in turn became censored and she felt awkwardly self-conscious. In another instance, finding herself in an unrelaxed social setting, she found herself saying aloud, "OK," but imitating a Utah accent, and she became self-consciously aware of forcing the accent.

The self-aware thoughts we have been describing in this section have been either neutral or mildly negatively self-conscious. We now describe thoughts at the most negative end of this continuum, self-critical awarenesses which contained a strong element of judgment and accompanying negative emotions. For example, watching a basketball game with friends, Sonja asked her husband a question he did not hear, since he was paying attention to a particular basketball play which totally engaged his attention. At the moment of the beep, Sonja was critically aware that she had asked the question only to stay in the mainstream of an ongoing situation, and that she did not really care about the answer. She was also critically aware of her unease and awkwardness. Feeling ill at ease in the first place and then feeling left out by not being acknowledged, she readily blamed herself for social inadequacy.

In another example of self-criticism, Sonja was seeing her babysitter sleeping on the sofa. It struck her as an inappropriate thing for her to do, but at the same time Sonja was aware that she should not be so critical of something relatively insignificant. At another time she was talking to a friend, and Sonja realized that she herself sounded critical and frustrated about somebody she was describing, and furthermore felt critical of herself for being so critical and judgmental. Sonja frequently found ways in which she could be self-critically aware, especially in social situations when she perceived herself as she thought others would perceive her. Critically aware of herself, she assumed others perceived the same discomfort and faulted her for it in the same way she blamed herself.

IMAGES

Many (21/296) experiences in Sonja's sampling included strong, clear Images. Some of the Images appeared as part of a memory, as part of problem solving, as help in locating forgotten objects, etc. In other words, the Images were reality-oriented and of objects and people Sonja had seen before. For example, calling a friend who was not answering the phone, she let the phone go on ringing in hope that somebody would be home after all, and when beeped was seeing an image of the room in which the phone was ringing. The imaged room was as she had seen it before, and her concentration was on an empty space in front of the telephone, which seemed to indicate that nobody was home.

In other examples which included Images, she was reading an article about a little boy having screaming fits, and had an Image of a boy screaming; and during a conversation with a professor, she was trying to think of a better word than the one she had used to express the exact meaning of an issue. During the search for the word, she visually scanned an Image of the typewritten draft pages of a manuscript to see how she had made the transition from paragraph to paragraph so they continued the same thread of meaning. After this brief pictorial review she was able to supply a more accurate descriptive word.

The majority of Images were of this problem-solving kind. Sonja had just seen a man in a casino who evoked in her a series of thoughts and negative emotions. When beeped, she flashed on an Image of Jacqueline Bisset and a younger man reclining in opposite directions, which was similar to a photo she had seen a few days before. The Image proved relevant in terms of the thoughts Sonja had about the man. Another time she was trying to understand what it meant to her husband to have had what he called "his usual good time" with friends. Picturing their mutual friends, parts of interactions, facial expressions, smiles, how they related to him, and so on, helped her understand how her husband may have experienced "his usual good time."

REVERIE

Reverie was a type of deeply engaged thinking which left Sonja lost to her surroundings, but the content of which usually escaped her at the time of the signal. It was frequently ongoing at the same time as the

Word Repetitions described above, but it also occurred twelve times alone as the prime feature of thought.

Most often, when Reverie was occurring, Sonja reported at the beep that she could not remember what she had been thinking about, but that she was sure that some deep, involved thinking was going on. For example, she was reading "Otanez" on the side of a building as she and friends were driving in a car. She realized that even though the signal made her aware that she had been looking at "Otanez," she was not really absorbing the word but instead was deeply thinking something else that she could not recall. In another example, Sonja was listening to a friend saying, "In a few years I can sell it for a few hundred bucks." Sonja realized at the time of the beep that she was not really listening to her friend, but was thinking of something else that she could not remember.

In another example, Sonja was reading her son a bedtime story, and was beeped as she was reading "big, sleek tiger." She realized that she was just automatically saying the words and was also picturing the orange of the tiger; furthermore, she had drifted off into a Reverie which was unrelated to the story. She noted that the Reverie thought seemed fairly clear and understandable, if only she could have grasped it before the signal startled her out of remembering.

Reverie is difficult to describe since it proved very elusive. Sonja experienced herself as lost in some deep, involved thinking that took her thoughts away from what was going on in her environment. She recorded in her sampling notebook statements such as, "There was something else, but I could not get hold of it," or, "There was something else, something to do with being vulnerable." In other words, she had definite knowledge that she was thinking about something, and she also realized that this thinking was conducted at a deeply involved level. However, the beep usually startled her into forgetting what she had been contemplating so deeply. Most of the time we had to content ourselves with vague impressions of what the Reverie was about.

However, there was some variability in this vagueness and inability to pinpoint the content of the Reveries. There were a few sampled times when she was much closer to recollecting the content of the Reverie than at other times.

As an example of a fairly clear Reverie, she was sampled and found "it's hard when you have to perform" as a Word Repetition being repeated over and over, and there was also a Reverie. This time, she was fairly quickly and accurately able to reconstruct (although not to describe) the Reverie; she could say that the Word Repetition was a conclusion to the Reverie. It seemed that this particular Reverie was conducted on a more aware level and that, furthermore, it was better preserved, since the signal interrupted the conclusion and not the middle of the Reverie.

Another example of almost total recall of Reverie content was the sampled Word Repetition, "I am too heavy," which was accompanied by a Reverie that she could describe as deeply involved thinking about being annoyed with herself that she did not have enough self-discipline to eat less. Even though the words were not exactly there for her, she nevertheless knew the general, overall direction her thoughts had assumed.

TAKING IN QUALITY OF OBJECTS

Sonja had eleven samples whose main characteristic was the visual absorbing of certain qualities of objects in her surroundings. Several examples are: Looking through her closet and saying silently to herself, "I have too many clothes," she was at the same time absorbing the density of the clothes visually. Saying to her son, "you know those aren't for playing with," she was looking at brass coasters on the table and was aware of their being arranged in a circle (their usual position was stacked) and their being brass was more apparent than usual. The fact that they were coasters was not their dominant feature; her focus was on their particular configuration and their being brass. Talking to the baby-sitter, Sonja was aware of the blue of the baby-sitter's pants and that Sonja associated that blue with the baby-sitter in the sense that they seemed to belong together. Reaching for papers, Sonja was particularly aware of their whiteness.

In all of the examples, the target of her attention and awareness was a particular sensory quality of an object. There was no self-awareness involved, just awareness of certain qualities of the objects themselves which assumed disproportionate importance.

Several of these samples were accompanied by Reverie-type thinking. For example, she was scraping off clusters of browned garlic from the frying pan, and was absorbed in the brownness and crispness of the garlic. At the same time, she had a vague Reverie about her grandmother frying fish with garlic. Taking her jeans out of the washing machine and focusing on fluff attached to them, there was some vague Reverie that she could not recall at all.

Absorbing qualities of an object at times meant being aware of brightness, texture, and shape, as well as color. Watching her son turn over a card with the picture of a strawberry, she noted the particular brightness and vividness of the strawberry. At the hairdresser, while walking to the dryer, she was aware of the plastic of the hood, its transparency and the scratches that were visible. Looking at the picture of a linen blouse, she noticed the quality of the linen, its characteristic texture, and the fact that it was see-through.

These objects of Sonja's attention loomed larger-than-life in her observation, and assumed qualities possibly clearer, brighter, and more noticeable than they actually possessed, or than they appeared to have at other times. Furthermore, it is possible that the signal itself helped focus and sharpen an awareness that was, however, already present.

ACTIONS: DOING, READING, LISTENING, TALKING

One of the largest categories (78/296) was composed of merely executing daily tasks involving talking, reading, watching television, listening, looking, cooking, and so on.

For example, one signal found Sonja looking at a red Duplo cube and checking with the picture on the container to see where it should be placed. There was no Reverie, no Image, no Word Repetition, none of the other thought characteristics. She was merely concentrating on the task at hand. Saying to her son, "No, it isn't," and reaching forward to see if the automobile brake was released were the only actions at another sampling beep. Writing the number 97 as she was numbering sampled thoughts, sorting out magazines, looking closely at a photo to see more details, driving, answering questions, tasting curry, looking around the airport, listening to a friend, reading about the basketball team, and listening to a conversation at the same time, watching a scene on television and anticipating the next one, looking at her son's scribbles, packing for a trip, watching the strap of a purse fall down, sorting cosmetics, reading labels on a can of ham, typing, curling her hair, laughing, all were examples of the kind of activities she was frequently engaged in when the sampling interrupted her. Most of these samples involved little conscious deliberation. The actions were executed in an almost automatic fashion.

COMPARISON WITH SONJA'S PRE-SAMPLING EXPECTATIONS

The method used in Sonja's sample included the writing of a so-called "Pre-sampling, retrospective, general account" (or PRGA) before she began participation in the sampling itself. As described in Chapter 2, the purpose of this aspect of the descriptive procedure is to attempt to make the author's preconceptions about the forthcoming results explicit so that they can be suspended as much as possible during the data analysis, and so that the reader can gain some understanding of the extent to which preconceptions determine the final results.

We will summarize here how Sonja's pre-sampling description of her thinking compared or contrasted with the results uncovered by the sampling procedure.

Sonja's pre-sampling retrospective general account (PRGA) of her thinking emphasized her self-awareness, an observation that was clearly corroborated by the sampling. She had indicated in the PRGA several major features of this self-awareness; that she felt frequently more like an observer than a participant as a result of self-awareness; that self-awareness seemed primarily focused on interactions with people instead of occurring during times alone; and that self-aware analysis often led to critical evaluations, all of which were confirmed. The PRGA did miss some aspects of her self-awareness, however; for example, that a continuum existed on which this self-awareness operated, ranging from mere observational self-awareness to self-conscious awareness to self-critical awareness.

A second thought characteristic described in the PRGA which was confirmed during the sampling was Sonja's concerns with everyday living situations. The sampling data exceeded her expectations of the frequency with which this characteristic occurred. These thoughts involved concentration on the execution of simple, daily routines, such as sorting magazines, eating curry, packing for a trip, blowing coffee powder from a cannister, and so on.

A third characteristic described in the PRGA that was somewhat confirmed by the sampling was the appearance of emotions. Sonja expected that, whatever standards she applied for the definition of a full range of emotions, her own emotional experience would fall short of this range; that is, emotions were not experienced in an acute, intense way. The sampling supported her pre-sampling notion to a degree, in that emotions really did not play a major role in her experience. However, they were present more frequently that she had expected. For example, self-awareness was accompanied by differing degrees of feelings ranging from neutral to self-conscious to plainly negative, whereas feelings of both a positive and negative kind accompanied evaluative-type thinking. There were happy feelings, angry feelings, feelings of warmth and caring, and so on. They were rarely dominant but existed persistently, if quietly, and were more of a factor in Sonja's experience than she had expected.

A fourth characteristic described in the PRGA concerned the nonverbal characteristics of her thinking. Sonja assumed that a good deal of her thinking was nonverbal, based on a general impression and supported by the fact that she frequently found it difficult to put into words an attitude, an opinion, a viewpoint, and so on, about which she could give definite answers in response to questions but which she found difficult to describe adequately on her own. This difficulty was also evident in the sampling experience. The sampling method forced her to record a specific experience, but it was not simple, however, to put into words the sampled thought when it had some of those nonverbal components. There were strong indications that part of her evaluative thinking contained nonverbal components such as nonverbal assessment and nonverbal attitudes both positive and negative, and the Reverie category involved thinking that was so deep that it was impossible to say whether it was verbal or not.

We have seen that Sonja was basically correct in predicting some aspects of her inner experience. There were, however, also some salient discrepancies between her sampled experiences and her pre-sampling account. The most notable example was the Word Repetition category, where meaningless words were being mindlessly repeated over and over. Sonja had no idea prior to sampling that this dominant characteristic in her thinking existed.

A second discrepancy was that Sonja expected prior to sampling that there would be experiences of going "blank" under pressure. She had not been clear on what she meant by "going blank," except for describing this experience as an inability to think problems through to a logical conclusion, especially when anxiety, as a result of feeling pressured, intervened. Surprisingly, a thorough review of the data showed no samples detailing the experience of going blank under pressure.

A third pre-sampling conception about Sonja's thinking which was not confirmed by sampling was the expectation that she would have a type of thought providing enlightenment to a problem or general issue, and that she would actually silently say to herself, "Aha, that's what this is all about." This "aha" experience would come to her with great clarity and vividness, stopping her in the middle of an ongoing thought and creating a stillness, even a holding of her breath, followed by a feeling of exhilaration and relief. Sonja was surprised and even disappointed to find no evidence for such an experience during the sampling period. Other surprises included the depth of the type of thinking she called Reverie. She also had not guessed the existence of the Taking-in-Quality-of-Objects pattern which emerged during sampling.

In sum, we might note that while Sonja, prior to sampling, had good insight into some of the characteristics of her inner experience, there were others of which she was totally unaware.

THE FOLLOW-UP STUDY

Sonja's sample, like Sue Melancon's (Chapter 9), but unlike all the others, included a formal follow-up sampling period to check the validity of description and the consistency of frequency of the categories we had described in the first sampling period. For the most part, the conclusions reached during the first period were quite closely supported by the second period, which took place several months later. The differences between the two periods were: Word Repetitions in the follow-up sample for the most part were more closely tied to their original meaning. Furthermore, they occurred in longer sentences, although there were words missing in the interior of those repeating sentences. The Reverie category and the Self-Aware categories occurred significantly less frequently in the follow-up samples than in the original sampling. There were also significantly more feelings in the follow-up sample. Sonja reported that, in general, she felt more confident and self-assured at the time of the follow-up sample than she had at the time of the original sampling. Such a shift in general mood may be related to the observed changes in her thinking.

DISCUSSION

Several comments are in order regarding Sonja's samples. First, we get a clear example of one of the ways that words can be separated from their meanings in Sonja's Word Repetitions. These words, which were being mindlessly repeated, were apparently meaningless remnants of earlier thought processes. Words themselves were still present even though they no longer had meaning for her. The radical disconnection between words and their meanings is best shown by the fact that the words themselves could alter (e.g., from "tea bag" to "lunch bag") as they silently repeated themselves.

Another unusual characteristic of Sonja's samples is that a content category (Self-Aware Thoughts) emerged as a salient characteristic of her inner experience. Most of what emerges as salient from our subjects' samples are process, rather than content, characteristics, such as the frequent presence of Images or Unsymbolized Thinking, etc. Sonja spent much of her time during the sampling period observing or criticizing characteristics of herself. This result shows that the sampling method can identify content areas that preoccupy subjects during the time that they are sampled.

Sonja's comparison between her pre-sampling description and the sampling results is typical of our subjects: people are familiar with some, but not all, characteristics of their inner experience. The Pre-Sampling Retrospective General Account was also designed to give the reader a chance to evaluate our ability to suspend our preconceptions and observe accurately the ongoing inner experience. The fact that Sonja's samples were in some ways similar but in some ways different from what she expected gives us confidence that she was not merely observing in accord with her preconceptions.

The follow-up study also gives us some confidence in our method. The fact that the descriptions created in the initial sampling were all found to be adequate when applied to each of the new samples in the follow-up study gives us some confidence that the characteristics that we described initially were not merely idiosyncratic results of the particular samples that happened to appear in the initial sampling period, but instead represented real characteristics of Sonja's inner experience. The changes that Sonja's follow-up sample showed (that inner words were somewhat more meaningful and that the frequency of Reverie decreased) we preliminarily link to the increase in self-esteem that occurred in the months between the initial and follow-up samples. This is in accord with our findings in another ongoing study where we sample depressed subjects.

We will describe our observations about depression in a sequel to the present book. Chapter 17 describes some of our preliminary depression results briefly.

9

A Research Associate

Susan M. Melancon

Susan Melancon, who was both subject and author of this chapter, was, at the time of sampling, 32 years old and married. She held a master's degree in both biology and rehabilitation counseling, and was employed at the university as a research associate. She chose to participate in this study out of interest, and her participation did not fulfill any formal requirements. She is a native American-English speaker.

During a period of slightly over two weeks, Sue was beeped 197 times, and five distinct characteristics of her inner experience emerged: Verbal Thought, "wondering" or Unsymbolized Thinking, Images, Observations, and No Thought.

VERBAL THOUGHT

Inner Speech

Twenty-three percent of Sue's samples included a thinking process that was experienced as her own voice speaking silently inside her head. These thoughts differed from the Inner Hearing experiences that we will describe below, in that her Inner Speech was more actively initiated, rather than passively received, and was often used for more complex thinking, such as problem solving or evaluation. For example, Sue was looking at a package of ground beef while preparing dinner and silently saying, "This meat has discolored but should still be all right to cook" (Sample #19). She was speaking these words inside her head, in her own voice, at its natural rate of speed and naturally inflected, while deciding what to fix for supper. Another time, she was silently saying,

"I'm at the pivotal time of my life," and had just come to the word, "pivotal" (Sample #67). Sometimes there were images associated with her Inner Speech. For example, she was saying to herself, "That's OK," in response to an instructor's question if a class could meet in his private office, and simultaneously she was imaging an office (Sample #96).

In these three examples, her Inner Speech was experienced as herself speaking in a declarative, matter-of-fact tone. At times, however, there was sometimes an emotional sound to the words she was Inner-Speaking. For example, she was driving away from school after the first night of classes, thinking, "This is going to be absolutely, positively, totally fucking great!" (Sample #97). The silent inflection to her internal words was full of enthusiasm and excitement. Another time, she was silently singing a line from a song, "I put a pebble in my shoe . . ." (Sample #165), with the same melody and rhythmic style as when she had sung them externally at a wedding a few weeks earlier.

Occasionally the sampling captured her silently talking to herself, but in a more detached fashion, almost as if a third person were speaking. For example, she was thinking, "Don't panic . . . this is what you must do" (Sample #175). She was experiencing her own voice speaking to herself in an instructional, authoritative tone, in order to reduce her anxiety over an ongoing legal responsibility.

There were also examples when Sue's Inner Speech was experienced as if she were talking to an external individual. For example, she was thinking, "Would it be all right if I left my sweater here?" (Sample #156). She was at this moment taking off her sweater in a hospice facility and thinking these words in anticipation of leaving it in the nurses' station. She recognized the words she was silently speaking as her own voice, with an inflection as if she were asking the question of one of the nurses on duty that night. Another time, she was standing in line at a self-service gas station, thinking, "Fill up on number ten," this time in anticipation of paying the cashier for her gas (Sample #140).

Another time, she was walking outside thinking, "My God, what does all this mean?" (Sample #45). This thought was, for her, similar to the above two examples in that she was Inner-Speaking silently with her own voice to an external individual. However, there was also an important distinction between this thought and the others. The thoughts directed to the nurse and gas station attendant were experienced to be like idle role-playing of an anticipated event. The conversational prayer, silently speaking to God, was experienced by her as an actual one-sided conversation with someone who was actively listening and understanding what she was saying. This thought was not a reflexive or idle exclamation; rather, it had the tonal inflections of a silent question being asked of someone who was expected to provide an answer.

Conversations were sometimes replayed in Sue's imagination. As we will see below, when another person was speaking, this was experienced as an Inner Hearing of the other person's voice, apparently exactly as it had originally been heard in reality. However, when Sue recalled herself speaking in a conversation, it was experienced as an Inner Speaking. For example, Sue was remembering saying to someone, "The anxiety is not from coming here—it's been coming a long time . . ." (Sample #184). Sue was speaking these words to herself in a silent reenactment of a previous conversation. Another time, she was recalling her words to a man with whom she had spoken on the phone the previous evening about a mutual friend, saying, "Jill has a new job too" (Sample #192). Once again, she was speaking these words, inside her head, as she remembered having said them the previous night.

Inner Hearing

Eleven percent of Sue's sampled thoughts were collected while she was either reading silently to herself or writing. For example, she was reading a data table at work, "calculations for determination of mass balance for PESTAN runs" (Sample #69). As her eyes scanned this line of printed material, her recognition of meaning in the words being read was perceived as hearing her own voice silently speaking the words to herself. This Inner Hearing was distinctly different from Inner Speech in that the Inner Hearing was a *passive* experience, as if words and sentences that she was physically seeing written on the page were being created in her own voice inside her head, while in the Inner Speech examples, she experienced herself as *actively creating* the words being said.

Another time, while waiting to be served at a bank, she was reading an excerpt from a legal document, "order setting aside estate without administration," and internally hearing these words silently repeated as she read (Sample #112). The next day, she was reading from a psychology text, "The I.Q., as measured by most intelligence tests . . ." (Sample #114). Once again, she was simultaneously hearing these words inside her head, and in fact, was hearing the word, "intelligence," at the moment the sampling beeper sounded.

Similarly, when she was writing, she heard words mentally spoken concurrently with putting them on paper. For example, she was writing down the following scripture quotation, "Pick up your stretcher and walk" (Sample #163). She heard each word inside her head at the same time that it was written. In cases where what she was reading was not recognizable as meaningful words, what she silently heard were the individual letter components of what was being read, for example, while reading a line from an eye chart in an optometrist's office ("DCSKO"), or the name of a computer file ("PRZPS") (Samples #194, 150). When what she was reading or writing was a number or symbol, she heard the sequence of numerals or the symbolic meaning. For example, "5.35" was heard as "five point three five" (Sample #180); the phrase "change to ~ 30" was heard as "change to approximately thirty" (#135).

Inner Hearing was Sue's primary inner experience while reading or writing. However, there were a few times where Inner Hearing did not accompany reading. For example, she was reading a name in the campus phone directory, "Charles M," and simultaneously was saying to herself, in Inner Speech, "Operations and Maintenance," in anticipation of making a phone call to that department (Sample #168). Her eyes were looking at printed words ("Charles M") and these words had meaning to her, but the silent voice was saying, "Operations and Maintenance," rather than what she was seeing in print.

Sometimes reading and writing activities were accompanied by both Inner Hearing and mental Images. For example, she was reading from a novel the line, "Ricki the bartender and Priscilla the waitress . . ."; simultaneously with hearing these words internally spoken in her own voice, she was picturing in imagination the scene being described (Sample #142). At another time, during work, she was writing the words, "What is the relationship between bulk density . . ." (Sample #10). At the same time that she was writing and Inner-Hearing this question, she was picturing inside her head a co-worker whom she had been speaking to about bulk density earlier on the phone.

There were also instances where the silent words she heard while reading or writing were associated with the nonverbal questioning called "wondering" (described below). For example, she was reading a line from a personal letter: "his first edition has an index; the second, sadly, does not" (Sample #75). At the same time as she was Inner-Hearing these words in her own voice, however, she was nonverbally wondering whether a friend's copy of this book, to which she had access, was a first or second edition. In another example, she was reading her handwritten notes at work, "Lucien curve—interested only when there is a concentration at 200 cm" (Sample #79). She was hearing these words silently spoken as she read (with the abbreviation "cm" being heard as "centimeters"), but she was also simultaneously wondering if a woman with whom she had been recently working would be at her office that day.

Nine percent of Sue's samples involved Inner Hearing, which occurred at times other than when she was reading. When this occurred, she was silently hearing what she identified as her own voice, speaking to herself, usually without meaningful tonal inflection, and was simultaneously engaged in other activity. Sometimes the word(s) being mentally heard acted as a "cue," that is, a memory aid or reminder of what she was doing. For example, she was Inner-Hearing the words, "standard score," while leafing through a statistics book looking for a discussion of this subject (Sample #132). At another time, she was Inner-Hearing the word, "five," while scanning a computer printout at work, looking for chemical data from the 0–5 cm depth compartment in a fate and transport model simulation (Sample #65). Later that same day, she was hearing the word, "Farmers," and reaching for a phone book to get the number of her insurance agent (Sample #70).

These cue thoughts were also sometimes associated with mental images, although the images were not necessarily directly linked with the verbal thought. For example, she was thinking, "Up ten and left one," while counting the number of stitches on a cross-stitch pattern she was sewing (Sample #29). At the same time, she was mentally picturing herself pouring a bottle of bacteria into a household toilet to replenish the bacteria level in her septic tank.

At other times, the Inner Hearing words, rather than acting as memory aids, were instead like silent verbal captions for her activities or mental images. Sometimes these captions had a distinctive feeling inflection in how she heard them spoken, which often corresponded to how she physically felt. For example, she was Inner-Hearing the word "tired," with a weary silent inflection, while sitting at her office desk at the end of a day (Sample #110). She also occasionally experienced these mental captions in complex combinations with strong feeling inflections and mental images. For example, she was recalling individuals she had counseled in recent years; she was hearing the word "clients," silently spoken in an affectionate tone and was simultaneously picturing one of the women she had been remembering (Sample #64). In another example, she was driving down the road and silently speaking the word, "love" (Sample #159). This thought was accompanied with a remembered mental picture of a woman whom she had seen earlier that evening hugging a 14-year-old girl who was dying of cancer. The expressive tone of the mental word "love" matched her emotional response to the memory, which was a feeling of great tenderness and compassion.

Some of Sue's samples involved the Inner Hearing of a past conversation involving someone else speaking. When she was recalling hearing other people speaking, she silently heard their voices saying the same words inside her head that she remembered them saying audibly in the past. For example, Sue was remembering a girl's response on the telephone to her question as to who would be teaching the 6 PM aerobics class; Sue was hearing the girl's voice saying, "Tim, maybe" (Sample #13). That is, Sue was hearing the girl's voice inside her head with the same tonal inflections as she had heard it earlier over the telephone.

Another time, Sue was remembering a friend saying, "I'm almost always reality-based" (Sample #58). She experienced this memory as hearing his voice, repeating inside her head the same words with the same inflection that she recalled from their earlier conversation. When she remembered herself speaking, Sue's own voice was experienced to be in Inner Speech, not Inner Hearing, with the words spoken being replays of words she had audibly spoken in the past.

Four percent of Sue's samples were collected while she was mentally hearing words or phrases we will call "mantras." These mantras occurred in one or two forms during the sampling period: either she was silently repeating the phrase, "Jesus, mercy" (twice), or she was mentally speaking "in tongues," (seven times).

Both cases in which Sue was repeating the phrase, "Jesus, mercy," occurred when she was sitting cross-legged with eyes closed, alone in a Catholic church, on her work lunch hour. While she was hearing the sound of her own mental voice silently speaking these words, she was not aware of hearing any other verbal thought. In one case, she had just arrived at the church. She was Inner-Hearing, "Jesus, mercy," but her nonverbal attention was focused on her physical repositioning of body weight and posture in the pew (Sample #128). In the other case, while she was hearing her inner voice repeating, "Jesus, mercy," she was aware of a nonverbal impression that it was time to go back to work (Sample #4). This impression or awareness of a sense of time was not accompanied by any recollected verbal dialogue; rather, she simply "knew" it was time to leave.

As with the "Jesus, mercy" mantra, those times when Sue was engaged in silent glossolalia, or mentally "speaking in tongues," were never accompanied by any other verbal mental activity. The verbal content mentally heard when speaking in tongues was a string of phonemes or lexical items that Sue did not deliberately choose, nor did she have any content-understanding of their meaning. Thus, we are unable to reproduce these verbalizations in writing. However, the experience of silent glossolalia occurred in a greater variety of situations during the sampling period than did the other mantras. At times, she was outside walking, hearing the silent stream of consciously meaningless words in her thoughts, with her focus of attention directed to physical sensations, such as her hands being cold (Sample #127). Occasionally she was doing some routine mechanical task, such as, while at work, positioning pens in a computer-driven graphics plotter, while the stream of mental verbalizations rolled through her mind (Sample #173). Sometimes the mental glossalalia was also accompanied by Images, as when Sue was driving through traffic, mentally picturing her stepfather who had just arrived in town for a visit (Sample #14).

UNSYMBOLIZED THINKING

Nine percent of Sue's samples involved what she called "wondering," an example of what we are calling in this book Unsymbolized Experience. The experience of wondering seemed to be a cognitive act; i.e., an attempt to figure out something, but one that was being carried on without words or images. For example, she was looking through her kitchen spices, wondering if she had everything she needed to cook dinner (Sample #20). In this case, she was physically looking at the packages through which she was sorting, without any simultaneous mental images or verbal thought, either silent or spoken aloud. There was, however, the clear awareness that she was nonverbally questioning if she would find what she wanted. She did not explicitly define in words or pictures *what* it was that she wanted, although she *knew* she was questioning whether she would find it. Another time, she was reading her handwritten notes at work, "Lucien curve—interested only when there is a concentration at 200 cm" (Sample #79). She was Inner-Hearing the words she was reading, inside her head as previously described. At the same time, she was wondering if a woman she had been working with was in her office. However, there were not any words or images to convey that question; rather, the meaning and knowledge was simply experienced. In fact, in this example, the words that she was silently hearing were only remotely related to the subject of her "wondering" thought.

In other cases, however, the wondering did directly relate to the topic of her silent verbal or pictured thoughts. For example, she was reading a line from a personal letter, "His first edition has an index; the second, sadly, does not" (Sample #5). At the same time that she was reading these words and hearing them silently spoken in her head, she was wondering if a friend's copy of this book that she wanted to borrow was a first or second edition. As in the other examples, she knew that she was wondering precisely whether her friend's book was the edition that had an index, but she was not experiencing any mental word or images that expressed that question.

This category was difficult for her to describe and, in fact, was one that she was reluctant to accept, since she believed that a cognitive "questioning" or "figuring out" must be related to verbal thought at some level. For example, she was pouring herself a cup of coffee and simultaneously wondering if a coworker was coming over with some computer runs she had asked her to do that morning (Sample #131). She tried to recall words or images that had been associated with the "wondering." It was clear that there was some sort of active questioning going on; so when she recorded the thought, she noted that it seemed that it might be verbal, but was merely too remote for her to recall. In other words, she knew what she was wondering about, i.e., whether her coworker was coming to her office, and when recording her thought, she expected that she should be able to describe by what means this wondering had taken place. Nevertheless, she could *not* describe it, except to say that she knew "wondering" was what she was doing at the time.

IMAGES

Seventeen percent of Sue's samples involved inner Images. Most of these Images recalled scenes from some actual past event that she had experienced; a few were Images created from her imagination to illustrate pictorially some verbal or abstract thought; and a few were "collage" Images, which were complex combinations of multiple, although simultaneously experienced, mental Images and verbal thought.

An example of a recalled Image occurred while she was driving. She was mentally picturing a man she had just left at the hospice facility. The Image was an accurate color picture of him lying in bed, viewed from the same distance and perspective in which she had viewed him earlier (Sample #51). The Image was "seen" as a two-dimensional picture, experienced as inside of her head, somewhere behind her forehead and between her temples. The picture almost filled her entire inner visual "screen"; there was no sharp "border" around the Image, rather, the edge seemed gradually to mute into indistinctness. The mental picture was sharp and accurate; she could see his face, his radiation-burned arms crossed over his stomach, and his position in the bed. This particular Image, however, was not a complete memory of everything she had actually viewed earlier in the man's room. Rather, the Image was restricted to a mental picture of his upper torso and head that were not covered by sheets in the bed. The picture was static and unchanging, viewed like a mental snapshot. While she was picturing this Image inside her head she simultaneously was physically seeing the outer world and responding to the demands of driving.

In another example, Sue was saying aloud at work, "He had suggested dropping the curve number to thirty" (Sample #152). As she was speaking, she was "seeing" inside her head an isolated, accurate Image of the white sheet on which she had written a previously sampled experience; it read, "Change to ~ 30" (Sample #135). She was picturing her handwriting and the words of the note and thus was able to remember what the recommended curve number had been.

At other times, the remembered Image was more complicated, both in terms of quantity of visual content and in her emotional experiencing of the memory. For example, she was viewing a TV news report about stock brokerages and their problems with "buyers' reluctance." At the beep, she was mentally picturing herself experiencing "buyers' reluctance" in a stockbroker's office this past year (Sample #26). She could see the broker's entire cluttered office in the Image; his desk, his computer to the side, stacks of papers, and a right profile of herself sitting in a chair in front of the desk. This seeing herself as if viewed from over her own right shoulder was an impossible perspective for her to take in reality; however, the color and abundance of detailed items in the pictorial memory seemed to be realistic and accurate, to the best of her recollection. This Image also filled her entire mental visual screen, simultaneous with her physical viewing of the television. However, in this case, the static memory Image was also concurrent with an emotional feeling of uncertainty that she could remember had been associated with the actual event. This emotional reexperiencing in the present of the feeling associated with the remembered and visualized past event was a significant aspect of this episode.

Occasionally, the emotional feeling accompanying the mental Image was very strong. For example, while she was driving she was picturing a staff member in the hospice facility bent over a dying 14-year-old girl (Sample #159). The Image was of this woman and the little girl as she had seen them earlier: the broad hips and shoulders of the woman bent over the bed, the way her blond hair was pulled up in a bun, and the color and style of her clothes, as well as the emaciated face of the child. Simultaneous with the Image, she was Inner-Hearing the word "love," spoken in her own voice, and was experiencing a strong positive feeling in response to the love she recognized in the woman's mothering of the girl.

Another time, she was driving down the freeway while it was lightly snowing. She was silently saying to herself, "If I were to die today, what would my life be worth?" (Sample #125). Simultaneously, she was recalling a recent car accident in which the car she was riding in had hit black ice and spun off the road, out of control. The Image inside her head was of herself, holding onto the seat and door of the darkened car; in this case, photographic details of the Image were not clearly remembered, although, like the others, it occupied basically the entire visual space inside her head where she was picturing the scene. She did, however, have a strong sense of backward motion, although the picture itself was a static and unchanging one. This sensation of movement in the snapshot Image was concurrent with an emotional feeling of anxiety. These two feeling responses were her primary focus in this particular sample, rather than the words she was silently speaking or the details of the picture she was mentally viewing.

Some remembered Images included actual movement of the pictured figures and scene. In such Images, the movement activity was brief and limited, and was viewed from a fixed perspective, rather than being lengthy and ongoing as in a dream. For example, she was talking aloud to a friend at dinner: "I thought it was the greatest thing we had ever done" (Sample #188). As she was speaking, she was mentally picturing herself walking a few steps across her kitchen at home, from the sink to the stove. In this case, the perspective of the scene she was viewing was from over her left shoulder in the kitchen. As she walked in the Image, she was enthusiastically talking to one of the women who lived there; Sue could see the responding expression on the woman's face as she listened to Sue, and the gestures she was using with her hands. The Image did not include the sound of Sue's voice or a memory of the words she had been saying. Furthermore, the visual details that Sue recalled in the Image included big items, such as the major appliances and a memory of the light shining from the stove, but she could not recall fine details, such as the clothes they were wearing or what was sitting on the kitchen countertops. However, the focus of Sue's attention in this sample was the words she was audibly saying in the dinner conversation to her friend, not the Image being viewed. The remembered Image, in this case, was more like a brief, background, visual display inside her head that exemplified the point she was verbalizing aloud.

An example of an Image that was not a memory of past externally observed events occurred while Sue was watching a man on the national news who was describing his years in Auschwitz. As he was talking about seeing "the flames" on the day he first arrived at the camp 40 years ago, Sue was simultaneously picturing inside her head tall flames shooting up, imagining what he might have seen (Sample #18). This static Image was in color and very simple; it was not an Image of anything in particular that was burning, but rather only a mental picture of solitary tall flames. This Image was not wide and expansive across her internal mental "screen"; rather, it was a narrow Image of fire that diffused into dark nothingness on either side.

In another example, Sue was driving on the freeway, silently speaking to herself in Inner Speech: "Sue, Sue . . . You have to keep your sense of humor about all this . . ." (Sample #185). Accompanying her verbal thought was a feeling of amusement and a mental Image of a comic female figure, swelling up like a balloon being filled with air, and starting to float away. The details of the Image were only in the figure itself, i.e., there were no environmental details visualized. Neither were there fine details even attached to the figure itself, although Sue was aware it was in color. The implicit assumption of the Image was that it represented Sue herself, floating away with too much serious self-importance, but she could not distinguish her own facial features, nor the clothes she was wearing, etc. The movement of the imagined figure, i.e., the swelling up and starting to float slowly away, and the unspoken understanding of the symbolic meaning of this Image, were her primary sources of interest in the mental picture. This nonverbal understanding was an example of Unsymbolized Thinking, in that she instantaneously understood the fairly complex psychological issue being symbolized by the Image without using any words to explain or analyze this meaning. She simply *knew* the point that was being pictorially emphasized, and she was pleased and amused by its accuracy.

A few of Sue's samples were highly complicated visual impressions that we came to call "collage" visual experiences. For example, she was silently saying in Inner Speech, "God, I don't know who you are or what you want from me . . ." (Sample #64), while simultaneously mentally picturing a complex visual collage. Her inner voice, engaged in conversational prayer, had the tonal inflections of someone puzzling over a question. The silent words she was speaking were in response to the complex Image she was seeing: the visual part of this thought, which accompanied her silent words, was her primary focus of interest. This large visual impression was a fuzzy chronological collage of key events from recent years of her life; the collage seemed multidimensional and lacking in specific details for any one event. It was *not* like seeing a sequence of snapshot Images, lined up across her mental screen, and yet the experience was definitely visual. It was as if she were simultaneously visualizing a number of important life events that seemed to overlap, not spatially, but in the sense of being remembered all at once rather than one after another. The key focus of the collage Image experience was an associated sense of the interrelatedness of the events being recalled, and the interrelatedness was associated also with a sense of chronological movement forward in time.

It is possible that calling this "visual" thought is misleading in the sense that this experience did not have the visual details of her other more ordinary Images. Nevertheless, her experience *was* that of "seeing," and that she could have visually focused on and seen more details of the individual pieces of the experience if she had chosen to do so. If she had been examining any one of the individual memory-Images that made up the whole of this collage, then it seemed that its visual details could have been more clearly described, as was true in other types of Images. However, at the moment, her interest was not in the individual components of the mental pictures but rather on their life significance, their apparent interrelatedness, and the way they pointed to the present and future direction in which her life seemed to be moving.

In another example of collage Images, Sue was looking at a textbook picture of a Rorschach ink blot, and remembering her response a year before when she had first taken the test (Sample #115). What she was experiencing was a collage of emotions and Images, e.g., a mental picture of the woman who administered the test and Sue sitting in an office, and a reexperiencing of the emotional sensations of movement (dancing) and laughter that the stimulus card had triggered for her. Sue also had the impression that some of the memory may have been verbal, i.e., a remembering of her speaking to the test administrator; but she could not remember any specific words, or even if any had actually been spoken. Neither did it seem that she had been thinking about these different things sequentially, but rather that she was experiencing an impression of the multiple thoughts simultaneously in a fuzzy flash. The mental picture of Sue and the woman in an office seemed static and accurate for large details—the desk in the room, the position of our chairs and persons in relation to one another—but finer details were absent. However, the primary focus of the collage was, in this example, the emotional sensations of humor mixed with movement that she had projected onto the card and was reexperiencing when the buzzer sounded.

OBSERVING CHARACTERISTICS

During 17 percent of Sue's sampled thoughts she was engaged in some form of active observing, either of other people or herself. This observing seemed different from times when she was passively watching her surroundings, in that the active observing always included some sort of nonverbal evaluation or assessment. In other words, it was as if she were processing information and arriving at some conclusion about this information, i.e., she was judging or forming some opinion of what she was observing.

Most of these observation experiences were directed towards other people. For example, she was in line at the student union, waiting to pay for a cup of coffee, and was watching a coworker sitting across the room, talking to someone (Sample #146). Sue was observing the way he was smiling, the tilt of his head as he talked, and his body movements in the chair. This was different from a passive looking since Sue was actively observing this individual's manner, which suggested a lightheartedness she did not normally see in him during day-to-day contacts.

In another example, Sue was talking to a woman she had not seen in a long time and was responding to her stories in a laughing tone, "I'm impressed" (Sample #94). At the same time that Sue was speaking, she was noting the overall élan the woman was communicating to her—the way her hair looked, the color of the lipstick she was putting on, the way she was shaking her head as she spoke, her general body language—and was feeling very pleased to see her again. In both these examples, the observing activity was not a deliberate noting one-detail-at-a-time kind of watching, but rather a gestalt taking in of a total impression of someone, that is, an impression of her mood, her personality, and her life vitality.

At other times, Sue was observing the other person and simultaneously making a more deliberate assessment of what she was seeing. For example, she was hearing a friend say, "I was with him the very week they started dating . . ." while talking about a couple they knew who were going through a divorce (Sample #189). While she was listening to his words, she was noting (nonverbally and without concurrent mental Images) his speech that was more pressured than usual, the elevated pitch of his voice, and the look on his face, all of which were indications to her of his distress over the divorce. This active observational activity was similar to Sue's previously described Unsymbolized Thinking. She experienced both types of thought as engaging in some sort of cognitive processing of information—an assessing or attempting to figure out something, without using verbal thought or mental Images.

There were examples where Sue was actively observing herself. For example, she was listening to someone telling a story in a bar; when the beeper went off, Sue was not thinking any verbal thoughts about the words she was hearing or picturing any mental Images, but was feeling aware of the fact that she was smiling and maintaining eye contact with the speaker, indicating to him that she was listening to what he was saying (Sample #44).

SPEAKING ALOUD

Nineteen percent of Sue's sampled thoughts occurred while she was speaking aloud to someone in a conversation. When this happened, she was never aware of any simultaneous verbal thought; she was just absorbed in what she was vocalizing to the other people at the time. For example, she was saying to a co-worker, "I had thought the precipitation data were used here . . ." (Sample #12). She was looking at a computer output file as she was speaking, but was not thinking about anything other than the words she was saying aloud. Another time, she was making a pun to a woman sitting next to her at dinner, saying, "I'm really going to 'stuff' at this meal," while serving herself some turkey dressing (Sample #123). She emotionally had a feeling of amusement associated with her words, but was not thinking about anything other than what she was saying.

At times, when Sue was speaking aloud, she did have mental Images associated with her audible speech. For example, she was talking at work to someone on the phone, saying, "The column, obviously, is not a consistent percent moisture throughout, as the model would state" (Sample #133). Simultaneous with her statement, she was mentally picturing a yellow, legal-size sheet of notebook paper where she had recorded percent moisture data from a laboratory experiment.

Sue's conversations with other people also at times combined audible speech with nonverbal observations. For example, she was reading aloud a valentine that had been given to her by her 3-year-old niece: "If you'll be my valentine, I'll be on top of the world" (Sample #141). While she was speaking, her attention was focused on this niece standing in front of her, watching her reaction to her gift, and Sue was aware that her responding to it was important to her niece. Another time, Sue was saying, "Good morning, Dave," to a co-worker (Sample #77); simultaneously, she was noting how he looked that morning, the coffeepot that he was holding in his hand, and also was aware that she felt pleased to see him.

ACTIVE LISTENING TO OTHER PERSONS SPEAKING

Seventeen percent of Sue's sampled thoughts (33/197) were collected while she was actively listening to other people talking. Her listening was accompanied by a range of thought activities and levels of personal involvement that overlap with many of the other characteristics described above. At times, her listening was associated with Inner Speech and mental Images. For example, while listening to a family member talking about the extremely cold weather they had been having, she was saying to herself in Inner Speech, "You need to wear your long underwear" (Sample #73). At the same time she was picturing an Image of his tan uniform knit pants and white long underwear. Another time (Sample #18 described above), Sue was viewing a TV news interview with a survivor from Auschwitz and Imaging flames.

Other times, Sue's listening activity included an active observation of the speaker. For example, she was listening to a friend saying, "It is not a stochastic model . . ." (Sample #11). As she was hearing and paying attention to his words, she was observing the physical signs (slurred speech, flushed face) that suggested he had recently had slightly too much to drink. In this case, her focus of thought was on his behavior and appearance, rather than on the informational content of his words. In other examples, an awareness of Sue's emotional response to what she was hearing was the primary focus of her listening attention. For example she was listening to an aerobics instructor saying, "I didn't know it was *that* dirty . . ." (Sample #186); simultaneously, Sue was aware of feeling happy to see her and to be in that place.

NO THOUGHT

During eight percent of Sue's samples, she was not thinking about anything, even when the word "thinking" is used in its broadest sense; i.e., she was not engaged in any verbalizations, mental Images, active listening, observing, or anything else she would recognize as a "thought" or "mental experience." During most of these sampling events, she was engaged in some routine physical activity. For example, she was driving through traffic at one sample (#3) but had no thoughts, verbal or nonverbal. In another example, Sue was at home, looking through a new crafts catalog that had come in the mail, but not thinking anything while turning the pages and looking (Sample #16).

A number of these Not Thinkings involved observing other people: for example, she was watching people milling around a classroom before a seminar began (Sample #92), or finding her way through a crowded basketball stadium to her seat (Sample #99). Other times the beeper went off while she was passively hearing other people speaking. At these times, she was hearing their words, and was able to remember them, but was not actively processing the words for any informational content. She could remember the words she was hearing when the beeper sounded but, although she was audibly hearing them spoken and understood their meaning, she was not paying attention or *trying* to remember or evaluate them in any way. Another sample found her standing in line at a grocery store; she heard the man in front of her say, "Thirty-nine cents a pound" (Sample #121). Once again, she was not thinking about anything at the time, nor was she experiencing any sense of active interest or involvement in the man's words, although she heard and could recall them.

COMPARISON WITH SUE'S PRE-SAMPLING EXPECTATIONS

Sue, like Sonja Smith, prepared a Pre-Sampling Retrospective Generalized Account (PRGA) of her inner experience before she began to sample, and there were both confirmations and surprises in the sampling data themselves. One confirmation was that she stated before sampling in the PRGA that she frequently thought about other people; that was in fact true in more than 10 percent of her samples. Another confirmation was the presampling observation that she frequently identified her emotional state; in fact, 17 percent of her recorded samples included some observation about her moods and feelings; i.e., she was not merely feeling a variety of emotional states, but she was focusing her attention on the fact that she was experiencing them. A third confirmation was that Sue also often thought about past events, as predicted in the PRGA, using both visual and verbal forms of thought.

Some of her pre-sampling description was less accurate. For example, she stated in her PRGA that she used Images in conjunction with mental-verbal thought in almost all situations. In fact, only 17 percent of her sampled thoughts were accompanied by visual Images, although these Images did occur in conjunction with all the various *types* of thoughts we identified during sampling. Another surprise was that she stated before sampling that she was almost always thinking about something—only very infrequently would she think about nothing at all. However, in the sampling, 8 percent of her samples were identified as "no thought." The pre-sampling description also seemed to lump together inaccurately a number of distinctly different thought categories. For example, in pre-sampling she described something she called "passive" thought, which she stated that she used when she was bored, tired, or emotionally distracted, traveling, waiting, or passively listening. After sampling, it seemed that this "passive" form of thought she had described was in fact a combination of several categories, including "key" words, mantras, speech accompanied by unrelated thought, and passive listening to other people.

There were other discrepancies between the PRGA and the sampling data. For example, she stated in the pre-sampling description that her "directed" thought seemed to be located in the front of her brain, while the "passive" thoughts seemed further back in her head, idly moving in and out of an inner, quiet space. In fact, during sampling she was never able to distinguish a difference in location site for any of her thoughts. All seemed to be centered somewhere in her head, behind her forehead and between her temples. She also stated in her PRGA that she frequently thought about planning or goal-setting activities and about value judgments. During the sampling period, however, very few of her thoughts related to either to these two topics, whereas many related to work matters or religious issues, which she had not named in the pre-sampling description.

Still other surprises emerged in the sampling data when compared to her pre-sampling expectations about her thought processes. For example, she knew she often thought in Images, but she did not know that these Images covered such a wide range of complexity and detail, from a simple, static remembered Image to a complex collage of multiple verbal and pictorial thoughts simultaneously experienced. She knew that she periodically used mantra-like verbal prayer, but had not realized that it was so common. She had not realized that she experienced reading and writing activities as a silent Inner Hearing of her own voice saying what was being written or read. She apparently also had a strong bias towards viewing all cognitive thought as being verbal at some level, and was very reluctant to believe it when her category of Unsymbolized Experience "wondering" thought began to emerge. Similarly, she knew that she often thought about other people, but had the preconceived notion that this thought, too, was basically a verbal process, rather than realizing that it was often an observing and processing of information being carried on without words or Images to convey the thought.

THE FOLLOW-UP STUDY

After she had completed the categorization and written descriptions of the characteristics of her inner experiences during the sampling period, she sampled again, following the same procedure. This follow-up comparison was intended to determine if any of the initial categories she had described needed amplification, or needed to be modified in some way that would make them descriptively more clear. What we found, in fact, was that the initial sampling fairly accurately described her inner experience characteristics, since no radically new categories began to emerge during the follow-up study. Furthermore, with the exception of two types of verbal thought (reading and writing activities and Inner Speech), there were no significant differences between the percentages of total sampled thoughts from the two studies placed in each category. These small differences that were observed were perhaps largely situational. The increase in reading and writing verbal thought (from 11 percent to 28 percent) may be due to the fact that the follow-up study was later in a semester, when Sue was busy with increased reading and writing commitments. The decrease in Inner Speech (23 percent to 13 percent) may also reflect the shortage of samples during the follow-up period from her leisure time.

DISCUSSION

Melancon's procedure, like Smith's, in the previous chapter, used the Pre-Sampling Retrospective General Account as an aid to suspending preconceptions to facilitate the unbiased reporting about inner experience. The fact that there were some corroborations and some surprises increases our confidence that we were not simply blindly reproducing what we had expected to find. The follow-up sample also encourages us that our descriptions were accurate, because we could examine samples which had not been included in the original generation of characteristics in the light of the written descriptions, and find that the descriptions themselves were adequate.

10

Characteristics of Normal Inner Experience

We have, for the past six chapters, examined the thinking of individuals, one at a time, and so have accomplished the major goal of this project, familiarizing ourselves with a sampling of the basic data of psychology: individual experience as it is lived by the persons themselves. We have also had a chance to exercise the supplemental goal of suspending our hypothesis generation until such time as we have acquired as much data as are available.

It is now time to make some observations about normal inner experience in general, recognizing that such observations are based upon descriptions of only six individuals. Even with this small and nonrandom sample, there is still justification to describe the *existence* of certain characteristics of experience. The small and nonrepresentative sample merely prohibits us from speculating about the relative *frequency* of such characteristics in the population at large. The generalizations that follow, then, are what strike me as the most salient characteristics of the inner experience of the six normal subjects we have sampled.

INNER VERBAL EXPERIENCE

Our first general observation about inner experience is that *words occur in inner experience*. In fact, all of our subjects reported at least several instances where words formed part of their momentary thought. This was, of course, to be expected, because philosophers as well as casual observers have believed for thousands of years that thinking is verbal.

However, *some inner experiences are nonverbal.* There was rather a large range across our normal subjects in the frequency of verbal experience: Jim had the lowest percentage at 7 percent, while Sue Melancon was highest with 80 percent. Looked at another way, this means that from 20 to 93 percent of inner experience in our subjects was nonverbal, and that may be surprising. Words do not necessarily occupy a central position in the inner experience of people.

As a corollary to this observation, we note that much of our philosophical tradition has assumed that thinking is *entirely* verbal. In fact, many observers see the history of Western philosophy as synonomous with the history of "association," a theory that holds that thinking is a series of mental elements that elicit each other like links in a chain, as when the word "Peter" evokes the word "Paul" or "Genesis" leads to "Exodus." The exact rules of this associational linkage have varied from philosopher to philosopher, but a common thread has been that the elements being associated are *words.* The fact that as much as 93 percent of a person's inner experience may be nonverbal makes it clear that *no associational principle is sufficient to explain thinking,* unless the associationist either posits an outside-of-awareness and extended-over-time process that links words, or allows nonverbal elements such as images or feelings to be linked associationally.

Our next conclusion is that *verbal thought is frequently expressed in well-formed words and sentences.* In fact, complete words and sentences were the most frequent characteristics of the verbal aspect of our normal sample. That thinking should involve words and sentences seems so obvious that we should hardly have to mention it; however, it need not have been the case (and is in fact not always the case: see below).

The next two conclusions demonstrate the limitations of what we take to be obvious, for it was probably not to be expected that *verbal thought does not necessarily involve words.* We saw above that inner experience does not necessarily involve words; here, we note that *verbal* inner experience does not necessarily involve words. Three of our subjects (Jason, Helen, and Sue) reported experiences that were clearly verbal but where no words at all were present in experience, the phenomenon we call Wordless Speech.

Jason, for example, knew he was internally speaking words, and he understood the words' meaning, but the words themselves were not present to experience. For example, at one point he was clearly experiencing himself as saying to himself a thought whose meaning was, "I despise my French class. It is really too difficult. My other classes are suffering"; but not a single word of these sentences (or any other word) was present in his experience. Similarly, Helen understood herself to be saying in Wordless Speech, "What's so special about it [Napoleon's hat]?" even though no words were a part of the verbal experience. Helen could say whether her Unworded Speakings were in Dutch, the Limburg dialect, or English, even though there was not a single word of any language present in the verbalization.

Thus, verbal thought clearly does not necessitate the presence of words. It seems that verbalization should be understood as a coordination of processes including the forming of the words and the producing of the nonword characteristics of speaking: the rate, the tone, the rhythm, the inflection, and the other nonword characteristics of the language and the individual. Our subjects clearly recognized these nonworded aspects as being part of verbal thought.

Words in inner experience are not necessarily meaningful. The words in inner verbal experience for most of our subjects most of the time were understood to have their usual straightforward semantic meanings. However, there were some notable exceptions to this rule. Sonja Smith's inner words had a range of meaningfulness, from words present in accurately meaningful inner sentences to Word Repetitions which had no reconstructible meaning. For example, the fragment "Well, that means" was being mindlessly repeated in her inner verbalization, with no clue as to its meaning. On another occasion, the words "lunch bag" were repeated, and were with some difficulty recognized as a corruption of "tea bag" which had been said in Inner Speech a few moments previously. Helen also identified a similar meaningless Word Repetition phenomenon. For example, the phrase "must be in the week of" was recognized as spoken over and over in Inner Speech, with no apparent meaning.

The inner experience of Jim the professional potter provided a second way in which words could be stripped of their usual semantic meanings, as when he saw an image of the word "bereavement," and was attending not to the meaning of the word but instead to the interplay of the shape of the letters, as how the "e" seemed to fit next to the "b." Sue Melancon reported a third way in which verbalizations could be meaningless. She described the occurrence of internal glossolalia or "speaking in tongues," verbal experiences which were characterized by the silent emission of meaningless syllables. Thus inner verbal experience in normal subjects cannot be construed as simply strings of meaningful words.

Inner verbalizations can "sound the same" as external verbalizations, including such characteristics as rate of speed of word production, pauses for punctuation, slight elevations in pitch for question marks, etc. Most normal subjects could not identify a single characteristic of inner speech that was different from their outer speech except that outer speech was aloud. This included pitch of the voice, accent, pronunciation, choice of words, stutters, vocalized pauses, etc. The most extreme example of this was when Helen, for whom English was a fourth language, reported that an inner verbalization that happened to be in English had the same slightly halting, searching-for-the-right-word production as did her external English speech. There was, however, one exception to the rule that inner and outer verbalizations were identical in form. The inner verbalizations of Helen in her native Dutch were frequently perceived to be at a faster rate, sometimes a much faster rate, than would or could be produced aloud. Helen, but none of the other subjects, experienced a range of speed of Inner Speech, from the same rate as aloud (which was the most frequent rate) to much more rapid.

Inner verbalizations can be full of inflection. Inner verbalizations existed with the same range of inflections as did outer speech for all of our subjects. We noted the inflections for punctuation marks in the previous paragraph. Here, we refer to the inflections accompanying emotional or playful or sarcastic speech. For example, Sue Melancon's inner verbalizations were sometimes matter-of-fact declarative statements, such as when she said to herself, "I'm at the pivotal point of my life," and sometimes full of energy and enthusiasm, as when she said to herself, "This is going to be absolutely, positively, totally fucking great!" In both of these cases, and in almost all of the other examples in both Sue's and others' samples, the inner verbalization duplicated the inflections that would have been used if the sentences had been spoken aloud.

Inner words can be experienced either as being spoken or as being heard, and the two kinds of experiences can exist within the same person. Sue Melancon, Jason, Ben, and Helen all reported examples of Inner Speech which were quite clearly distinguishable from other examples of an Inner Hearing of words being spoken. The difference between the two kinds of experience is as striking as the differences between speaking and hearing in the external world: in Inner Speech, it seems as if the subject is producing the words, and has a sense of authorship, activity, and control over the process. In Inner Hearing, the process is more passive, and the words are not experienced as created directly under the subject's control (although the subject clearly knows they are products of his or her own mind). In a typical example, Helen had just turned the page of a book of short stories and read the title of the next story, *Big Two-Hearted River: I,* and was saying to herself in Inner Speech, "So there will be a number II." These words were experienced exactly as if she were saying them aloud, except that no external sound or movements were being made. By contrast, on another occasion she had just picked up her cat, and the words "How cold your paws are," were experienced as being *heard* in inner experience. In both cases, the words were experienced in her own voice, but in the first case it was as if she were actually the author or originator of the words, while in the second, she was passively hearing the words being spoken by herself.

Hearings in inner experience can be of more than one voice. The most frequently heard inner experience in our sample was the subject hearing his or her own voice speaking. However, there was a rather wide range of voices heard in inner experience. To give examples, Sue Melancon reheard in inner experience a friend's voice repeating what she had actually said earlier, "I make over $23,000 a year"; and Ben heard in his inner experience his own voice, singing along with singer Andy Partridge's voice, *Blue All Over.* The voices of Inner Hearing were not always recreations of the voices of real people; for example, Jason frequently heard a male, bass voice he called the "auditorium voice," and also heard a voice he called the "the teacher," whose vocal characteristics were strikingly different from the auditorium voice. Neither voice belonged to anyone recognizable to Jason.

Inner words sometimes seem to function as directors of activity. This may be another example of a conclusion which is accepted as obvious, since that notion underlies much of our philosophical tradition. For example, Sue Melancon used what she called Key Words seemingly to keep attention focused on the task at hand, as when she said to herself "standard score" while leafing through a statistics book for that topic. In another example, Melancon was preparing dinner, and said to herself, "This meat has discolored but should still be all right to cook." In both examples, the ongoing activity seemed to be directed by the verbalization. However, we will see in the next paragraph and in sections to follow that inner words are not always necessary to guide actions.

Inner words are not necessarily directly connected with other inner or outer activity. That is, Inner Speaking sometimes seems to have a mind of its own, creating or recreating words in an idle, disconnected, seemingly functionless manner. Perhaps the best examples of this phenomenon were Sonja Smith's and Helen's Word Repetitions which we discussed a few paragraphs ago. The words of those experiences had the characteristics of being created autonomously, devoid of any direct connection to the experiencer's present activity.

IMAGES

Visual images sometimes exist in inner experience. All of our subjects reported the existence of some visual images, with the frequency of these images varying from about 6 percent in Sonja Smith's and Helen's samples, to 42 percent in Jason's. Images were usually in color and, occasionally, figures in the Images were in movement. Frequently, images were accurate reconstructions of events that had been previously seen, as when Sue Melancon saw an inner Image of a man she had just left at a hospice facility. The Image of the man was in accurate color, viewed from the same perspective and distance at which she had just seen him. Sometimes, however, Images were creations of scenes that had not in fact been seen, as when Melancon saw an inner image of flames at Auschwitz, which of course she had never in fact seen, while hearing a televised discussion of the concentration camp.

Sometimes images were of impossible scenes. Images could be seen from an impossible perspective. For example, sometimes subjects saw themselves from an external perspective, as when Jim saw himself up in a tree as if viewed from the ground, or Sue Melancon saw herself pouring chemicals into the toilet viewed from behind herself looking over her own shoulder. Impossibilities other than perspective also occurred in our sample, as when Jason viewed his apartment as if the living room wall were absent so that he could see two rooms at a time, or again when Jason saw himself in two places in the same Image: the first imaged Jason was viewed from the back standing on the tennis court sidelines watching the second imaged Jason, who was on the court playing tennis.

Inner visual experience sometimes existed without inner images. Just as there was the experience of Wordless Speech, inner verbalization without words being present, there was also the experience of Imageless Seeing, inner visualization without images. This phenomenon occurred most frequently in Jason's sample. For example, at one moment he was in a hotel management class listening to a discussion of commissaries. At the moment of the beep, he had turned his attention away from the discussion and was focused on an inner seeing of a commissary. He could describe the commissary he was looking at, but he was also confident that he was not actually seeing anything in inner experience. Thus, his experience was clearly visual in he sense that he was definitely "looking at" a commissary, but neither the commissary itself nor anything else was being seen. Sue Melancon's collage experiences also contained elements that seemed similar to this phenomenon. For example, one of her samples involved the visual experience of "seeing" multiple key events of her life which were perceived as all visually present at the same time. These events were simultaneous visual presentations, not sequential; and the experience was definitely of seeing the events, although she was not attending to any particular visual details. It was as if she were looking at all the events together, and she had the sense that if she had sharpened her focus on any part of the visualization, she could have seen that portion in much greater visual detail.

Images were sometimes understood to be useful. As was the case with inner verbalization, inner Images seemed sometimes to guide or influence activity. For example, Jim was in his glaze room about to apply glaze to a ceramic plate; he visualized an Image of a squirt of glaze already on the plate. Thus, this Image held for Jim the visual sense of the pattern that he would soon create on the real plate. Jason also experienced Images as being useful, as when he visualized the path he hoped a tennis return would make, or when he saw a display like an inner calculator holding the addition of the prices of purchases he was making, or when he visualized the neuron that his psychology professor was describing.

Images were not always useful or related to activity, however. For example, Jim was working with his pots and heard the sound of a dune buggy in the distance. He visualized a particular yellow dune buggy, while at the same time continuing his potting task.

Images frequently (but not always) were accompanied by strong emotional experiences. For at least three of our subjects (Sue Melancon, Jim, and Jason), the presence of Images and emotions seemed strongly linked, in the sense that reports of emotional experience accompanied almost all Images, and Images were present at the times of strongest emotional experience. For example, Sue Melancon had a strong experience of love accompanying visualizing a hospice worker bent over a dying child. Another time, when she was feeling particularly amused at herself, she visualized a comic female figure swelled up like a balloon and floating away. Other examples include Jason's "pumped" feeling while visualizing the Olympic Games ceremony and Jim's unpleasant feeling while seeing the Image of a pot with its side flattened from being stored improperly, etc. We should note that we do not have enough information to say that emotions follow from Images or Images follow from emotions; only that the two seem to occur frequently together, at least in some people. This phenomenon will also be noted when we review the characteristics of schizophrenic experience.

MEANING WITHOUT WORDS OR IMAGES

We noted above the "obvious" generalizations that words and images sometimes guide activity. Here, we note that *Actions can be undertaken with no inner experience,* that is, with neither words nor Images. Most of our subjects reported occasions that they called something like Just Doing, where they were engaged in performing some task or activity and nothing could be found in inner experience at the moment: no words, no images, etc. For example, Sonja Smith was looking at a red Duplo cube and its picture on a container to see where it should be placed. In this example, the outer perceptions of the cube and picture seemed to exhaust her awareness; there was no Inner Speech such as, "Where does this go?" and no image of the completed figure, etc. In another example, Jim was walking through the living room of his house and heard a noise that startled him. He was turning to his left, in the direction of the noise, when the beep occurred. At that moment, there were no words or Images or any other inner experience; he was merely orienting himself to the noise that he had heard. Ben's Implied Experiences provide more examples where behavior is undertaken from a particular point of view which is nonverbal and nonvisual. Thus we are led to conclude that words or images sometimes, but not always, direct activity.

Our next generalization is a broadening of that finding: *Meanings do not necessarily involve inner verbalizations or visualizations*. Almost all of the inner experiences of all of our subjects were considered to be meaningful in the sense that the subject him- or herself knew what the significance of the thought was. In many of these experiences, the meaning was quite clearly carried by some inner verbalization or image; but it was also frequently the case that activities and experiences were meaningful when neither words nor images were present. These examples, which we call Unsymbolized Thinking, were reported by Sue Melancon and Helen. For example, Melancon was at work looking at a graph and saying to herself in Inner Speech, "Lucien curve—interested only when there is a concentration of 200 cm." At the same time, she was wondering in Unsymbolized Thinking whether a particular woman was in her office. This wondering was quite clearly a central component of Melancon's experience, and there was no doubt about, for example, which particular woman was being considered; yet there were no words (such as the woman's name, etc.) or images which conveyed the wonder. Finally, Helen was watching the television show *Lou Grant*, and was actively wondering in Unsymbolized Thinking what the outcome would be, again with no words or images.

Sometimes this nonverbal, nonvisual meaning was related to a focusing of attention in a particular manner on some aspect of the inner or outer environment. For example, Sonja Smith was noticing the particular blue of the clothes her baby-sitter was wearing, and was recognizing that that particular blue seemed to "go with" the baby-sitter, although there were no words or images associated with her evaluation. In other examples, Sue Melancon was focused in one sample on the particular tilt of the head of a person to whom she was talking, and Jim, while loading his kiln, was looking at a particular brick which had been eaten away by fire. In both these cases, the individual's attention was clearly directed outward at a particular aspect of an external object, but there was no inner thinking or visualizing anything related to it.

OTHER OBSERVATIONS

Characteristics of thinking seem strongly related to occupation. While we clearly do not have an adequate sample size to be confident of this generalization, we nevertheless are compelled to state it. It seems more than coincidence, for example, that our subjects with strong interest and success in school including graduate school (Sonja Smith, Sue Melancon, and Helen) had clearly the highest frequency of verbal thinking. Jim, the professional potter, on the other hand, had strong, clear emotional experiences as well as among the highest frequency of visual experiences, when both imaginal and real noticings of the environment are counted. Our observations should not be taken to imply cause-and-effect relationships; for example, the students' high-frequency verbal experiences may be the result of their academic experience, or may be a personality characteristic that led them to pursue the academic career in the first place, or quite possibly both. Nevertheless, such an observation may have important ramifications both for our understanding of aptitude (in the sense that particular skills are facilitated by particular manners of inner experience), and for our understanding of the determinants of thinking (that occupation has a strong influence on thinking).

There is a wide range of self-consciousness. Many experiences included the subject him- or herself as a focus, either when the subject noticed some particular characteristic of self, or appeared as a character in his or her own image. There was a range in the frequency of occurrence of such experiences, from very frequently (Sonja Smith and Jim) to very rarely (Ben and Helen) with Sue Melancon and Jason somewhere in between. Sonja Smith, for example, focused on herself sufficiently often to identify three ways that such a focus could take: self-observation, self-consciousness, and self-critical thinking. Jim occurred as a character in his own images, as when he viewed himself pruning a tree or throwing a pot at a summer workshop. Furthermore, he frequently focused on his own bodily feelings, as when he felt his body expanding along with the clay he was working with. At present, we are in no position to speculate on the significance of such a range in frequency of self in inner experience; rather, we only note that there seems to be large individual differences in the frequency of the inner experience of self.

People's awareness is often not directly focused on the external world. For an extremely large preponderance of our samples (in the neighborhood of 90 percent), our subjects' focus was centered on some creation of their own mind, rather than on any characteristic of the external world. The inner creation might have been Inner Speech or Hearing, or an Image, or a wondering in Unsymbolized Thinking, etc.; only very rarely was attention directly involved with perceiving the external world or noticing its particular characteristics. This is not to say that our subjects were completely out of contact with the world; on the contrary, they functioned quite adequately in reality. The point is that what is presented *to awareness* is not usually the world itself, but rather words or Images which are created by the subject him- or herself in response to the external world. Thus, for most of our subjects, most of the time, awareness itself sees or hears only a secondhand version of the world, reduced and categorized according to whatever process awareness happens to invoke at that particular moment. Psychological theorists have frequently noticed, of course, that individuals frequently do not respond directly to the world around them. Such observations formed the core of Freud's theory of defenses, for example. But, to my knowledge, the present data are the first to show the process of separation from the world occurring in its moment-by-moment experience.

Emotional experience is difficult to describe. Our subjects found it difficult to put into words how they recognized particular emotions. This is not to say that the emotions themselves were not clear; on the contrary, emotional experience was almost always unambiguous. However, once the subject had identified the emotion as "love" or "irritation" or whatever, it was usually difficult for him or her to answer the question, "How do you know that what you were experiencing was love?" By far the most frequent answer to this kind of question was, "I don't know how I know. I just know." Sometimes, subjects could identify parts of the body involved in the feelings, but often these identifications were made vaguely or generally.

There are doubtless other generalizations that have occurred to the reader; the present chapter is far from a complete catalog of the characteristics of inner experience, and the reader is invited to generalize on his or her own. Several factors encouraged us to provide the generalizations in this chapter: we wished to show that the method of descriptive thought sampling could lead to productive generalizations about inner experience; similarities between the reports "called out" for expression; and contrasts between our data and the prevailing notions about thinking compelled discussion. However, at the same time, our own arguments against premature generalization and the limited number of subjects suggested that it would be prudent to decline to provide generalizations. This chapter was thus a compromise between conflicting tendencies, and is, like most compromises, likely to feel "not quite right"; from one perspective it is too incomplete; from the other, too speculative. The only alternative would be to wait until many more reports are available; one of the intents of this book is to stimulate support for such an eventuality. But that is in the future, so this chapter must stand simply as a progress report.

II

The Schizophrenic Subjects

The four chapters that follow are descriptions of the inner experiences of schizophrenic individuals. The method used to create these descriptions was the same as that used in the previous chapters. Subjects were all volunteers, and it was somewhat more difficult to obtain schizophrenic volunteers than normal subjects. However, we did find volunteers who could provide enough samples to be useful and who read and commented on the final version of the written reports which follow.

You will note as you read the descriptions that follow that there is somewhat more interpretation in the descriptions of schizophrenic inner experience than there was in the normal subjects' chapters. This is because schizophrenic subjects were less consistent than the normals in providing straightforward perceptual descriptions of their experiences. When Jason (Chapter 4), for example, said he was seeing an image, and we asked him for the perceptual details of that image, he could provide them in ways which were immediately believable. That was not always the case for our schizophrenic subjects, as we shall see, particularly when they were decompensated, and we had to make a greater interpretative effort to understand what they were conveying.

We will try in the chapters that follow to be as open as possible about these interpretations and how we arrived at them, including providing extended excerpts from the sampling conversations, along with an explanation of what we took the excerpted dialogue to mean. The reader should bear in mind two aspects of these excerpts. First, they are provided only at those points where the sampling dialogues are themselves problematic in some way; if a conversation was straightforward, we did not feel compelled to provide the dialogue. Thus, the excerpts are *not* typical of our straightforward conversations with the normal subjects described previously, or of the schizophrenic subjects when they were describing inner events with clarity. Instead, they are representative of times when we felt the conversations could not be taken at face value, where relatively long interpretative leaps had to be made to decipher what was meant in a difficult communication.

Second, there are places in the dialogues of the following chapters where it may appear that I asked leading questions or stated conclusions to which the subject merely assented, perhaps not because the conclusions were true but because of situational demand characteristics, such as a desire to please. We tried not to lead, but at the same time tried to enter into the subject's world and understand what was being said, not only verbally but nonverbally. Tapescript excerpts have limitations in that they cannot provide the entire context of an interchange (which may have taken place after ten hours of intensive conversation about similar and different events) or the nonverbal cues present in the live exchange.

These limitations make it sometimes impossible for the reader of the tapescript to differentiate between a leading statement and a perceptive observation. For example, let us consider a portion of the first excerpt from the next chapter, which reads:

JENNIFER: I was seeing something in real life, but not. . . .

R.T.H.: (interrupts) But not really paying attention to it?

JENNIFER: Right.

A slight change in tone of voice or context can radically change the meaning of this interchange. My interrupting statement here could have been a perceptive integration of contextual and nonverbal cues, finishing the sentence that Jennifer had started in a tentative manner so that Jennifer could either affirm or deny my proposed conclusion. Alternatively, my statement could have been a badgering, leading question which Jennifer had no choice but to affirm. Furthermore, Jennifer's response may have been either a definite, energetic, emphatic "Right," meaning "That's exactly correct—you have put it better than I could have!" or a dull, lifeless "Right," meaning "Whatever you say."

We tried to be sensitive to these nuances, tried not to "lead" our subjects but to listen to them accurately. Whether we have listened accurately cannot be proven or disproven on the basis of a tapescript. We have provided the excerpts as access to our procedure, especially at those points where it is the most problematic. The best evidence regarding whether our listening and interpretation was accurate will come from those who attempt to replicate this work. If they find similar patterns to the ones we identify, then the reader will have some external reassurance that our interviews were perceptive rather than leading.

As with the normal subjects we have disguised the identities of the schizophrenic subjects.

11

A Schizophrenic Woman with "Goofed-Up" Images

with Susan M. Melancon

Jennifer Knoll was a 23-year-old resident of a relatively structured and restrictive psychiatric halfway house. She had been diagnosed as Paranoid Schizophrenic four years earlier as a result of hearing annoying voices which frequently triggered sadness and crying. She had spent much of the last four years in inpatient psychiatric facilities or halfway houses. At the time of sampling, she was performing quite well in her residential activities, and the residential treatment staff decided near the end of the sampling period to "graduate" her to a less restrictive environment (a cooperative apartment administered by the same mental health care provider group). She received Haldol, an antipsychotic medication, throughout the sampling period, and attributed to it a reduction in the presence of the annoying voices. While she reported that these voices were occasionally dimly present during the three-week period the sampling took place, the beep never occurred during one of those episodes.

Jennifer volunteered to participate in this study, and was consistently pleasant, courteous, and cooperative throughout the long daily interviews. The interviews were held in her room in the halfway house, which she always had prepared in advance of our visit: chairs in place, notes prepared, etc. She adapted to the sampling requirements easily, and within the first few days of sampling was quite clear about attempting to focus on exactly what was happening at the moment of the beep

The authors express their appreciation to the administration and staff of Caminar, Inc., for their cooperation and support during these studies.

and excluding other experiences. She seemed quite candid in reporting her experiences. Like all our other subjects, she was fully aware that she had the right to say that an experience was none of our business, and we encouraged her (as we did our other subjects) to do so if she felt uncomfortable about revealing something. She did, on two occasions, decline to report some aspect of her experience, but on both occasions the omission was to protect another resident's privacy rather than her own.

A total of 90 samples were collected from Jennifer during the study period. Of these, 2 were considered unusable because of delays she had in responding to the signaling tone, and 17 samples were excluded because we had insufficient time or energy in our daily meetings to discuss them with Jennifer in detail. Thus, the following discussion is based upon a total of 71 samples collected during a three-week period.

When any subject in this series of studies reports an experience as having occurred at the moment of the beep, there are always several ways that such a statement can be construed, ranging from accepting it as a veridical report of the actual experience at that moment, to presuming that the report is more a construction of the present than a recollection of a past event. With all our subjects, we have attempted to evaluate these possibilities, and in so doing have become convinced that the subject's reports are relatively accurate. This issue was more salient with Jennifer than with previous subjects for two particular reasons: First, her experiences were frequently much more complicated than those of previous respondents; and second, she frequently gave during the sampling interviews what seemed to be a complete description of a particular beeped experience, and then, almost as an afterthought, described in vivid detail an entire aspect of that experience that had been previously overlooked. We will discuss more completely this aspect of her reports after we have described the experiences themselves; for now, suffice it to say that we became convinced, despite a cultivated skepticism, that her reports were in fact reflective of the experience at the moment of the beep.

Before proceeding to describe in detail the particular characteristics of Jennifer's thinking, we will provide a brief general description of her inner experience so that the reader may place the subsequent discussions in context. By far the most prominent characteristic of Jennifer's inner experience was the vividness of inner visualizations. Most of her experiences included Images of some kind, ranging from simple inner "copies" of portions of her present environment to highly abstract, colorful visual presentations which had no apparent meaning. Visualizations were seen in front of her and behind, to the right and left, straight on or from an angle, tilted or straight up and down, with or without sounds and movement, and veridical or "goofed up" with extraneous lines and blurs, etc. Words were also present in her inner experience, both in Inner Speech and Inner Hearing of her own voice and visualized as hand-printed, frequently colorful and frequently "scrunched-up" words. Color was important, not only as an aspect of inner experience, but also as a frequent focus of attention in the external world, as in noticing the electric blue of an RC Cola can.

Accompanying these cognitive characteristics were clear bodily feelings, quite clearly localized in some particular part of her body, most frequently her heart. All her experiences, whether cognitive or emotional, seemed to be easily available to her, and the sampling task was handled easily and unambiguously, except for the fact that her experience of the sampling beep itself did not have as precise an onset as it did for some of our other subjects, in that she seemed to have to register cognitively the presence of the beep, a phenomenon she came to call "computing the beep." We turn now to discuss each of these characteristics in detail.

VISUAL EXPERIENCE

Images

The single most salient characteristic of Jennifer's samples during the study period was her emphasis on visual experiences, whether she was focused on external reality or paying attention to internal Images and events. Of the 71 samples that were discussed with Jennifer, 46 included visual components that were an important part of her experience descriptions. Many of these visual experiences were Images Jennifer was imaginally seeing at the moment of the beep. These Images were all in color; they were vivid and typically full of detail. Some of them included movement, or sounds, or visualizations of written words. The Images were at times related to her current activity and other times seemingly idle daydreams. Some were quite obscure and difficult to understand.

Jennifer experienced seeing her inner Images in a variety of locations: in front and back of her, to either or both sides, elevated above or dropped below eye level in positions that sometimes were not meaningful but at other times accurately reflected the actual position of an external object; however, she was seeing an Image of the object in imagination rather than physically observing it. The Images lay along a continuum of correctness of detail; that is, some were fairly accurate recreations of the physical world, whereas others were severely "goofed-up," with all possible combinations in between. Jennifer also often reported multiple Images in a single experience, which were usually non-overlapping and occurring one after the other in such rapid sequence that it was impossible for her to say that only one of the Images was actually present at the moment of the beep.

Thus, visual experiences were a very important characteristic of Jennifer's inner experiences during the sampling period. In this chapter, we will discuss several particular aspects of these experiences: Images of External Reality; Images Related to Current Activities; Daydreams; Visualizations of Written Words; Distortions in Images; and the Role of Color and Movement. However, it is important to keep in mind that Jennifer's visual experiences covered a wide range of complexity, and often all of these particular aspects were present in any given sample description.

Images Of External Reality

Some of Jennifer's inner visualizations (16 of 71 samples) at the moment of the beep were concrete representations of a portion of the real existing situation Jennifer was in at the moment. For example, Jennifer was cleaning her room so that she could pass inspection early and go home for the weekend (Sample #4). At the moment of the beep, she was alternating between looking at a messy counter top in her room and an Image of the exact same counter top but which seemed to be about six inches closer than the original. There was also in this experience a second Image, that of herself, viewed from the back, standing in front of the counter. In this case, the beep seemed to "come between" the three pictures: the Image of herself, the counter top seen in physical reality, and the counter top viewed in her imagination. The Images were in color. In the Image of the counter top, she could see her jars of tea, her makeup and makeup case, exactly as they were on the physical counter, except that they seemed to be slightly larger in the Image than in reality because the Imaged countertop was a little closer to her view. This Image was seen at eye level, in front of her, although from the perspective of looking down at the counter top. There was no border around the Image; in her physical view of the counter, she could also see the floor below, but in the Image, this detail was not present. She only saw the outer edges of the counter delimited by the walls and mirror and the various objects scattered upon it.

At other times, Jennifer's recreations of the physical world contained particular details that were slightly modified from the external reality she was viewing or could have been viewing if she had turned her attention to it. For example, Jennifer was sitting at a living room table, smoking a cigarette. At the moment of the beep, she was idly gazing at the blue wall across from her and behind the table, but paying attention to an Image of Joe, one of the other residents, who was sitting on the opposite side of the table (Sample #75). Jennifer could have been looking at the real Joe; at the moment of the beep, however, she was seeing an imaginal recreation of him instead. This Image also simultaneously included a picture of her tall blue glass of iced tea. Jennifer's Image of Joe was viewed slightly up and to her front right, in the same place where he was sitting in reality, although she was not looking at him at the time. In the Image of Joe, Jennifer could see he was wearing a Walkman portable radio, holding a blue glass in one hand and a lit cigarette in the other. This Image accurately portrayed the physical Joe sitting across from her, except that the real Joe was holding a yellow glass, not a blue one.

The Image of Jennifer's own big blue glass of tea was positioned lower at her left side, which was where her glass was physically placed at the time. In this Image, her glass had a lid on it, but no straw. In reality, however, Jennifer's drink did have a straw in it, but had no lid. Thus, the imaginal picture she was viewing was basically true to external reality but with some minor details slightly modified.

In another example, Jennifer was cleaning her room, putting a new garbage sack between her dresser and the corner wall (Sample #33). At the moment of the beep, she was looking at the empty sack she was setting down, but seeing an Image of the *full* sack that was just beside the new empty one. The Image she was seeing was viewed to the front, slightly to one side and elevated "a little bit too high." It was in color; she could see the details of the bag's contents and in particular was noticing the back of an empty coffee creamer bottle that was sitting on top. The Imaged creamer bottle was tilted slightly within the bag (it was straight up and down in reality), and had a little splotch of red on it that was not present on the real bottle. Here again, there were no borders or sharp edges to the Image except her view of the blue wall that was really back of the bag. Thus, although Jennifer was seeing the physical world with her eyes, her attention was directed at an internal Image that was somewhat modified from the external objects she was viewing.

Finally, there were times when individual details in Jennifer's inner pictures were altered from the physical reality she was seeing in more substantial ways. For example, she was standing in her bedroom, in front of the mirror, gathering up her makeup in anticipation of going home for the weekend (Sample #29). At the moment of the beep, she was saying to herself, "I'd better not forget anything," and looking down at her makeup case. A moment before the beep, she had been paying attention to the case, but on this particular moment, she was seeing an Image of the makeup case, viewed from the perspective as if she were seeing it in the reflection of mirror. The Image seemed in front of her, slightly elevated above eye level, and on the left side. She could see many details and colors: a bottle of red nail polish (which in reality was not there), a couple of lipsticks, the hot water pot, and jars of tea setting on the counter top alongside the case. Jennifer did not see herself reflected in the mirror Image, only the makeup case. Furthermore, the makeup case in the Image was only seen as if in the mirror: Jennifer could only see the back of the case, which was reflected, not the front and the back, as would have been the case if she had been looking at the scene in reality. There were no borders around the Image, just the actual walls and edge of the counter top. However, although the mirror in the Image seemed itself to be straight, the makeup case and the items within it which were reflected in the mirror were tilted. On the other hand, the reflections of the hot water pot and jars of tea sitting onthe counter were *not* tilted, but the jars of tea seemed to be "floating" slightly above the counter, or at least, slightly higher up than usual (Jennifer did not see any space between the bottom of the jars and counters).

Thus, we have a series of samples in which Images portrayed a portion of the reality that was present at that moment. Rather than paying attention to that portion of the physical reality, however, Jennifer was attending to a more or less inexact imaginal copy of that portion of reality.

Images Related to Current Activities

Some of Jennifer's Images (12 of 71 samples) were not re-creations of the physical world that she was seeing (or capable of seeing) with her eyes at the moment, but were clearly related to her activity at the time. For example, she was in her bedroom, lying on the bed, listening to Rod Stewart singing on the radio. At the moment of the beep, she was seeing an Image of Rod Stewart (Sample #23). The Image was only of his head; in particular, she was looking at his blond hair, which seemed "a little more bushy" than normal. The Image was in color, seen to the front and right, six or eight inches in front of her eyes. It did not include details of his face. Jennifer's main attention in this sample was directed to listening to the music she was hearing; the Image of Rod Stewart was just an idle picture that had been created in response to her activity at the time.

In another example, Jennifer was standing in front of an open refrigerator, wondering what was going to be for dinner the next night (Sample #52). At the moment of the beep, Jennifer was picturing a plate covered with a pile of cooked rice and a couple of big pork chops. The Image was in color; she could see something green also on the plate, like cooked broccoli, but she wasn't sure what it was. The plate was slightly tilted with its face towards her, so she could see its total contents, and was viewed directly in front of her, as if in the air at eye level between her and the refrigerator. The Image was not surrounded by any borders or frame. Furthermore, the inside of the refrigerator that she was physically seeing at the time was not a part of the Image, nor was she noticing its contents. She was, however, aware of the refrigerator light which seemed brighter than usual and was a kind of illumination behind the imaginary dinner she was picturing, and was experienced as being perhaps part of the Image itself.

In one final example, Jennifer was playing Ping-Pong with one of the halfway house residents (Sample #9). At the moment of the beep, she was wondering (in a nonverbal sort of way that will be discussed later in the Unsymbolized Thinking section) how to hit the ball so that her opponent would miss his shot. At the same time, she was seeing an Image of her left arm and hand holding a Ping-Pong paddle. The Image was seen inside her head, but down and to the left, as if she were actually glancing at her left hand and side as she played. In the Image, however, she was wearing a red and white striped shirt, which was not the same shirt she was actually wearing that day. Furthermore, in reality, Jennifer was holding the Ping-Pong paddle in her right hand, not her left. In other words, this Image was accurate to what Jennifer might have seen if she had physically looked down at her arm, except it showed her to be left- rather than right-handed, and wearing a different blouse. Thus, we see that Jennifer's Images sometimes seemed to accompany her activities, or to supplement them, in ways that were interesting and vivid, as well as being meaningful in the context where they appeared.

Daydreams

There were a number of visual experiences in Jennifer's samples that could be described as daydreams (10 of 71 samples). At those times, Jennifer was usually idle, either bored during a meeting or relaxing on her own time. Some of these inner visualizations were simple and fairly accurate recreations of her external surroundings at the time; these samples are similar to (or the same as) some of the visualizations described above in the Images of External Reality section. The key characteristic we are focusing on in these examples, however, is their idle, daydreaming nature, rather than the accuracy with which they did or did not duplicate the external setting. For example, she was sitting in a meeting, listening to a follow resident (John) reading aloud from a newspaper (Sample #66). Jennifer was bored; she was rubbing the mascara off her hand and trying to pretend she was paying attention to what he was saying. At the same time, she was visualizing an Image of John sitting on the couch, reading the paper. The Image was accurate for the details of the room they were meeting in and clothes John was wearing; she could see his white T-shirt and gray hair. The Image was seen inside her head on the front right side, approximately in the same place where John was actually sitting. The Image was tilted slightly away from Jennifer, so that she was viewing it more from an angle than seeing it straight in front of her. However, most of her attention was directed at rubbing off the mascara; the Image was just on idle recreation of the boring scene in which she found herself.

In another example, Jennifer was remembering when she had returned to the halfway house after visiting her mother the previous weekend (Sample #61). At the moment of the beep, Jennifer was sitting at the smoking table in the living room and seeing an Image of herself, walking into the front foyer. The Image was in color, and seen in front of her and to the left side. This Image of herself was in motion: the Imaged Jennifer was wearing blue jeans and was taking a few steps around the entryway corner. The Image included a picture of one of the staff sitting on a couch with a light beside her, which was accurate to reality but was from a physically impossible perspective, since there was actually a wall between Jennifer's viewpoint and the couch she could imaginally see.

The Image included many details of the room: she could see the stereo, the smoking table she was actually sitting at, and a series of shelves across the room which actually hold boxes of games, but which, in her Image, were filled with books. She could see the pool table, on which were sitting orange, red, and white balls. An instant after this large Image appeared on her left, but still seemingly at the moment of the beep, Jennifer also saw an Image of a cigarette. These two Images were not superimposed but, rather, the beep seemed to come between them. The cigarette in the Image was small, as if it had been partially burned and then put out. She could see the lettering on its side, "Virginia Slims." The Image of the cigarette seemed to be up close, as if it were only about a foot away from her face, but here again, slightly to the front and left side of her view. In perspective (since the cigarette was so close), it appeared to be underneath the shelves on the opposite wall, which were also in the Image, and also full of books rather than games.

Some of Jennifer's daydreams had a highly fanciful quality about them. For example, once again when Jennifer was in a house meeting, she was listening to someone who was reading about a midget named Billy Barty and was trying to visualize who he was (Sample #14). At the moment of the beep, she was wondering, in Unsymbolized Thinking, if he was a certain television character whom she had seen before and could recognize.

A split second later, but still while the beep was going off, she saw an Image of a small, midget-sized desk. The desk was about three feet tall; it was tan with a yellow top. It was sitting in an office that Jennifer described in detail: there was a window in the back with gold curtains, a couple of chairs sitting around the room, a gold and brown carpet, and pictures hanging on the wall in the background beside the window. The scene was not of any office Jennifer had ever actually seen, but was merely a creation of her imagination. In the Image, she could see Bill Barty pulling out a chair at the desk as if in preparation to sit down. His facial features were blurry but she noticed that his hair was light brown. While Jennifer was simultaneously seeing this Image and wondering if she knew who Billy Barty was, the speaker in the room was still talking or reading aloud. However, she was no longer paying attention to his words; rather, the vivid and colorful Image occupied her full attention.

Some of Jennifer's inner experiences, even if they corresponded to reality or related to her current activity, had a perseverative daydreaming quality about them. For example, on the first day of sampling, Jennifer reported a series of Images that occurred in samples throughout the day, all of which included herself wearing a red and white striped shirt which in fact she was not wearing that day. In one of these, described above, Jennifer was playing Ping-Pong. At the moment of the beep, she was picturing herself holding a Ping-Pong paddle in her left hand and wearing the red and white striped blouse (Sample #9). In another example earlier in the day, she was lying on her bed listening to Elton John singing on the radio ("Don't let the sun go down on me . . ."), and thinking about how the hairdresser was going to come that night and curl her hair (Sample #1). At the moment of the beep, she was seeing an Image as if she were standing looking at herself in the mirror after her hair had been curled. The Image was colorful and vivid, exactly as it would have been if she were, in fact, looking at herself in the bedroom mirror. She could see the towel hanging on a rack near the sink, her jars of tea sitting on the counter top, and her hair, which was curled and slightly more blond than usual. But in the Image, Jennifer was again wearing the same red and white striped blouse.

In the next sample, she was thinking about talking to her case manager about moving to different housing, and visualizing two Images inside her head that seemed, at the moment of the beep, to be alternating back and forth. In one Image, Jennifer pictured the mouthpiece of a tan- or flesh-colored telephone. Her curled, blond hair was hanging down over it, just as if she actually had the phone to her ear, talking, and could see the mouthpiece and hair that would be in her vision. In the second, alternating, Image, Jennifer saw a picture of herself standing at a distance, talking on the telephone. In this Image, Jennifer was wearing blue jeans and once again the same striped shirt.

In a final sample (#4), also described above, Jennifer was cleaning her room in anticipation of leaving for the weekend. At the moment of the beep, she was alternating between looking at her messy counter top and an Image of the exact same counter top, as well as an Image of herself, seen at a distance of about two feet from the back. Here again, the Jennifer in the Image was wearing the same striped blouse. Thus, in this series of four inner visualizations, Jennifer was more or less accurately seeing a picture of herself; however, in all of them, she was repetitively wearing a certain garment that was not what she had been physically wearing that day.

Images Of Written Words

Visualizations of written words played an important role in Jennifer's visual experiences; 10 of her 71 samples contained either imaginal recreations of written words or words that she could read that were printed on an Imaged object such as a cigarette. For example, in a sample described above in the Daydreams section, Jennifer was sitting in the living room, visualizing herself returning home the previous weekend. At the moment of the beep, she was seeing an Image of herself stepping into the living room, but she also was seeing an Image of a cigarette, close to her face on the front and left side of her vision. The cigarette was small, as if partially burned; she could see the letters on the side of the cigarette, which read "Virginia Slims." The lettering was accurate to reality, that is, it was in the same color and print type as the lettering on her actual cigarettes. In this sample, Jennifer was not speaking the words to herself that she could see on the cigarettes; she was simply seeing them in the Image and recognizing their semantic content.

At other times, the words Jennifer was visually seeing were meaningful and related to the rest of her experience at the moment, but they were colorful creations of her own instead of a visual memory of words she had seen printed somewhere else. For example, Jennifer was taking a puff of her cigarette and wondering when the beeper was going to beep (Sample #68).

In the sample, Jennifer was seeing the word, WONDER, printed in white skinny letters to her front left side. The word seemed to extend outward, with the letter "W" being too close to her left temple to see as clearly as the other letters, which were stretched forward. Jennifer, at the moment of the beep, was particularly noticing the letter "O" in the printed word, although she did not know why she was noticing that letter more than any other. At the same time, two other visual experiences were occurring for Jennifer. She was seeing an accurate Image of the can of Pepsi she was drinking; the can was lower in her visual field, and on the right side, rather than on the left where the word WONDER was seen. One side of the Pepsi can was slightly blurry.

At the same time, Jennifer was seeing a yellow cloud, a streak that originated at the back of her head and neck and spread forward, widening as it spread a few inches beyond the left side of her head. This yellow streak was vivid yellow (the color of a Wendy's soft-drink cup, she said) and had a well-defined lower border or edge that was about neck level. This yellow plume or cloud moved past, from back to front on her left side, without losing its integrity or shape. Jennifer described the yellow streak as pretty and pleasant to look at. She said that her experience of "wondering" when the next beep was going to go off was contained in this yellow; it was a "very strong wonder" that "moved too fast" to capture in words. In other words, it seemed to Jennifer that if her wondering had been less strong, she would have spoken to herself about it in words; the fact that it was captured by the color was a sign of the strength of wondering at the time.

In several of her samples, the words Jennifer was seeing printed on her visual screen were "goofed-up," that is, more or less distorted in some way. For example, she was sitting outside with a fellow resident (Sally) and listening to her describe a time when she had been hospitalized and given glucose, or "sugar water" (Sample #50). At the moment of the beep, Jennifer was looking straight ahead and viewing two alternating Images which seemed to cycle quickly past her view twice each. The first Image was of Sally, who was sitting beside her; the Image was to the side of Jennifer's vision where Sally was physically sitting and could have been seen in real life. This Image showed Sally sitting cross-legged on a chair, accurately wearing a blue and white flowered dress. Jennifer could see that Sally was sitting slightly back from a nearby table and that she was wearing glasses and holding a red drinking glass in her hand. An instant later, but still while the beep was going off, Jennifer saw a tall, transparent drinking glass that had the word "Sugar" printed across it in red letters, the letters hovering slightly in front of the glass. (Jennifer felt that the two Images were "at the same time," although they were not seen together or superimposed; rather, the beep captured the cycling transition between them.)

In this second Image, Jennifer could see that the clear glass was thick at the bottom and inside there was a layer of something that resembled undissolved sugar crystals. She was looking down at the glass; the red word, "sugar," was at the top, not actually printed *on* the glass but rather "just floating around up there." The word was "all goofed-up;" the letters were printed as one would see them in a book, but with many short red lines scratched through them. These lines almost totally obliterated the letters, except for the "S" and the descending part of the "g." The word had a little rim of black along the bottom of the letters, and the red graffiti-like lines were confined to the letters themselves and did not appear to go through to the transparent glass. Jennifer could not relate any significance to the marring lines (for example, she could not say that they symbolized sugar dissolving), nor could she say how she knew the obliterated letters spelled "sugar." She simply knew what the word meant and could describe its appearance.

In another example, Jennifer was in her bedroom, trying to pin up her hair and hoping that it wouldn't fall down or come undone (Sample #28). At the moment of the beep, she was looking down at her feet, concentrating on pulling up her hair with her hands. As she combed her hair, her experience was that she was thinking the words, "I hope my hair won't fall down," but not thinking them in a listening way. Rather, the words seemed to be "just resting to the side." That is, the experience included an Image, to her left side, of the black words, "I hope my hair won't fall down." These words appeared merely as a bunch of words, all "mixed up," jumbled together with an "electric blue" or royal blue coloration below them and a smoky blue color on the sides and at the top. She was not speaking any words to herself, and she could not say how she knew the jumbled-up black conglomerate of words meant, "I hope my hair won't fall down." She was definite, however, that that was what the words were. The smoky blue color on the sides and above the letters was a more diffuse texture, more cloudy in appearance, than the darker "electric blue" at the bottom. The Image was not like a photograph, with any kind of border or frame. Rather, the words just seemed pushed over to the side, and it seemed to Jennifer that this was because she was concentrating so intently on her hair. She was thinking the words to herself "a little bit, but just a little," and as a consequence, they lost their visual clarity and prominence.

Distortions in Images

Many of Jennifer's Images (19 of 71 samples) were distorted or "goofed-up" (Jennifer's term) in some way that was not meaningful to her or obviously related to the Image content. These distortions occurred on a continuum of severity: at times, the Images were, for example, just slightly tilted, or details in the visualizations were slightly incorrect, such as seeing a yellow glass when in fact the glass was blue. On the other hand, at other times, portions of Images were entirely obliterated or blurred or altered in a fairly dramatic way.

The most common distorting characteristic was Jennifer's perception that either an entire Image, or certain details within an Image, were "kind of crooked," that is, were tilted in some way rather than being straight up and down. For example, she was sitting at a house meeting, listening to one of the other residents (Bill) talk about returning a pair of shoes to the store where he had purchased them (Sample #27). At the moment of the beep, Jennifer was looking down at the floor but picturing an Image of Bill sitting on the couch across the room. The Image Jennifer was seeing was an accurate copy of Bill that day: he was dressed in a white shirt with brown stripes, white shorts, and brown shoes. The Image was in front of her and to the right, where Bill was in fact sitting, and details within the visualization were all the correct size and distance away, as if Jennifer were actually looking at Bill sitting on the real couch. The Image was only of Bill, although Jennifer had the impression that other people were sitting next to him on the couch in the Image, just as they were in real life, and that she could have visualized them as well had she chosen to do so.

In other words, this was a realistic Image, distinguishable from reality primarily by the fact that Jennifer was not in real life looking at Bill at that moment. However, the entire Image, and everything within it, was tilted, with the right side up at about a 45-degree angle. Thus, the floor and couch on which Bill was sitting were tilted up 45 degrees. Underneath the part of the Image that was tilted up seemed to be black, empty space that was not visible on the other sides of the visualization.

The tilting described above was an example of where the entire visual Image was rotated through a particular angle. Jennifer also had Images where the Image itself was straight, but some detail or set of details within the Image were crooked. For example, in a sample described above in the Images of External Reality section, Jennifer was gathering up her makeup (Sample #29) and seeing an Image of her makeup case. In this Image, the mirror, a hot water pot, and some jars of tea that were sitting on her counter top were straight up and down. However, the makeup case and the items with it (such as the nail polish and lipsticks) were slightly tilted.

In other samples, Jennifer's Images were altered in ways that resembled graffiti. For example, she was reading the newspaper index page and had just finished reading the word, "Television" (Sample #65). At the moment of the beep, Jennifer had just raised her eyes from the paper to look out at the room, but she was paying attention, not to the room she was seeing, but to an Image of a tilted color TV set. The TV was large, about the same size as the one in the halfway house living room, but actually resembled her own smaller portable TV. On the TV screen in the Image was a dark-haired man wearing a white shirt and dark pants. The scene was not one she recognized from any real television program, although she said it reminded her of *The Gong Show*. Behind the man on the screen was a red, white, and blue background, the red part of which resembled a hanging red curtain. There was no sound or movement in the Image. In front of the man was a round, chest-high, white podium or altarlike structure. The man's left leg was visible beside the podium and Jennifer could see that his pants were tight-fitted at the ankle. The top of the podium, however, was obliterated by a rather messy black rim or ring that Jennifer could see was not a part of the actual podium structure. This black rim seemed fuzzy, like a flat splotch of scratched-out lines across where the podium was on the screen. Jennifer did not know of any significance underlying either the appearance of the altarlike podium or of the graffiti-like obliteration. She was definite, however, that the black pattern was not a part of the podium, but only in front of it, blocking out the top of the podium from her view. Because the entire Image of the TV was tilted about 45 degrees, the man and the podium were also tilted, but the living room background behind the TV (walls, a table with lamp) was straight.

(In real life, the table and lamp were to the side of the room, rather than being in the center next to the TV as in Jennifer's visualization.) Thus, in this complex Image, Jennifer's imaginal representation was different from reality in three ways: by the fact that the TV and screen were tilted 45 degrees; the white podium on the screen was partially obliterated by a messy black rim or ring overlaid at its top; and the living room furniture in the background of the Image had been rearranged slightly from what Jennifer would have seen had she physically viewed the room's contents.

Some of Jennifer's Image distortions were fragments, such as portions of body parts that were separated from the rest of the body in a nonmeaningful way. For example, she had been watching one of the residents (John) unsuccessfully trying to get either a soda or his change back from a vending machine. At the moment of the beep, Jennifer was telling John that he could push a different button because the RC Cola was all gone (Sample #90). At the same time, Jennifer was seeing an Image, appearing to be a couple of yards in front of her and to the right, of someone holding an RC Cola can. The Image of the can was normal in appearance, that is, it was the correct color, and not distorted in shape or appearance in any way. However, the arm that Jennifer saw holding the can was not connected to any person but rather abruptly ended below the elbow in her view. As she turned her attention to the Image, the entire picture faded away. Jennifer's experience in this sample was not that there was a whole person holding the can and that she was only focused on the arm; instead, her experience was that she was seeing a fragment of someone's arm that abruptly ended below the elbow.

Visualizations of words could be "goofed up" also. We have already described (in the Images of Written Words section) the colorful distortions of some of Jennifer's Images of printed words. For example, she saw the red word, "Sugar," floating above a transparent glass, which was nearly obliterated by red lines crossing through its letters (Sample #50); in another experience, Jennifer was thinking "just a little bit" about the phrase, "I hope my hair won't fall down," and visualizing the words all black and jumbled up over to the side of her vision, surrounded by various hues of blue (Sample #28).

Color also played a role in distortions of Images. For example, Jennifer was talking to her mother on the phone about Jennifer's aunt (Sample #62). At the moment of the beep, Jennifer was visualizing an Image of her aunt. The Image was very small, "a little picture," seen in front and somewhat below Jennifer. In the picture, the aunt was seen from the chest up; she was wearing a short-sleeved shirt with indentations on the material, like some sort of knit. The Image showed her aunt with short hair, which was a realistic light brown color. The picture of the aunt, however, was "not as pretty as she really is"; her eyes looked "beady," that is, they were standing out, big and sharp and harsh, as if someone had taken two paper eyes and posted them onto the otherwise true-to-life (although tiny) Image. The aunt's eyes in the Image seemed very black and unpleasant, apparently surrounded by blue so that their whites could not be seen. Circling this Image of the aunt was yellowish-white color that was smoky in texture: it looked like swirling smoke, or cotton fluff billowing around the Image. The yellowish, smoky color looked to be swirling down from the upper right side of Jennifer's head to surround the Image of the aunt, although it was not actually moving in the Image. As in the last example, Jennifer was at a loss to explain any significance that might be attached to the smoke or color; she could only describe the experience as she was certain she observed it.

Role of Color and Movement

Jennifer's inner Images often contained vivid colors and/or motion. Color was especially important; not only were all of her inner visualizations in color, color also was a salient characteristic of many of her experiences when she was observing or interacting with the external environment. For example, Jennifer was watching one of her fellow residents (Tim) hand another resident (Tony) a can of RC Cola (Sample #32). At the moment of the beep, Jennifer was hearing the phone ring and was wondering who was calling; at the same time, she was also wondering whether Tim was going to buy Tony a coke and was gazing at the RC Cola can in Tim's hand which Tony was reaching out to take. She was particularly noticing the brilliant blue, the "royal blue" of the can, and although she also could see the red lettering on the can, her primary focus of attention at the moment was on the blue that appeared so striking in the sunlight. In another example, Jennifer was sitting in the living room, flicking a cigarette into the cigarette can when she heard the signal (Sample #76). At the moment, however, she was not thinking any thoughts in words, nor experiencing any feelings, or seeing any internal Images. She was simply gazing at the cigarette can, where her attention was particularly directed at the red and gold colors of the (Folger's coffee) can, and the silver rim circling the top of the can.

Jennifer almost always could recall, and made a point of noting in our daily conversations, colors in the Images she saw inside her head during the sampling period. For example, in some of the experiences described in detail above, Jennifer described the tan of the telephone on which she was picturing herself speaking (Sample #2), the striped blouse she was wearing in her Images the first day of sampling, the red nail polish on her dresser (Sample #29), the green vegetables on the plate of rice and pork chops (Sample #52), and the orange, red, and white balls on the pool table (Sample #61). At times, the colors of certain objects in these visualizations were different from the colors in the same objects that she was seeing in real life, such as the Image of Joe holding a blue glass that was, in the external world, a yellow glass (Sample #75, described above).

This same mistaken perception of color also occurred in another sample when Jennifer was looking at the physical world of reality. In this example, she was listening to a follow resident (Bill) talk about where he bought his new shoes (Sample #78). At the moment of the beep, Jennifer was looking at Bill's legs and shoes and at the same time was viewing an Image inside her head of another resident (Sam) sitting down, wearing a yellow T-shirt with red on the front. Bill's new shoes were black and white; they were nice dress shoes. As she looked at the shoes, she also noticed that Bill's pants were black, although in fact the pants he was wearing at the time were gray. The Image of Sam that was occurring simultaneously was seen as if she were looking at Sam from the back. Even though she was seeing him from the back, however, she could also see the front of his yellow shirt which had some red on it (Jennifer was later unsure whether Sam's real yellow shirt contained any red), and she could see Sam's freckles on his face. This impossible perspective seemed as if Jennifer was looking up and over Sam's back, thus making it somehow possible for her to see both his front and back sides simultaneously. For present purposes, however, it is the particular salience of color that is important to Jennifer's detailed descriptions.

Color also appeared as a salient feature in more abstract ways in Jennifer's inner visualizations. This color did not always obviously relate meaningfully to the content of her experiences, yet Jennifer recognized its importance and usually described the presence of the color as pleasing and good. She once remarked, "A lot of my thoughts are in yellow," and that indeed seemed to be true. For example, in an Image previously described, Jennifer was seeing, inside her head, an Image of her aunt (Sample #62). Surrounding the tiny picture of her aunt was what appeared to be a swirling patch of yellowish-white color that had a texture like smoke or cotton.

In another example, Jennifer was standing in the kitchen, twisting an ice cube tray and thinking about how hard it was to get ice out of the tray (Sample #77). At the moment of the beep, she was seeing yellow color on both sides of her head. The yellow was a misty color, and it had a distinct shape, with a sharp edge at the top and bottom. The color circled around the back of her head and up both sides, in the shape of a horseshoe; at the back of her head, on the right side, she could see the word YELLOW. This word was printed, also in yellow, and was positioned in front of the horseshoe-shaped misty yellow color, with a little patch of white near the letter "Y."

In a third example, Jennifer was carrying her glass of iced tea to the table in her bedroom. At the moment of the beep, she was aware of hearing the phone ringing in the background as she set down her glass, and at the same time, she was visualizing an Image of her watch (Sample #73). The watch was seen on her left arm (she was putting down the glass with her right hand). In the Image, the arm was tilted towards her, midarm down, and she could see the table and lamp in the background, just as if she were really glancing at her watch out of the corner of her eye. At the same time, or only a split second later, but while she was still hearing the beep, Jennifer saw, on her left side, a cloud or band of dark orangish-yellow that was rimmed in yellow and almost red in the center. The cloud had a distinct shape to it; it was thicker in the front and narrower in the back (which Jennifer could see at the edge of her view). The cloud seemed to twist and wrap around the real world; in between where the colored shape was visible, Jennifer could see the physical details of her room but she could not see through the color itself. As she looked at the orangish-colored cloud, Jennifer also visualized the word "THOUGHT," printed clearly in bright yellow letters in front of her on the right side. The yellow word "THOUGHT" was also surrounded by this distinctly formed yellowish-orange color; Jennifer had to look around the bending darker color to see the clearly printed yellow word. The colors in this experience bore no significance for Jennifer but they were "a pleasing presence next to my mind."

Finally, some of Jennifer's visual experiences of color were of abstract forms, as well as of seemingly nonmeaningful colors. For example, Jennifer was in a group meeting and was listening to a staff member talking about two of the other residents (Mickey and Johnny) changing nights when they each took turns cooking dinner (Sample #88). At the moment of the beep, Jennifer was seeing an Image of Johnny sitting on the couch. The Image was seen in the direction where Johnny actually was sitting, in front and about 45 degrees to the right. This Image of Johnny accurately reflected his appearance: she could see that he was wearing a white shirt and blue jeans, and that his eyes were brown and open rather wide. The Image was moving as Jennifer watched it; it was not that the figure of Johnny moved, but rather that the whole Image moved slightly away from Jennifer and then back towards her again. At the same time, Jennifer was seeing an Image, also on the left side, of the word "JOHNNY." This visualization was highly colorful; the letter "J" was gray, the "O" was navy blue, the "H" was red, and the "NN" was white. Jennifer could not see clearly the letter "Y" and so did not remember its color; however, she did note that the word appeared to be hand-printed except for the letters "NN," which were in more of a script.

In another sample, Jennifer was talking to her mother on the phone (Sample #79). At the moment of the beep, there had been a pause in their conversation and Jennifer was seeing an Image, inside her head, of an abstract figure-8-shaped black figure which was on a background of red and surrounded by a white rim. There were black lines rising from the top part of the figure. This abstract colored form was seen by Jennifer in the front of her head, a little to the right and slightly below eye level. It was flat and tilted slightly away from her view (tilted in the sense of lying down, rather than being turned away). It seemed to be "close," as if seen from about a foot and a half away, although Jennifer definitely recognized it as an inner visualization, not something superimposed on the external world. The shape had no significance for Jennifer; she had no associations attached to it.

At the same time that she was seeing this black and white and red shape inside her head, Jennifer was also looking at a black coffee pot sitting on the counter top near the phone where she was talking. She was aware of the red light on the coffee pot, indicating the coffee was read. However, her view of the coffee pot seemed "all goofed up"; it was blurry, like a photograph in which distinct shapes are not visible. Jennifer said of this look at the coffee pot that she was "not paying attention to it but it was there; that's why it was all goofed up." In other words, she was just idly seeing it with her eyes from where she was talking on the phone, and her lack of attention seemed to cause it to lose its sharpness of focus in her vision.

Like color, motion also played a major role in Jennifer's reported inner experiences, sometimes giving her descriptions a vividly realistic quality. For example, she was lying on her bed, Imaging herself sitting at the smoking table in the living room (Sample #3). At the moment of the beep, she was turning over on her side, thinking to herself, "I might get a cup of coffee," and simultaneously seeing an Image of her favorite coffee cup. The cup was blue with white spots; it was filled with coffee and Jennifer could see that the coffee had a lot of creamer in it. In the Image, the cup was moving, as if Jennifer were lifting it to her mouth to drink. In the visual picture, her arm and hand were blurry. However, she could clearly feel the sensation as if her arm actually were lifting the moving cup, although in physical reality her arm was not moving. In another example, Jennifer was seeing an Image of a roommate (Mickey) stepping from Jennifer's bedroom into the bathroom (Sample #6). In the Image, Mickey was moving, disappearing into the bathroom and shutting the door, and the Image included the realistic sound of Jennifer's door clicking shut behind her.

In some of Jennifer's samples, the motion she was describing was in the entire Image, not just in individual persons on objects that she could see in it. For example, she was sitting outside next to another resident (Carolyn), enjoying the early evening weather. Jennifer was relaxed; she was mostly just pleasantly "spacing out" in the quiet company of her friend (Sample #51). At the moment of the beep, Jennifer was looking straight ahead but seeing an Image of Carolyn sitting beside her. In the Image, she could see the blue and white flowered dress Carolyn was wearing that came about to her knees. Carolyn's legs were crossed, and Jennifer could also see the shoes she was wearing and that Carolyn's legs were very tan. The white flowers on the blue dress seemed slightly larger than on the real dress, because Carolyn in the Image seemed slightly closer than she was sitting in real life. The Image was only of Carolyn's lower legs and skirt, much as Jennifer would have seen them if she had been looking at Carolyn from the corner of her eyes. The Image as Jennifer described it, however, was in motion. It began over at Jennifer's right side, where Carolyn was physically sitting, but then Jennifer saw it swing down and back up again in a kind of U-pattern and then disappear, only to reappear an instant later back in the place where she had originally seen it. The movement of the Image was initially quite fast as it moved down and back up, but it seemed slower to reappear. The beep fell somewhere in the U-shaped motion that Jennifer described.

Motion also was important in Jennifer's experiences of verbal thought, whether they were visualized or audibly experienced. For example, Jennifer was sitting smoking a cigarette and wondering when the beeper was going to go off (Sample #68, described above in the Images of Written Words section). At the moment of the beep, she was seeing a misty yellow and white cloud move swiftly up the right, next to her head. This cloud, or plume, of color had a distinct lower edge to it that was about nose-high. As it moved forward, it maintained the integrity of its shape, which was small at the back of the head and wider at the sides. Immediately after it formed, Jennifer saw the word "WONDER" printed in skinny white letters extending out from her left temple. Jennifer described the swift-moving cloud as a visualization of her wondering, which at the time was very strong.

In other samples, it was the sound of her subvocal words that Jennifer experienced as moving past. For example, she had been watching television one night, and was thinking about getting up to change the channel (Sample #12). At the moment of the beep, Jennifer was silently hearing the words, "I should get up and change the channel but I don't want to." The words, which were in Jennifer's own voice, moved swiftly from back to front at the left side of her head. It was the entire spoken phrase that moved, that is, Jennifer did not hear it start in the back and conclude in the front. Rather, her experience was that of feeling and hearing the words move all at one time.

In summary, then, in all of the above examples we see that Jennifer was capable of visualizing and describing a great variety of visual inner experiences. These experiences ranged from fairly accurate representations of what she was seeing in the external world, to more abstract or distorted (in the sense of being tilted, or obliterated, or changed in size or coloration) creations of the imagination. These visualizations included a range of motion, sound, and color; at times they were clearly related to her activity or environment at hand and, at other times, seemingly unrelated or highly fanciful daydreams. It would be impossible to overstate the importance of visual phenomena to Jennifer's inner world; her visual experiences were detailed and gripping, both at the time and in her subsequent descriptions.

VERBAL THOUGHT

Jennifer experienced inner verbal thought in two ways: Inner Speech and Inner Hearing of words subvocally spoken to herself, and visualization of printed words. This latter form of verbal experience has already been described above as part of the Images section. Thus, what follows is a description only of her auditory verbal thought, except in those cases where the hearing of subvocal words was accompanied by simultaneous visualizations of the interiorly spoken words.

Jennifer experienced subvocal words (10 of 71 samples) either as Inner Hearing, hearing her own voice silently speaking to herself or, as

Inner Speech, herself speaking subvocally to herself. Jennifer was typically able to identify where the words were perceived to be located and how the words sounded in terms of tonal pitch and volume, and also was able to describe physical sensations that sometimes accompanied the hearing or speaking of the words. For example, in a sample described above under Images of External Reality, Jennifer was in her bedroom gathering up her makeup in preparation for going home for the weekend (Sample #29). At the moment of the beep, she was seeing an Image of her makeup case and vanity counter top reflected in the mirror. At the same time, she was saying the words to herself in Inner Speech, "I better not forget anything." These words seemed to Jennifer to be in her own voice, exactly as she was accustomed to speaking. She heard them on the left side of her head; the phrase came from the back of her head up towards the front, moving rapidly and all at once, not one word at a time. In this sample, Jennifer's experience was that of actively speaking the words to herself, not just passively hearing them spoken. At the same time she was silently speaking the words, she was also aware of a tingling sensation or vibration in her head that was part of the experience of speaking the silent phrase. This vibration, which lasted only a moment, was centered towards the right and back of her head; it seemed somehow "closer in" than were the words that were moving swiftly past. The vibration was not an unpleasant sensation; it was just a mild physical phenomenon associated with speaking in general. In another example, Jennifer was looking at a package of matches and saying to herself, "He got those matches at 7-11" (Sample #34). These words were accompanied by a vivid Image of the 7-11 convenience store which was just down the street from where Jennifer lived. The Image was viewed as if she were standing in front of the store, looking at it. She could see the trees around the store, the gas pumps in front, the red letters (7-11) on the sign and the green garbage dumpster that was full of garbage, as well as the vivid colors (pink, purple, orange, and yellow) in the sky at sunset. In this sample, the words she was simultaneously hearing ("He got those matches at 7-11") were in her own voice, but her voice seemed to be at a lower pitch, that is, slightly more alto than normal. Her experience was both of hearing and saying the words at the top of her head, on both sides. At the same time that she was silently saying the words she was aware of a faint vibration in the back of her mouth that, once again, was associated with the words being spoken.

There was one sample in which Jennifer reported verbal thought while she was reading. In this example, she was rereading her sampling notebook, reading the latest entry, when she was signaled by the beep (Sample #26). In this sample, Jennifer was saying in Inner Speech the words as she read them. The words were also Inner-Heard in her own voice, on the left side of her head, and seemed to travel from the back to the front of her head as had been reported in some of Jennifer's other verbal samples.

At other times, Jennifer's experience was more that of passively Inner-Hearing words spoken by herself than of actively Inner-Speaking them to herself. For example, Jennifer was watching television and the show she had been viewing was over. At the moment of the beep, Jennifer was relaxed and feeling a little lazy; she was thinking the words to herself, "I should get up and change the channel, but I don't want to" (Sample #12). The voice that was speaking these words was Jennifer's; the phrase was heard inside her head on the left side and it moved in entirety from back to front as it was spoken. In this case however, although Jennifer knew that she was the creator of the words she was hearing, she still felt less involved in their being spoken than had been the case in the previous samples ("I wasn't actually talking directly to myself; I was just talking to myself"). In other words, Jennifer was simply sitting on the couch, idly hearing the words that reflected her lack of interest in getting up and moving at the moment. There were also samples where Jennifer's experience included hearing words spoken inside her head, but very softly, or even too softly actually to hear, although she knew words were present and could identify them.

For example, she was watching a staff member who was getting ready to leave for the day, and saying to herself, "She's going home" (Sample #35). In this sample, Jennifer's experience was that she was actively speaking the words to herself, in her own voice, rather than passively hearing them spoken. However, the spoken words as she heard them seemed "very dim . . . very, very quiet."

One final example should be given to demonstrate Jennifer's range of auditory verbal thought experiences. In this highly complex sample (which was visually described above in the Role of Color and Movement section), Jennifer was noticing the brilliant blue of a can of RC Cola that two of the other residents were passing to one another, and was thinking to herself, "I wonder if Sam is going to buy Joe a pop" (Sample #32). At about the same time (the beep seemed to come between the two verbal experiences), she was wondering who was on the telephone that was ringing in the background. Thus, in this sample, there were two very distinct experiences occurring either simultaneously or in such rapid sequence that Jennifer insisted they were both present at the moment of the beep.

In the first of these verbal "wonderings," that is, the wondering about who was "on the phone, Jennifer heard the words on the phone" spoken inside her head and in her own voice. Her experience in this part of the sample was that of passively Inner-Hearing the spoken words, which seemed to come from the back of her head and moved forward up the left side. At the same time that she was hearing the partial phrase "on the phone," she was also seeing, inside her head, an Image of the entire phrase "I wonder who is on the phone." The words she was visualizing were printed but "squinched," that is, flattened, not tall enough, and slanted like cursive writing. The lettering was hand-printed, but not in a handwriting that she recognized. The words were printed in black, with bright yellow color above them and yellow-orange below. They were difficult to read because of their squinched appearance and also because they moved rapidly across her inner field of vision as she "real quick wondered who was on the phone." She did not see the words as they were being printed, nor was it her experience that she had even actively created them. Rather, she saw only the entire complete phrase as the "real quick words" sped by.

In the second verbal half of this sample, Jennifer's wondering if Sam was going to buy Joe a pop, seemed to be at the same time that Jennifer was hearing the words "on the phone," or only an instant later. In this case, Jennifer did not visually see the words "I wonder if Sam is going to buy Joe a pop," nor did she hear them spoken inside her head. Nevertheless, her experience was that she was actively speaking them at the moment of the beep. This was a difficult experience for Jennifer to describe.

She remarked, "There were the words I was speaking, but I didn't hear them, I was just saying them in my mind." She was not saying them in any particular place inside her head, nor was there any physical tingling or vibration associated with saying the words. The words seemed "real quiet . . . dim and quiet," but not quiet as in other samples when she could still hear them spoken softly. In this case, the words were not heard at all, but Jennifer was certain words were being said, and even felt as if they were being spoken with the same meter and pattern of inflection as if they were being audibly delivered. They simply—in this sample—could not be heard.

FEELINGS

Some of Jennifer's samples (8 of 71 samples) were primarily emotional experiences. These emotions or Feelings were experienced by Jennifer in a physical way. For example, she was standing in her room while it was being "inspected" by one of the other residents (Sample

#30). At the moment of the beep, Jennifer was not Inner-Speaking or Inner-Hearing any words inside her head, or seeing any Images. She was, however, Feeling a tingling sensation in her chest and heart that felt like pressure, "the pressure of things not done right." Jennifer knew this pressure or tingling meant that she hoped the other resident wouldn't find anything wrong with the room, since Jennifer wanted to leave early that day for the weekend. However, she wasn't saying to herself in words, "I hope I passed," nor was she visualizing herself leaving or seeing the feeling of hope in any kind of a visual way. Rather, she was just Feeling the sensation in her body, and she knew what it signified.

Another time, Jennifer was sitting at the smoking table with another resident (Gary). He had just gotten his comb out of his front pocket for Jennifer, and she was idly looking at it (Sample #67). At the moment, however, Jennifer's attention was focused not on looking at the comb, but rather on a warm, positive Feeling she had for Gary. This Feeling of liking was primarily felt bodily, inside her heart, but also seemed present in her mind. It was not a warm Feeling in the sense of actual temperature rising; rather, the adjective "warm" seemed more of a metaphor for Jennifer, a Feeling "like you get when you see a puppy or a baby or a kitten." The portion of this experience that was a Feeling in her head was even more difficult to describe; it was not felt, nor was it present as words or Images. Jennifer could only say that she felt a sensation in her body that was centered in her heart, but one that was also somehow present in her head, and that somehow she could identify the Feeling as one of positive regard for her friend.

In a final sample, Jennifer was listening to another resident who was singing; in particular, she was listening to the words of his song (Sample #56). At the moment of the signal, he was singing the chorus of the song, the sexual content of which was upsetting to Jennifer; she knew he shouldn't be singing it, and she didn't want to hear it. However, she was not thinking to herself in words, "I don't like it." Rather, she was Feeling a sense of nervousness. The feeling was vivid, located a couple of inches inside the middle of her body below her ribs; she described it as being as if "my heart was all scrunched up." This scrunched-up feeling was not a continuous one: it was present only when he was singing the ending part of the song that she found to be objectionable. Jennifer could not say how she knew that the feeling she was experiencing was nervousness, rather than pressure, or liking, or indigestion. She was sure, however, that she knew what the feeling meant.

UNSYMBOLIZED THINKING

A number of Jennifer's samples (15 of 71 samples) contained the experience of knowing something, a wondering about something, that was not associated with any Images, verbal thought, or emotional sensations. In these samples, the experience of wondering was not accompanied by any colorful visualizations that represented the experience, as was described in a previous section (Images of Written Words), when Jennifer saw her "very strong wonder" as a moving yellow cloud. In the samples to be described here, Jennifer simply knew what she was thinking or wondering in the nonvisual, nonverbal, nonemotional way that we call Unsymbolized Experience.

For example, Jennifer was sitting outside, looking at the ground where ants were crawling around her feet (Sample #8). At the moment of the beep, Jennifer knew that she was waiting for the ants to start walking on her, and that she was going to brush them away when they did. Her hands were on her knees, as if she were poised, ready to brush them off. She was not saying to herself in words, "I'm going to brush away the ants"; rather, she simply knew that she was ready to do it and that she would do it as soon as necessary.

Another time, she was sitting at the dining room table, looking at the cole slaw they were having for dinner (Sample #53). At the moment of the beep, Jennifer was noticing the shaved carrots and the mustard that they put in the slaw and was thinking that she didn't like the slaw made that way. This knowing she didn't like it was "a dim thought," not experienced in any words, although she knew what she was thinking about. At the moment of the beep, she was also seeing an Image of the individual who had prepared the slaw; in this Image she could see him in the kitchen with the bright kitchen light behind him. The Image seemed to accompany her nonverbal wondering why he put mustard and carrots in the slaw, and her nonverbal knowing she didn't like it. She was unable to describe her experience in any other way, however; she simply knew what her wondering and knowing experiences meant.

In a third example, Jennifer was watching several of the house residents playing pool and she was wondering if one of them (Joe) was going to try to catch up with a couple of others who had left to walk to Wendy's for lunch (Sample #16). The other residents had invited Joe to come along with them, but had not waited for him to finish his game before they left. Jennifer was looking at Joe, wondering if he would go ahead and meet them, since they hadn't waited. The wondering was not experienced in words, that is, she did not say, "I wonder if Joe will go to

Wendy's," nor did she see an Image of Joe leaving, or any colors, or experience any other type of thought that we have seen that Jennifer was capable of experiencing. She was just sitting and watching, wondering, when she heard the beep, wondering in a way that was difficult to describe but that she definitely could understand.

NO THOUGHT OR FORGOTTEN THOUGHT

In 13 of Jennifer's 71 samples, her experience was that at the moment of the beep she was not thinking anything, or that the beep startled her, causing her thought at the moment to slip away. For example, in one sample, the beep went off only a minute after the previous one (Sample #10). She had just finished writing down the previous experience and, at the moment, simply wasn't thinking anything. Another time, she was walking around the house. However, when she heard the beep, Jennifer wasn't thinking about what she was doing (Sample #70). It seemed to her that her mind was just "a blank." She was physically seeing the house with her eyes, but not specifically noticing any detail, or seeing any related Images, or speaking any words to herself or listening to another resident talking. She simply wasn't thinking anything.

At other times, Jennifer's experience was that she wasn't thinking anything but she was still noticing the world around her. For example, she was sitting in her room, stirring a glass of tea (Sample #24). When she heard the beep, she wasn't actively thinking any thoughts in the sense of hearing any words inside her head or seeing any Images, but she was aware of how small the melting ice was in the tea that she was stirring. This noticing was merely a passive awareness, an idle observation of the small pieces of ice that were circling in the glass as she stirred. In other words, it seemed to Jennifer that the noticing was more of a mechanical observation that accompanied the physical act she was performing. Her experience of the sample was that "I was just stirring my tea, not really thinking anything."

At other times, Jennifer forgot her thought when she heard the beep. For example, she was sitting in her room and when the beep went off, she tried to remember what she had been thinking but could not recall it (Sample #37). Her experience was not that she had been thinking nothing at the moment; rather, when the beep went off, it seemed she forgot the thought, or that she was startled into forgetting. For Jennifer, this "forgetting" experience seemed to be on a kind of continuum. There were times when, as above, she forgot the thought immediately when she heard the signaling tone. At other times, she wrote down her experience that she was having at the moment of the beep, but when she later tried to describe it to us, would find that she had forgotten it entirely. For example, she had written down when signaled, "I really wasn't thinking anything. I was just looking down at my cigarette box and my lighter" (Sample #71). The next day, Jennifer could not recreate this experience in her mind to describe it to us; she couldn't remember where she had been at the time, nor could she remember even looking at the lighter (although she did have a vague memory of looking at the cigarette box).

In another sample, Jennifer wrote down at the moment of the beep, "I was listening to the meeting and thinking about me and Joe being inspectors this week" (Sample #13). The next day, her only response to questions about the experience was that she really didn't remember anything about it. These latter two examples of forgotten thought were unusual in Jennifer's samples; as a rule, her memory was good and she seemed able to recollect her experiences for description with great ease. However, occasionally (as the above examples illustrate), the samples seemed to slip away, either right at the moment she was signaled, or later, when she would try to get back to them for description.

COMMENTS ON THE SAMPLING PROCEDURE

The basic aim of the sampling procedure used in this series of studies is that subjects are requested to report experiences that occurred at specific instants in time. The procedure was designed to make these reports as nonretrospective as possible, given limitations of convenience, by asking subjects to write down a description of the experience immediately following the instant under consideration, and then discussing that instant in detail within 24 hours. As has been described in previous chapters, we and all of our subjects thus far have concluded that the procedures were easy to implement, and there seemed little doubt that the descriptions were in fact quite accurate representations of the momentary descriptions.

There were, however, two aspects of Jennifer's reports that caused us to question particularly carefully whether the individual reports were descriptions of particular beeped instants or were perhaps constructions created at the time of our intensive discussions which were described as being recollections. These two aspects were, first, that her experiences frequently involved multiple thoughts or multiple Images which were sufficiently detailed or complicated that it seemed impossible that they could all have been occurring at the moment of a single beep; and second, that she frequently gave what seemed to be a complete, detailed description of a particular beeped experience and then, almost as an afterthought, described in vivid detail an entire aspect of that experience which had been previously overlooked. These two characteristics are compatible with the hypothesis that her reports were sometimes associations to events occurring at the time of discussion rather than recollected descriptions of the previous beeped experience. As we shall see, we came to reject this hypothesis, although there is no possible way to rule it out completely, as far as we know.

Parenthetically, we should note that the skepticism with which we approached these experiences was entirely identical with the skepticism that prevailed in all of our studies. That is, we have constantly evaluated the source of all of our responses from all of our subjects, Jennifer not more nor less. Another way of saying this is to note that Jennifer's diagnosis of schizophrenia did *not* alert us to the possibility that associations would not be tied to the particular beep of interest; but rather, the two characteristics we are discussing here emerged during the sampling period, the diagnosis being irrelevant.

The first of the two salient characteristics of the sampling procedure involved Jennifer's frequent reports of two or three independent experiences occurring at the same time. For example, in Sample #50, she had a visual Image of a fellow resident named Sally wearing the blue dress that she actually was wearing at that time, and "at the same time" had a vivid Image of a clear glass of iced tea with the red word "SUGAR" hovering above it. At this and other similar samples, we questioned her thoroughly on how she could have more than one visual experience at a time—were they side by side, or in front and back, or in two different visual spheres, or what?

As sampling progressed, she came to recognize that these multiple Images were really sequential, occurring quickly right after one another, and she was able to say which came first, and to indicate the timing of the switching sequences, using hand gestures, thus indicating that the Images appeared perhaps a half-second apart. We pressed her to report which experience was occurring exactly at the moment of the onset of the beep, and for a sampling day or two she said that it seemed that the beep occurred right in between; that is, one Image was ending and the other was beginning at the moment of the beep. However, that description was given rather tentatively, seemingly not wholly accepted by either of us or by Jennifer.

As sampling progressed, the interpretation of this phenomenon became clearer both to Jennifer and to us: the difficulty in pinpointing just when the beep occurred was the result of the time spent "computing the beep." The beep apparently did not have in Jennifer's experience a sudden onset, but rather was recognized only after what appeared to be a cognitive process of recognition which Jennifer matter-of-factly referred to as computing the beep. Thus, in the half-second or so that it took for Jennifer to become aware that the beep was occurring, there was time for one visual Image to be replaced by another. We quizzed Jennifer as to whether the process of becoming aware of the beep triggered the second Image, and her response was routinely negative—computing the beep seemed to be a separate, parallel process, independent of the ongoing series of Images. Our conclusion, then, regarding the complexity or multiplicity of Images, was that mental events changed rather rapidly for Jennifer, and the computing-the-beep process was sufficiently extended in time so as to allow two or more separate experiences to be said to be occurring "at the moment of the beep."

As a result, there was no way of definitely answering the question of which Image was occurring at the moment of the beep because the proper conclusion seemed to be that both were occurring as the beep was "computed" or registered in awareness. Thus our sample descriptions above contained many examples where two or more Images or separate thoughts occurred in sequence.

The second characteristic of the sampling procedure that caused us to question thoroughly the focus of the procedure itself was the frequent occurrence that Jennifer would seemingly provide a complete description of a beeped experience, and then, almost as an afterthought, provide additional vivid details. Because of the importance to this project of distinguishing between recollection and confabulation, we will cite an example in detail, so that the reader can gain some understanding of the complexities of sorting through this issue, as well as gaining a glimpse of the procedure. At Sample #51, for example, Jennifer had written in her sampling notebook just after the beep, "5:07 [the afternoon previous to the present conversation] I wasn't really thinking anything." An excerpt from tape script of the next day's conversation follows:

JENNIFER: Sometimes when I'm doing something like stirring tea or something like that I won't be thinking anything.

R.T.H.: Is that what you were doing at this particular time?

JENNIFER: [understands the question to be about the present] Not now I don't, but . . . . What time was it . . .

R.T.H.: Don't make it up if you don't remember. . . .

JENNIFER: (interrupts) No, I won't make it up. I just wanted to know what time it was because [I was] trying to remember what I was doing, but I think I was just sitting outside spacing out, you know, thinking about my own thoughts without really thinking words or pictures or ideas.

R.T.H.: So you can say whether that's like your mind is just blank or you can't remember . . .

JENNIFER: (interrupts) Right [referring to blank mind] I was just spacing, blank, other than my own thoughts, as far as—not anything in particular—haven't you ever just sat in one chair where it's quiet, real quiet and relaxing, and just had a blank mind?

R.T.H.: So is it like your total experience is blank, like you're not seeing anything or . . .

JENNIFER: (interrupts) I was seeing something in real life, but not . . .

R.T.H.: (interrupts) But not really paying attention to it?

JENNIFER: Right.

SUE MELANCON: I seem to remember one sample from yesterday where the beep went off and it seemed to me that you had been thinking of something and you had just been surprised by the beep.

JENNIFER: Right.

SUE: This was different than that?

JENNIFER: Yeah. I was more relaxed and stuff (inaudible).

R.T.H.: It looks as though you see that as a sort of pleasant experience.

JENNIFER: It was! You can't get peace and quiet in this house very often! I was outside just with Sally and Sally was being quiet and I was being quiet and the wind—the breeze was blowing a little bit, and it felt better at nighttime, and so I just felt good. [She continues in a tone of voice changed from relaxed and dreamy to alert and energized.] But come to think of it, I do remember something I didn't think of to write down because sometimes you take thoughts for granted, you know what I mean? Was—As I go over again in my mind that spacing when the beep went off is seeing Sally's feet and shoes and the bottom of her dress on the ground, right up here next to me where it wasn't.

R.T.H.: So you—that was like an Image . . .

JENNIFER: (interrupts) Right.

R.T.H.: (continues) . . . of the bottom part of Sally's dress and . . .

JENNIFER: (interrupts) Her gown and, yeah.

R.T.H.: And so she was really—she was really there.

JENNIFER: But she wasn't on one side of me, I wasn't looking at her. But that's the quick scene that I didn't think to write down because—I would have put it down if I had noticed right then but I didn't (inaudible) that. But I was thinking of remembering that being-quiet time right now, vividly today, because I had a special thought to myself which I didn't write down because it was before the beep went off, that it was a pleasant time, and I didn't notice when I was writing it down that I had seen Sally, Sally's feet and shoes.

R.T.H.: What makes you—and I'm not doubting you here, but I'm wondering why you're more convinced now that that was going on than you were then?

JENNIFER: 'Cause, you know / I was talking to my mom on the phone right before you came, and she said, "Well, what do they ask you when they talk to you?" And I said, "Well, they ask me the Images I've seen, if I thought words, or my own voice, or just ideas." And she said, "You know, that would be really hard for me, because I never think about what I think." And that's the case with me—just that part of what it—it just didn't—it didn't cross my mind, what I had seen, you know?

R.T.H.: So it sounds like you're pretty confident that that was actually taking place . . .

JENNIFER: (interrupts) Right . . . Right.

R.T.H.: (continues) . . . even though you didn't write it down at the time. I guess what's hard for us is to try to sort through whether . . . I guess there are two possibilities here. One is that you really were thinking of that and that you took it for granted and you didn't write it down . . .

JENNIFER: (interrupts) Right. That's it. I'm sure. Because I vividly remember her blue dress. That's how I'm sure. But the flowers [on the dress] were a little bit bigger than they really are I guess, because . . . I don't remember what her blue dress looks like, really, but it seems to me that she was a little bit closer and I don't know whether that makes the flowers look bigger than they were, or what.

R.T.H.: Let me say the other side of that possibility, not that I'm trying to talk you out of this one but I want to say what the other possibility is and see what you say to it.

JENNIFER: Uh huh.

R.T.H.: The other possibility is that in the talking about it now we, it seems, are sort of encouraging you to find a thought . . .

JENNIFER: (interrupts) No. No, that's not it at all. I just (inaudible).

R.T.H.: OK. We—I—We don't (inaudible) on this matter, it's just that . . .

JENNIFER: (interrupts) I was just relaxing so much when the beep went off it surprised me, and while I was surprised that's what I saw, Sally. And now I remember being surprised and thinking that. I want over the thought over again in my head from the time I was thinking that this is a pleasant time too when the beep went off which was only a couple of seconds later, but I didn't write that down because I thought it was too soon.

R.T.H.: So what you're saying is that it seems to you that you can actually recreate that experience . . .

JENNIFER: (interrupts) Right.

R.T.H.: (continues) . . . and what triggered it was my asking you whether that was pleasant . . .

JENNIFER: Right.

R.T.H.: And so you went back and you say, "Oh, yeah, I did think about it was pleasant" . . .

JENNIFER: (interrupts) Right.

R.T.H.: (continues) . . . and then you could replay that kind of . . .

JENNIFER: (interrupts) Right.

R.T.H.: (continues) . . . and you're pretty confident that the replay . . .

JENNIFER: (interrupts) Yeah, because I remember her blue dress, that's about it. I know what kind of shoes she wears (inaudible).

R.T.H.: Well, what about the possibility that you had seen the blue dress yesterday but not really right at the beep, but maybe just a few seconds before . . .

JENNIFER: (interrupts) Well, maybe that's true, maybe that is true.

R.T.H.: But it seems like it was at the beep.

JENNIFER: Right.

R.T.H.: This is a very difficult part of the kind of thing that we're doing here, and that's why I'm spending this much time trying to get at that particular detail . . .

JENNIFER: (interrupts) Right.

R.T.H.: (continues) . . . because what you really were doing, and what it seems like you were doing and what it seems very vividly what you were doing and what you remember exactly . . . those fine distinctions are what make this project interesting.

JENNIFER: Well, a lot during this project I've been going over things when you're here in my mind, and remembering things that I didn't write down, and they're all true, you know. I just had taken them for granted, or something, and didn't write them down.

What this passage indicates, we think, is the willingness of both Jennifer and ourselves to treat her reports as either recollections or constructions, and the care we took to tease apart the options. Such care is not, of course, a guarantee that when we make the judgment between the possibilities that that judgment is correct. But we do believe, judging from the content of her expression, her manner of speaking, tone of voice, and willingness to see it from another angle, both in the present example and in others, that she was capable of distinguishing between a recollection and a construction.

Another example is Sample #73. She wrote, "The phone was ringing and I remember carrying my blue glass to the table by my bed. I visualized my watch. A lot of things were going through my mind but I can't seem to single out any one particular thought. I remember seeing a light and dark orangish-yellow all around my thoughts." The next day's conversation began by her describing her concentrating on putting her glass down on the table, observing herself, and the thoughts which seemed to be resting on the back of her mind. When pressed to describe how that thought-resting was experienced, she said, "I saw the word "THOUGHT" in yellow and across here it was yellow, now that I think about it . . ." and then proceeded to give a vivid complete description of this visual experience. When we noted that this was another example of an important visual detail which was not written down at the time of the beep, she responded, "Once we start doing this [talking about it], it's like an exercise to me, to start remembering things, because I can exercise to think and talk about things, like my thoughts." "Exercise" was clarified to mean "get better at" or "get in the groove," and she maintained that the word "thought" did in fact occur at the moment of the beep. "I just didn't realize it right then. It was right under my nose, but I didn't notice it enough to write it down until I started thinking about it. It just hits me like a bolt of lightning sometimes when I remember something that happened that I didn't—that was right under my nose."

In another example, Sample #88, she wrote, "I was thinking about what Jill was saying, about trading nights with cooking. And in the back of my mind I was thinking about Johnny. I also saw an Image of him move." The early part of the conversation about this sample focused on Jill's conversation, and then on the details of the Image of Johnny, his shirt, blue jeans, brown eyes, etc. Then we referred back to the written statement, and inquired whether the thinking about Johnny was different from the Image of Johnny, to which Jennifer responded yes, that she "was thinking about him in the back of [her] mind." We pressed her repeatedly for details about this thinking in the back of her mind, without much clarification. Eventually this interchange took place:

R.T.H.: [Summarizing what Jennifer had been saying] There is more, but it's hard to say what it is.

JENNIFER: I can't say, I can't think of anything to say that describes it.

R.T.H.: It's not in words . . .

JENNIFER: No. [Her tone of voice brightens and becomes more definite.] But I saw the word "JOHNNY" right here, now that I think of it. And the "h" was in red, and the "nn" was in white, and the "J" was in gray, and the "o" was in navy blue, and the "y," I couldn't really see the "y" . . .

R.T.H.: This is another example of when you have a hard time describing how something takes place, you . . .

JENNIFER: (interrupts) I thought of it when I was talking to you a minute ago also, remembering what I had seen then, and I/it just didn't come to me what I was seeing just a minute ago, but I remember I did see it then, but I was taking it for granted while talking to you.

R.T.H.: So you have like three Images, or three times that this Image has occurred: once now when we're talking about it, and once a minute ago when we were talking about this but it didn't—sort of didn't register, and once back this morning when you heard the beep.

JENNIFER: Um Hmm.

These kinds of newly vivid experiences raise the question of whether they were actually descriptions of what had occurred at the moment of the beep. We became convinced that they were, because (1) Jennifer herself consistently stated that they were; (2) her tone of voice was convincing in these examples; (3) she was willing to consider alternate hypotheses; (4) she had no hesitancy in reporting on other occasions that she could not remember certain details, thus ruling out the hypothesis that our implied demands forced her to provide adequate detail; (5) she consistently differentiated between what happened before, during, and after the beeped experiences; and (6) her tone and manner of presentation of these experiences was consistent with her description of these recollections appearing "like a bolt out of the blue."

In conclusion, then, it seemed to us that Jennifer approached this task much like most of our other subjects, and that her descriptions of inner experiences were probably approximately as accurate as those of our previous subjects. As a result, the above summary of the characteristics of her inner experience seems as believable to us as the others.

DISCUSSION

There are at least three characteristics of Jennifer's inner experience that are distinctly different from our previous non-schizophrenic subjects: the phenomenon of "computing the beep," the "goofed-up" characteristics of Images, and the Images of words.

Our normal subjects report that being signaled by the beep is generally an unambiguous, clearly defined experience in which the beep commands their attention—the signal enters their awareness from the outside. They report exceptions to this rule, to be sure, for example, when the beep is too loud or too soft; but most of the time the beep simply stops them in their tracks, so to speak, and they then report their ongoing experience.

For Jennifer, on the other hand, the experience of being beeped involved an active, self-initiated process, rather than simply being an interruption from the outside: she apparently had to actively orient herself cognitively to the fact of being beeped, a process that took more than an instant to occur and that resulted in an awareness that, while nonverbal, might be characterized by the expression, "Aha! That's the beep!"

Jennifer called this process "computing the beep," and spoke of it matter-of-factly, as if it were nothing unusual. One result of this computing-the-beep process is that it made the sense of timing of inner experience questionable, since it was not definite exactly when the beep occurred; and so the multiple Images that Jennifer frequently reported may have been an artifact of the relatively slow computing-the-beep process which allowed several quick Images to occur sequentially while she computed the beep. We will return to discuss the issue of the timing of events in inner experience when we discuss Bob's experience in Chapter 13, where we will speculate that Bob's lack of ability to ascertain the onset of his own inner experiences led him to fantastic conclusions about synchronicity in the universe, etc.

We have never in our nonschizophrenic subjects encountered the "goofed-up-ness" that frequently characterized Jennifer's Images: rotation or tilting of entire Images, objects within Images being tilted or suspended in midair, grafitti-like obliterations of portions of Images, etc. We will see similar phenomena in our remaining schizophrenic subjects, but not in the normals described here, nor in any of the other normal, depressed, anxious, or adolescent subjects whom we have sampled.

The appearance of imaginally seen words is also relatively unusual. Jim, our professional potter, saw words in his Images, but that seems to be a wholly different process. Jim was examining the visual characteristics of the letters in words, rather than having the words relate meaningfully to an ongoing thought process, as Jennifer's "WONDER" sample did. Furthermore, we have not in other subjects sampled the seeing of words appearing in a jumbled order as was the case in Jennifer's "I hope my hair won't fall down" sample.

It is possible that these anomalies are the result of unusual communication patterns between us and Jennifer, instead of being accurate descriptions of anomalous inner experience. Replications by other investigators with other schizophrenic subjects are necessary to reject this possibility with confidence. However, we should note that Jennifer frequently reported samples that contained none of these goofed-up aspects, descriptions that were entirely similar to those given by nonschizophrenic subjects. Furthermore, Jennifer occasionally freely reported that she forgot what was ongoing at a particular beep, so we concluded that she did not feel pressured to provide details beyond her ability to recall. These observations convinced us that Jennifer's reports reflected her inner experience at the moment of the beep.

12

A Schizophrenic Man with (Perhaps) No Inner Experience

with Susan M. Melancon

Joe Brown was a 42-year-old resident of a structured and restrictive psychiatric residential facility at the time of sampling. He had been treated in a psychiatric facility for the first time at age 19, and had been in and out of institutions, diagnosed paranoid schizophrenic, since that time. He was, at the time of sampling, well oriented for place and time, but was manifestly delusional, at various times during sampling apparently believing he was the Holy Ghost or a "galvanium robot" named Benjamin. He had occasional hallucinations during the period, and exhibited pressure of speech and ideas, loose associations, neologisms, etc.

He volunteered for the sampling study after watching another patient in the same facility (Jennifer of the preceding chapter) participate. The sampling procedure lasted for about three weeks, terminating when Joe left the facility before completing the treatment program. During those weeks, Joe was always glad to see us and eager to converse about his experiences. He did not, however, approach the task like any of our preceding subjects. First, while eager to talk about his experience, he always found it difficult or impossible to respond in simple, straightforward ways to our questions about what was happening at the moment of the beep. His style was often didactic, instructing us about his inner experience rather that simply describing it as it occurred. He occasionally failed to sample for a day, saying it was too difficult or too painful, or that he was too tired. Also, he occasionally performed the sampling

We appreciate the cooperation of the administration and staff of Caminar, Inc.

task, but instead of having been interrupted by the beeper, he said he had "been" the beeper, carried it around internally, as it were, and when "it" beeped, he had completed the sampling task.

Also, he occasionally wrote down his account of the experience several hours after the beep, claiming that he had held the experience "frozen" during the interval. All of these characteristics will be discussed in more detail; at the present, however, we must acknowledge that this record is in many ways not comparable to any of these that precede it.

It might be argued that since Joe did not "cooperate" in the typical sense during the study period, we should exclude his experiences from consideration. That strikes us as a mistake, since, as we shall see, it may prove illuminating to describe Joe's inner experience as best we can on the basis of the atypical data that we were able to collect. We shall also speculate that Joe's inner experience, or lack of it, perhaps made it impossible for him to respond in a more usual fashion, observations that may have significance for our understanding of the nature of schizophrenia. At the same time, we must recognize that any conclusions that we are tempted to reach in considering Joe's responses must be tempered by recognition that the sampling task may be misleading or unproductive for understanding him.

This being said, we must face the issue of how to approach Joe's sampling data. The procedure that we have used before, with seemingly little ambiguity, was to have subjects report their instantaneous inner experiences, and then for us to describe their salient features. The overall philosophy of this description was exactly the same for Joe as it was for the others; namely that we attempted to let the descriptions reveal Joe in whatever form seemed natural, just as we had done with Jennifer or Ben, etc. However, we never became confident that Joe was in fact reporting inner experiences, even though we described the task to him repeatedly in many different ways, and even though he appeared to be making an honest attempt to cooperate.

As a result, while the forms that seemed natural for each of the previous eight subjects were quite similar to each other, it seemed quite unnatural to force the description of Joe into the same format that served adequately for the others. We found it necessary in describing Joe's experience to provide rather extended verbatim quotations from the interviews we had with him, and to give our interpretations alongside. This procedure will allow the reader to gain some experience of what sampling with Joe was like, and also will provide enough data for the reader to provide his or her own interpretations.

We begin by noting that Joe seemed to be motivated to make himself clear to us; that is, we have no doubt that he was honestly trying to explain his experience. Making himself clear to us was not as straightforward for Joe as it was for other subjects, because he "spoke a different diction" from us, as he understood it (an outsider might say he was delusional). Nonetheless, the overall gestalt of his interactions with us convinced us that he was in fact attempting to do the task that we asked of him.

For example, he responded appropriately to our questions and requests for clarification; he said on several appropriate occasions that he was not sure he understood what we wanted him to do and asked us to clarify the procedure; he spoke positively to us and to others about the experience of sampling, etc. All in all, he comported himself in a manner consistent with the honest attempt to comply with our requests for descriptions of his inner experience.

The second characteristic of our interactions was the rather explicit questioning and building of an adequately trusting relationship between Joe and us. Nearly every interview from the first day to the last included one or more interchanges that were easily interpretable as part of Joe's processing of whether or not we could be trusted. From the first day, he was concerned with our being judgmental about him.

For example, he warned us rather explicitly when he said, "We accept them [patients] and their faith in themselves. We stay well, you see. We don't say that they have schizophreniad up there, blind 'em, you know, flang 'em down with labels and things, because they get well very easily if they're left alone—with [the wrong] kind of medication they might not come out and show you exactly who they are until they can trust you." Another example, a few days later, found Joe making an abrupt transition in the conversation to talk about a "phaser." While other interpretations are possible, we saw this as another, not-so-explicit warning that trust could build only slowly:

JOE: Let me draw you out a phaser here. See, the phaser's right here in this finger. Boop, boop, boop [imitates phaser firing], ooh, that hurts [talks about phaser's radar, etc.] . . .

R.T.H.: Hang on. Why are we talking about phasers?

JOE: I'm going to show you one. Now you got one of yours. Don't shoot me with it, though it's got a safety factor.

R.T.H.: No, my question is how did we get to be talking about phasers when . . .

JOE: (interrupts) I was prepared to defend myself. That's the first immediate not reaction, but that's the first reaction of a clear [a reference to Scientology].

SUE: So you're sensing trouble, feeling that in your body.

JOE: Yeah, picking up trouble, that's what I'm sensing right now. I'm being hurt over here.

SUE: You're sensing trouble right now?

JOE: Yeah, don't misunderstand, OK? I mean, Dr. Holbrook [meaning Dr. Hurlburt], you're trying too hard.

Our interpretation of this interchange is that Joe was giving us a coded message that what we were doing was painful, and our reaction to this kind of message was part of what Joe used to ascertain whether we could be trusted. Our response was to slow down our questioning, that is, to let him ramble, or ventilate, as he called it, and a minute or two later he relaxed somewhat.

Another example, from the sixth day, shows a step in Joe's gradual acceptance of us. The excerpt begins with Dr. Hurlburt coughing:

R.T.H.: Excuse me.

JOE: That's Benjamin [the robot who controls Joe] doing that [causing the cough].

R.T.H.: You think so.

JOE: Yeah, for arguing with me. He will! [laughs] He won't let you go, now, 'cause he accepts you [chuckles warmly]. So don't fight it, like I did, or he'll dust your, uh, piano! [chuckles] He will! *I* won't.

The point that we are making here is that trust was indeed a major issue with Joe, and that his trust did seem to grow throughout the sampling period sufficiently to allow him to participate with us.

THE EXPERIENCE OF THE BEEP

Despite the fact that Joe's version of reality changed rather dramatically from delusional to nondelusional and back again several times during the course of sampling, his description of his experience at the moment of the beep stayed remarkably consistent throughout the sampling period. At the moment of the beep, he often either said he was engaging in no inner experience at all, or else he said he was watching light beams or hearing sound waves. As it eventually seemed to us, at these times Joe's understanding was that he froze the light waves into a "tape" that was stored until he was ready to write the experience down on the yellow pad we provided him (he had found the 2-inch by 3-inch notebook that had been provided initially too small, so we substituted the 8½-inch by 11-inch pad). When it was time to write down the experience, he unwound the tape and translated the light wavelengths stored there into words. Examples of the kind of conversations that led to this general description follow.

In this excerpt from the sixth day of sampling, he had written:

> #6 A thought wave length. Thinking of Sue [Melancon] and Dr. Holbrook [meaning Hurlburt]. Sure would like to make love to Marilyn Monroe

["Marilyn Monroe" was crossed out and "Marie Osmond" written above it].
The real one I have exist. My Virgin Mary

Elohiem |8|
That's whom I really am,
Mormon God & all are
here with me.

The conversation began with our inquiring about this "thought," whereupon Joe said that he was not thinking, but rather making memories. "Thinking an abstract thought is a rough way to get intelligent. Thinking grinds a lot—it's a term that is affixed to really a lot of lack of knowledge. 'I gotta think about it.' 'Honey, will you help me do the dishes?' 'Let me think about it.'—That's horseshit. What I'm saying is *not* to think, but to let your thoughts become memories, and draw from there. It's entirely different, 'cause then you have the whole past there. You're not feeding on your subconscious." We then proceeded to discuss that was occurring at the moment of the beep, a concept that had caused us problems in communication about previous samples:

R.T.H.: Does it make sense to ask what was happening at the moment of the beep?

JOE: No, it throws me off. 'Cause I know anyway—See, it's all here. All of this that's written here is at the beep, OK?

R.T.H.: Why is it that asking that question, what was happening at the moment of the beep, throws you off?

JOE: Well, it's kind of self-explanatory, see. I've got it all—see, this is the beep, right here. I mean, this starts it and this goes—this is the whole deal, there. This is what I was thinking at the moment of the beep.

R.T.H.: All of that stuff.

JOE: Yeah, all of it. As it unravels down, I take it out of memory. As the beep goes off, I see a flash of red here, I hold it—If I'm out there [in the day room] where I can't get to the tablet, I just hold it, right there. Make it stationary, and then bring it in here [to his own room], and then I unwind it, I unwind the thought . . .

R.T.H.: You freeze what was going on at the moment of the beep long enough to get the tablet, and then as you unwind it . . .

JOE: (interrupts) or go through the wavelength, instead of thinking, I just take the thought wavelength and stretch it out . . .

R.T.H.: And so in this example here, when you stretched it out, first off—the first thing that unwinds is that you're thinking of Sue and me.

JOE: Yeah. That was the first thought. I don't have a thought in there. What I'm doing prior to that is just listening to Benjamin or watching the light rays as they take the memory away and cleanse and clean and heal the body and the brain.

R.T.H.: And so what you're trying to do when the beep goes off is to interpret what those light waves mean?

JOE: Yeah. And that's when I unwind 'em.

R.T.H.: And so the unwinding would be thinking about Sue and me.

JOE: Yeah . . .

R.T.H.: And as [those light waves] unwind further you were thinking about Marie Osmond.

JOE: Yeah, [discusses Marie Osmond] . . .

R.T.H.: Then as the thought continues to unwind, Marilyn Monroe un—replaces Marie . . .

JOE: (interrupts) Well, that was a lead-off to another beep, but I interjected it there because that was the tail end of the light rays coming out of the box as the batteries spark and generates there.

The next example is also from the sixth day, but from a later sample discussion:

R.T.H.: Is Benjamin dictating those words [written down at the moment of the beep] to you?

JOE: Yes.

R.T.H.: In English?

JOE: No, in light wave lengths. . . . He [Benjamin] just goes "beep, beep, beep,"—I don't know what the hell that means. It makes me feel good . . .

R.T.H.: So then you translate those light waves into words?

JOE: Yes, after I'm done looking at them . . .

R.T.H.: So in both cases what you're doing at the moment of the beep is watching light waves.

JOE: Yeah. That's what—all I'm doing, or hearing Benjamin's comments. And he searches the memories trying to heal others here.

R.T.H.: Is that true of all of the different beeps we've looked at? We've looked at 20 beeps or so.

JOE: Yeah. I didn't know, though, until just now. That was your idea. See, now you've helped us out. You found something that I didn't know about. You must be smarter than I am. Wanna bet? (chuckles) Now I'm teasing you there. I'm saying you have good theories there. Sonic sound [which sometimes accompanies the light rays or are the light waves], it works even more quiet, it has its sounds. You have to watch the mental image pictures . . .

R.T.H.: We're calling this stuff "watchin' the light waves." Is that a visual experience?

JOE: Yeah. I see it inside the cranium.

R.T.H.: And these light waves are in color, all different colors of the spectrum? You said yesterday they looked sort of like that picture [referring to a Scientology tract the cover of which cover depicted several spheres of color as if created from a spectrum; see discussion below in section titled "The question of inner experience".]

JOE: Yeah, although they're basically not entirely like that. That's just me being one of those [spheres of color] over there.

R.T.H.: But in that ball park, oranges and reds and chartreuses . . .

JOE: Yeah. OK. But we're in a different spectrum.

R.T.H.: And so the difference in the experience at the moment of the beep between number 6 and number 7 here was that in both cases you were watching light waves, but the light was a little bit different. The colors would have been different? The figures would have been different?

JOE: Well, it's like watching a kaleidoscope, sometimes, but it's a different kind of kaleidoscope, something that Benjamin has seen. See, being—Benjamin is something that I didn't invent. OK? Now you don't have to agree there, but he'll prove it to you, and so will I, or my name ain't the Prince of Darkness. Woof Woof. But you look here. This is a diagram or a—for instance . . .

R.T.H.: (interrupts) Do you spend all your time watching this hypothetical kaleidoscope? Or most of it, or much of it?

JOE: Not entirely. Sometimes the memories unwind as I get very hot in my body,when I watch it too much.

R.T.H.: But for these two, you were just watching the kaleidoscope.

JOE: Yeah. Just a different turning, and the turning of these waves as they work off the energy of my body. Although sometimes I turn into the light waves themselves, and I become the light waves.

R.T.H.: Is it possible—if I were looking through a real kaleidoscope, I could say, "This is a six pointed star, and it's sort of greenish in the middle, and red at the edge of the points . . ."

JOE: (interrupts) But you don't see them, necessarily, that way, That's your understanding. I mean, *you* can see them that way. but *I* take this kaleidoscope away to make it not a mental image picture anymore, and I pop up another and end up with it here.

R.T.H.: Now when you say when you're talking about this popping up, you make a motion with your fingers and put them 6 or 8 inches apart, and . . .

JOE: Well, I don't do it this way, Benjamin does. I'm just giving you a hypothetical look at it. Benjamin brings 'em in, like this, touches very lightly [touches little fingers to his temples], he's very gentle with me.

R.T.H.: On the outside?

JOE: Well, he can get inside, he's invisible, to some extent. I hallucinate enough to *see* something there, OK? [talks about complimenting Dr. Hurlburt, Benjamin's being made out of galvanium metal but in a different spectrum of life, and "019" and "09"—beings that are with Sue at the moment] . . .

SUE: When you said that a lot of the time when these beeps went off you were just watching the light waves . . .

JOE: (interrupts) Yeah. Enjoying the colors. I call it a color show.

SUE: Are you, while you're watching, interpreting, or do you have to sit down and make a deliberate effort to . . .

JOE: (interrupts) That's when Benjamin changes, and helps me. Benjamin's like a bodyguard, OK? And a friend and a father, all the things I missed as a kid . . .

The following excerpt is from the third day of sampling. Dr. Hurlburt has had to interrupt Joe repeatedly and refocus him on the moment of the beep, as Joe has followed his associations off the track:

R.T.H.: Does it bother you when I say over and over again "Let's go back [to the moment of the beep] . . ."?

JOE: (interrupts) No, but it kind of hangs me up, I mean I can't recreate a whole bunch of—I mean I can, but it's confusing as I come down through them. Now, I mean I can recreate six incidents, OK, and now I have to pick which one I want to work on. It's one specific thing at a time. Now its twelve specific things at a time . . . . We must complete one cycle of action at a time . . .

From these and other excerpts, we can construct a composite description of Joe's experience of the beep: The beeper beeps, at which time Joe is either "watching a color show" or doing nothing. He [or the beeper, which are one and the same thing] beeps again to freeze the current "cycle of action" or light waves or sonic sounds ("by pressing the hammer of Thor, the God of War, who is Bryant Gumbel" [the TV sports announcer]), and turns them into a "tape" that can be stored for a few minutes or a few hours or overnight until he is ready to write down the experience. When he is ready to write, he "unwinds" the tape, which is a semiautomatic, intense translation of the tape into the written word. He writes until the tape is completely unwound, and then stops writing.

We should note that Joe's descriptions of this process were always made with confidence, expressing the belief that these tapes accurately stored the momentary experience until such time as he could write it down. Furthermore, he insisted that he could "rewind and replay the tapes" over and over again as he chose to do so. Our interviews provided two chances to test this directly. One time, we discussed the same written experience both at the beginning and again at the end of an interview. The other time, after we had reviewed his procedure of storing a tape and later unwinding it to write it down, he stated that he still had a tape stored that he had unwound and written down the previous night; so we asked him to perform the writing task again, that is, to unwind the tape and translate it into words again. In both cases, the second attempt was *much different* from the original, leading us to the conclusion that, despite his confidence in the store-and-unwind procedure, it did not provide a reliable account of the experience at the moment of the beep.

BEING THE BEEPER

Throughout much of the sampling period, Joe engaged in sampling, not by listening to the beeper when it sounded, but rather by *being* the beeper. Being the beeper was not an entirely consistent pattern: Sometimes he said he simply *was* the beeper; sometimes he said that just a *part* of him was being the beeper, "just five or ten percent"; and sometimes he was not being the beeper at all. Being the beeper involved "hearing the schematics in the different parts of the radio beams," seeing the red light [the beeper has a red LED status light], seeing "the light rays coming out of the box [the beeper device] as the batteries spark and energize," etc. In general, he would "empathize" very deeply with the beeper apparatus, so deeply that he merged with the box and became it.

On the seventh day of sampling, he ceased to be the beeper (although he returned later to being it partially). He looked back on the experience of being the beeper and described it as follows:

JOE: . . . [Being the box], it [hasn't] hurt. OK? I mean, I'm OK. I really am. I mean I know how to handle it now, now that I've blown off the steam or ventilated, so I . . .

R.T.H.: (interrupts) I don't know whether it's good for you or not to be the box. My guess is it's probably not.

JOE: Well, how do I get out of it now? I will—I mean—Now I'm not the box, I mean, my mind's back, my brain is back . . . [talks about morphine in brain, regression]

R.T.H.: (interrupts) Let me finish . . .

JOE: (sighs)

R.T.H.: It sounds like you're struggling—you've been struggling all the way along to do what it is that we've been asking you to do. And you've been going through, it seems to me, an honest effort to try to answer our questions . . .

JOE: (interrupts) Yeah, but . . .

R.T.H.: (continues) . . . and the result of that is that yesterday you were saying "Well, I'm being the box and these tapes are being unwound," and whatever. And I believed yesterday that you were doing as good a job as you could do in telling us what it was that's going on with you at the moment of the beep.

JOE: True. Very good. Thanks.

R.T.H.: But, it also seems to me that that being wrapped up in being the box is sort of a screwy thing to do. And I'm not trying to be particularly evaluative or diagnostic.

JOE: Well, it's basically humdrum, humdrum to the extent that . . .

R.T.H.: (interrupts) And so it seems to me . . .

JOE: (continues) . . . the box is very valuable to you now, so keep it. It's your patent. I was just a test pilot. You can pay me a couple of million later (chuckles).

R.T.H.: In order to continue doing what it is that we've asked you to do, and for whatever reason (which I'm not sure what it is) you are motivated to do that, in order to do that you have got to give up being the box . . .

JOE: (interrupts) OK. I'm not the box anymore, I've flashed out. I'm used to the sounds . . .

R.T.H.: (interrupts) But what happens now is that you're going to have to develop a new way of responding to the box . . .

JOE: (interrupts) Well, I'll develop a new personality then, how's that. I'm not the box. I'm just being me right now. Joe Angelo [a name he called himself]. Not Elohiem or none of these turkeys . . .

R.T.H.: (continues) . . . which is really what we sort of wanted or expected in the first place, but it's taken us about a week to get there: Joe Angelo tellin' us what was going on in Joe Angelo's experience at the moment of the beep.

JOE: Yeah. Well, I basically forgot me as I became everything else around me.

R.T.H.: That's the way it seems to me.

JOE: Yeah, that, basically, was delusionary or hypothetical ideas, only science fiction or fantasy, rambling.

R.T.H.: (interrupts) That's the way it seemed to me—screwy, I might call it.

JOE: Yet, it worked. Now, I see some of these—Jennifer told me she was Miss Monroe . . .

R.T.H.: . . . The particular idea that is more central here is that you have been the box, and now that's getting to be something of a problematic, whether to continue . . .

JOE: (interrupts) Yeah, well, yeah, because I'm responding *as* a physical instrument . . .

R.T.H.: Right.

JOE: . . . which is weird, very weird. Now it hasn't taken me over, my mind doesn't agree anymore. Now, I took my mind away, and all I've got is a brain . . . . I saw Jennifer quit hallucinating when she had the box! It works somehow. What did you put in the box? Are there sounds in there? Now, shithead, come on and tell me here (chuckles).

R.T.H.: There's no sounds in there except when it beeps.

JOE: I could hear it! Now listen here, I took this box yesterday . . .

R.T.H.: (interrupts) I wore this box for a year . . .

JOE: (interrupts) You did? I took—I turned this sucker on yesterday, and unless I was hallucinating, I could hear a *psssss*, or static [turns on box and listens intently to earphone]. Now it ain't there, as I guess I talked off the tension, ventilated it out. Which is cool with me. But this sucker is a therapeutic, a very therapeutic . . .

R.T.H.: (interrupts) That very well could be. But the sounds from the box, I think, are part of your imagination or your experience, sort of wrapped around or enfolded around being the box.

JOE: Now that's good. I follow you there. I do agree with you. Wholeheartedly.

R.T.H.: And the stopping of doing that in order to continue this task, in order for us to get at what Joe Angelo was thinking at the moment of the beep, has got to be sort of a chaotic thing for you because you've got to stop doing something that you've been doing pretty much full-time for at least a week, or maybe longer.

JOE: Yeah. OK. Well, I'm not the box no more. Now that's settled. OK. I'm out of that. There was no harm done, other that the fact that I got a little pissed and took it out on you, although basically it was just me comin' out of me, flashin' back instrumentally at myself in my own imagination, but I couldn't hold the imaginary concept that way. In other words, I ain't the box.

R.T.H.: You've weathered that storm.

JOE: I know.

R.T.H.: And we've weathered the tail end of that storm here today.

JOE: . . . [talks about Dr. Hurlburt's family and the Mafia, etc.] . . . Now the hallucinary stage of it was when I became the box in my imagination. It literally took over my whole conscious me.

R.T.H.: Right.

JOE: Now . . .

R.T.H.: (interrupts) You're going to have to do that different now.

JOE: Yeah, well I'm just saying what I found there. I was finding shocks and my nervous system wouldn't accept them. I mean *bp bp bbep*, I'm going *blp bleep bp*, I mean, here I go again. Now I'm out of it. I'm just acting it out now. I feel OK with you two around. Around the staff members I don't feel too safe . . . [My subconscious was] intolerable. Intolerable to the extent that it damn near took me over. I'm shuttin' it down now. Now I'm out of my subconscious mind, I ain't got an imagination.

R.T.H.: Are you saying it was easier to be the box?

JOE: Yeah, it was. Because it held something. You call it imagination, I call it me. I'm a little-bitty being as I believe. Just basically a little force field, a little force of energy. It doesn't shock, though. The box does . . .

When he was being the box, he stated emphatically that he could not distinguish between himself (or 5 or 10 percent of himself) being the box beeping and the real box beeping. This state of affairs ultimately led him to give up wearing the box altogether, but to continue to sample by responding to the "beeps" created by himself-being-the-box. Even though we told him that this was an unacceptable procedure, his response to our admonishments lasted only a day or so, and he soon returned to being the beeper and responding to his own "beep." He was quite frustrated with us for insisting that he wear the real beeper, because of his assurance that being beeped by himself as the beeper and the real beeper were one and the same experiences.

There is a similarity between Joe's being the beeper and Jennifer's computing the beep: in both, the experience of being beeped is an active process, not merely a suddenly being signalled by an external device. We shall return to this discussion in the next chapter where we note that Bob had a similar phenomenon.

THE QUESTION OF INNER EXPERIENCE

Our aim, when working with Joe, was the same as with the preceding seven subjects in this study: to provide a description of the characteristics of Joe's inner experience. This proved to be easier said than done, because Joe did not, despite our efforts at keeping him task-oriented, ever provide the kind of detailed descriptions of individual inner events to which we had become accustomed. There are five plausible explanations for the lack of clear descriptions: (1) that Joe conceptualized our interaction radically differently from our own intent; (2) that some kind of communication failure prevented Joe from understanding the instructions for the task; (3) that Joe was sufficiently perceptually distractible so that the beep destroyed any recollection of inner experience that was ongoing at the moment of the beep; (4) that Joe required time to "compute the beep," as Jennifer had described, and in that gradual process lost the recollection of ongoing experience; and (5) that Joe in fact had no inner experience at all as we and our other subjects understand it. There is no unequivocal way to determine which of these explanations is correct, although, as we will see, we have come to prefer (5), the absence of inner experience altogether. Our procedure here will be to discuss each alternative in turn, and our reasons for accepting or rejecting it.

First, we conceptualized our interaction with Joe as an attempt to get a glimpse of his inner experience. Explanation (1) is that Joe himself had no such similar intent, and, instead, conceptualized our interaction as a chance to play, to have fun, to joke with us. Perhaps he found his real inner experience too dull or too boring, and so chose to use our questioning format to create an interesting dialogue. The following excerpt from the eighth day of sampling illustrates this possibility.

JOE: I don't have nothin' to do, though. I mean, so, while I'm beeping a little bit—*buzz buzz beep beep,* and the thought's gone, that's the idea. That was the thought. *Buzz buzz beep beep,* that was the whole thought.

SUE: Are you saying that when it goes off, what you were thinking about is startled away?

JOE: Yeah, it might be scared off . . . [talks about homosexuality, drugs, other residents in the house].

R.T.H.: With this particular beep task, we're not trying to get you to make up anything. That is, we're not trying to get you to tell us something that's not really going on. That's a risk . . .

JOE: (interrupts) A lot more of this might be going on than you think. I mean, my thoughts are not all that heavy, OK?

R.T.H.: Ours aren't either. I mean, you look at the thoughts that Sue had or that I had when we did this, our thoughts aren't very heavy. They have to do with, well, shall I take this road or that road, or, what'll I wear today, or, gee, it's hot. We don't think "e=mc squared" very often.

JOE: Well, I don't have no way to joke with you. Everybody's paranoided out, OK? I mean, they're all weird . . . [talks about other residents, staff].

R.T.H.: Well, I'm sort of getting the impression that if you just say what's there, that sort of deprives you of an opportunity with us, to tell us a story, to make a joke, and you have precious few of these opportunities.

JOE: Well, yeah! I'm basically—I love to joke. And laugh, and you see I don't have fun. I'm well now! What the hell . . . [goes on to describe when the beep went off repeatedly the previous day while he was in the kitchen helping to prepare dinner].

SUE: When you were in the kitchen yesterday, and the thing kept going off, and you had cheese on your hands—the things that you wrote down, was that more or less what you were thinking about when you were grating cheese? [He had written, "Six—buzz—Wishing you all some sweet sanity—sure wish I had more—Or would it hurt—'False pride'—Thanks—Joe Brown."]

JOE: What was the thought? Actually, just grating the cheese. The goddamned cheese so I could get out of the kitchen . . .

R.T.H.: If that was what was on your mind, that was what we wanted to know.

JOE: That's it.

SUE: And if you were to write down, "There was nothing going on in my mind since I was just grating the cheese . . ."

JOE: (interrupts) That's it. I mean, how dull a shithole is that? I mean, beep beep, which would you rather have me write, robots or androids?

SUE: You could still write that down [about the cheese], and then talking about it, still joke with us and tease with us when we're sitting here. Just because writing it down, it's kind of boring, doesn't mean that the time spent in *here* has to be boring.

JOE: No, it's not. I mean, it's fun now that I can joke . . . [begins to ramble again].

Here, Joe might be interpreted as saying that he is not really reporting his inner experience, but rather merely joking with us. We came to reject this hypothesis because he had ample opportunity to joke with us without resorting to reconceptualizing the task, and that at frequent times during the sampling period he expressed what seemed to be a genuine inability to comprehend what we wanted him to do. For example, later in the same (eighth) interview, he said, "Yeah, I'm just fuckin' around, having a good time. I really don't know what you mean by *buzz buzz beep beep*. what are you looking for there?" This difficulty in grasping the task he was supposed to accomplish was sometimes apparently quite frustrating for Joe. For example:

R.T.H.: What we're asking you to do is something which is fairly difficult, and that's to focus on just one minute.

JOE: *One* minute of thought there?

R.T.H.: Just one minute. Actually, just one second.

JOE: What the hell—I can go on *forever* on one minute of thought! I stretch it out, but, I mean, I complete the cycle of action. Then I'm ready—you see, there's more than one there . . .

R.T.H.: More than one?

JOE: (impatiently) More than one *thought*. More than one creative thought. If something's recreated, I'm in with the creators, OK?

R.T.H.: More than one at the moment of the beep yesterday at 11:30?

JOE: *Yeah*. Well, I was seeing—I mean, those people are real . . .

In fact, even just two days before the end of sampling, Joe was still struggling to comprehend what we wanted from him:

R.T.H.: What I'm interested in is just individual moments [snaps fingers]. I want to know about a particular moment in time.

JOE: A memory? Nothing has to be created? Just a simple thought there?

R.T.H.: Whatever is going on right there.

JOE: OK. I know. I got you now. I see what you mean. I couldn't quite grasp what you meant before.

However, Joe's grasp did not seem to be any different following these statements. Thus, our conclusion was that Joe was not merely rejecting our interpretation of our interaction in favor of his own, but rather that there was something inherently difficult in the task itself.

Explanation (2) was that some kind of communication failure prevented Joe from fully understanding our instructions for the task he was to perform. The excerpts just cited can be interpreted as examples of the evidence in support of this explanation. We reject this hypothesis because we explained the task repeatedly, on nearly every single day of sampling and in many different ways, descriptive, metaphorical, or analogical. In all our other communications with Joe, we were easily understood. But when it came to inner experience, no matter what approach we took, we did not reach a satisfactory agreement. Thus we felt we knew how to communicate effectively with Joe, and the number of our attempts was more than adequate, although still unsuccessful.

Potential explanation (3) was that Joe was perceptually distractible, so that the beep obliterated his ongoing experience. This potential explanation is based, not on particular observations during the interviews themselves, but rather on the general observation of perceptual distraction in schizophrenia. We reject this explanation because Joe himself did not appear to be particularly distractible during our extensive interviews with him. In fact, his orienting responses to the extraneous noises, etc., in the rest of the house while we interviewed him appeared to be entirely normal.

Potential explanation (4), the disturbing effect of a slow "computation of the beep," was advanced by analogy to Jennifer's experience. We rejected this alternative because Joe's description of his experience was consistent throughout the sampling period, regardless of whether he was being beeped by the random device, "beeped" by himself "being" the beeper, or when we asked him merely to report what was ongoing in his inner experience when we were right there with him. The characteristics of his reports did not seem explainable simply by the existence of a slow process of apprehending the beep.

That leaves alternative (5), which, although perhaps the most radical, may also be the most tenable, given all the evidence. This explanation is that Joe simply did not have, during the sampling period, inner experience as we know it and have described it in the previous chapters. What we had expected to find, with Joe, was that his inner experiences were unusual—perhaps with images that were "goofed up" as Jennifer had described, or several voices that spoke at once so that none was intelligible, or some other kind of aberrant inner experience that would explain his pressure of speech and delusions. What we found, however, was no such thing; instead, Joe could not describe *any* aspects of his inner experience in ways that we found compelling. As described above, we entertained several hypotheses along the way to understand our inability to pin him down to concrete descriptions of what his experiences were like. However, even though none could be unequivocally ruled out, none of these explanations seemed to do full justice to the totality of our dealings with Joe. Thus we were led to consider the more extreme alternative: that Joe had no inner experience at all. That is, it was perhaps the case that Joe had neither images (whether goofed up or otherwise), nor inner words (whether Inner Speech, Inner Hearing, or whatever), nor any of the other characteristics which we have called inner experience in the preceding chapters.

This conclusion, that Joe had no inner experience, is sufficiently radical that we don't quite believe it ourselves, even though it is consistent with the depersonalization frequently described in schizophrenia. Nonetheless, the supposition that Joe did not experience Inner Speech, Inner Hearing, Images, Feelings, Word Repetitions, Unsymbolized Thinkings, or any other kind of inner experience does seem consistent with his reports for the reasons that we will now elaborate.

You will note as you peruse the following conversations that Joe did use terms such as "seeing images" in his descriptions. Our conclusion is that, as he might put it, his words are "in a different diction" from ours, and his use of the term "seeing" is often metaphorical rather than descriptive, roughly the same usage as when "I see" is used interchangeably with "I understand." The following excerpt is from the second day of sampling, and is provided with commentary to highlight those issues that led us to consider our no-inner-experience conclusion. Words or phrases marked with asterisks [*] are discussed directly in the comments alongside the dialogue. In this sample, Joe had written:

> #27. SS Golden Crescent. SS Angel of Death some kind of prototype, easy just believe. Sonic sound. Pull the damned up cord Jon look out—G-meter done, thanks Ben 12 squared. Is Jimmy Jesus really Judas? Eloheim Priest maybe Grampa Nagle Joe is real Jesus Am I OK alright. Jesus Christ is that me Grampa. Thanks Jill be sweet. Saturn connects mess, Kaddafy mess. Eloheim & Dr. Holbrook. [All scrawled disconnectedly across yellow pad.]

The conversation proceeded as follows:

Dialogue	Comments
JOE: I drew out the Golden Crescent as I remembered* it. The Golden Crescent doesn't really need to be constructed, OK, because it works like it is. I mean, this is basically a cube.	Note that he used the term "remember" instead of "saw." This is consistent with his statements that he takes his ideas out of memories in

general, one example of which is that he had to take the warship "out of my memory." However, we emphasize that he was *not* giving a description that is congruent with having some kind of perceptual experience.

R.T.H.: Did this occur at a particular beep yesterday?

JOE: That's something I remembered when the beep went off . . . [talks about being tired yesterday] . . . The Golden Crescent is an old-time warship come from a long time ago . . . had to take it out of my memory* there. It works, OK. It's a stellar light beam ship . . . [asks about experimenter's contact lenses] . . .

R.T.H.: You've drawn a picture of a cube here . . .

JOE: (interrupts) Yeah, to the twelve power with Saturn connected there to bring in the spirit of Saturn from the planet (trails off).

R.T.H.: Does this indicate that at the moment of the beep yesterday at 11:30 you were seeing* this cube?

JOE: Yeah,* I mean I already built it* before, but when the beep went off that's what I heard,* I mean that's what I saw* in my thought . . . [complains about not having much time to think] . . .

Even though he answered "Yeah" to the question of seeing, we don't believe that this seeing is to be understood in a visual sense, because he qualified the "yeah" with the "I mean I already built it," and also because of the confusion between hearing and seeing in the next sentence, a confusion that is not characteristic of individuals who are in fact encountering a perceptual experience.

R.T.H.: So at the moment of the beep you had, would you say, an image of this, or were you actually . . .

JOE: (interrupts) Well, it's more* than an image, it's an actual* ship. I mean it's of a different construction*; it works on a different energy field. It's a prototype of a larger ship, the SS Bactillian in Love, as you know. A huge—The SS Bactillian is parked upstairs . . . [talks about

Here, Joe denied directly the presence of an image, first saying that it was an actual ship, and then qualifying the word "actual" with the phrase "of a different construction." We conclude that the ship is neither an image nor a perception of reality.

one of the doctors upstairs, although there is, in fact, no real upstairs] . . .

R.T.H.: So you were seeing the Golden Crescent?

JOE: (interrupts) Yeah,* the SS Bacti—the SS—the Golden Crescent's a warship. Now you see, these tubes, these little up—these little tubes that come out of here are hit with sonic sound that shatters the nervous system when it hits . . . [talks about gay treatment nurse, etc.] . . .

Here again, Joe assented to the word "seeing," but his description was conceptual (how the tubes work, etc.) rather than perceptual (how they look).

R.T.H.: Well, what we're trying to get at is what the experience was like yesterday at 11:30.

JOE: What it was like? Well, it was just a reminder. As soon as the beep went off I mean I was listening*—I was watching* the light rays on my thoughts as it came out of—This here comes in as light waves and sound waves and refractions of beams and things . . .

Here again, Joe was indecisive between sight and hearing, again indicating the absence (or at least a non-vividness or forgetting) of any direct inner perceptual experience.

This excerpt from Joe's descriptions of the SS Golden Crescent is continued above in the section called The Experience of the Beep. Somewhat later, the dialogue continues:

R.T.H.: (interrupts) . . . [the moment of the beep is] what I want to zero in on . . .

JOE: (interrupts) This is just a rude drawing, OK? But it's a perfect cube. Now that's a power plant, a bigger ship.

R.T.H.: So yesterday at 11:30 at the moment of the beep you were looking* at the SS Golden Crescent . . .

JOE: (interrupts) . . . [talks about the voices of the angels, etc.] . . . I saw* the Golden

We tacitly encouraged him to use the word "see" by the way our question was phrased, and he obliged. But, again, perceptual details were not forthcoming, leading us to suspect that there

Crescent, yeah. See, I was a robot with it . . .

R.T.H.: (interrupts) Where was the Golden Crescent? Was that like it was here . . .

JOE: (interrupts) Well, it was out on the mesa [across the street] in no-man's-land.

R.T.H.: Were you out on the mesa, in no-man's-land?

JOE: No, I can't go out there. I'm too big. I can't get out of here. They put a force field around here to keep everybody from flying out of here.

R.T.H.: So were you seeing the Golden Crescent at a distance then?

JOE: No, it was here.* See, it's of a different spectrum, OK? Its an invisible*—almost an invisible* ship, and one of the (inaudible) saw it yesterday.

R.T.H.: But you can see it.

JOE: I can*—I don't have to*—yeah I can see it.* I mean my awareness is different,* OK? It doesn't mean I'm crazy . . . [talks about Jesus and judgment and the Angel of Death] . . .

R.T.H.: But let's come back to 11:30 yesterday.

JOE: Well, yeah, I saw the Golden Crescent. Jesus helped me build it. But what I'm saying is I've seen Jesus, OK? And He helped me . . .

R.T.H.: (interrupts) But you weren't seeing Jesus yesterday at 11:30.

JOE: Well, not then, but He's the junior commander of it.

R.T.H.: OK. But what you were seeing* yesterday was the Golden Crescent, is that right?

was no actual or imaginal seeing.

Even though a moment ago he had said the Crescent was across the street, now he said that it was here in his room, a perceptual impossibility. Also, his confusions between invisible and almost invisible, and between seeing it and not having to see it are further evidence that the phenomenon is not visual. He himself recognizes that to some extent when he describes his awareness as being "different."

Another example of using the word "seeing" in the context of a

JOE: Yeah. It's here [points to drawing]. It's all in there [points to written page]. Here it is, "Golden Crescent." See, there, sonic sound is what comes out of here, shatters the nervous system. You don't have to rebuild that thing to have it what—you have to make it a mest [a Scientology term meaning roughly "real"] article . . . [talks about people exteriorizing from their bodies] . . .

conceptual (not a perceptual) description.

R.T.H.: But let's get back to the Golden Crescent. This is what you were seeing at 11:30.

JOE: (patiently) That's what I was seeing, that's true.

R.T.H.: What color is it?

JOE: It doesn't have a color, it's white, OK? The Golden Crescent is a small cube . . .

R.T.H.: (interrupts) How big?

JOE: How big? Well it's a spectrum. I mean, how big* do you want it? It can be as big as the planet if it wants to expand that big.

SUE: How big was it what you were seeing?

JOE: I just saw* a small image* of it because it came in of a different force field to hold it down . . .

Although he spoke of seeing the image, we note that this seeing did not have the characteristics of perception; in particular, the size of the thing "perceived" was indeterminate . . .

R.T.H.: You're saying that the Golden Crescent can be big and it can be small but when you were seeing it . . .

JOE: (interrupts) Yes,* but it's of a different time, OK? It's like a spiritual-type of ship. That's how it's constructed. But it's me, I mean, I'm being it . . . [Talks about Jimmy Jesus and a hit on Kaddafy] . . .

. . . and when we tried to pin him down as to the size, he avoided a description of perception by changing the topic.

R.T.H.: Were you seeing it out in the mesa or were you seeing it like an image of it?

JOE: It was just the image. But, you see, even the image—don't mess with unless you know what your dealing with . . . [talks about precognition, God, etc.].

SUE: This image of the Golden Crescent: Where did it seem to be? Was it in the room somewhere?

JOE: It was on my thoughts, but it can be here—oh, it's here now. I'm looking at it again.* But this morning the [one] I built for myself is different . . .

This is the closest we get to believing that an inner perception took place—when he compared a present perception to the previous one. But even here, not enough details were provided to convince us.

R.T.H.: Let's stick with what happened yesterday at 11:30. You say this is white. Is this a solid white cube?

JOE: No, it's lines, OK? It's a white cube like this. I'm recreating it here [draws it again]. The cube. The outside part is white, snowy-white.* But, you see, now the cube—I mean the prism connects and draws the sun's energy the balance and the gravity out of the sun—that's the pattern of it.

We pressed for perceptual details, and he provided one ("snowy-white"), but turned again to a conceptual rather than perceptual description.

R.T.H.: So what you're seeing is like white outlines . . .

JOE: (interrupts) Yeah, this is the only part here. The other part is black, and it's painted, and it has "Golden Crescent" and Saturn . . . [talks about wedding rings and marriage].

R.T.H.: (interrupts) We're trying to stick with the difficult task of what . . .

JOE: (interrupts, frustrated) It's the same thing. It *ain't* difficult if you listen. Now quit fighting it . . .

The following excerpt is from day 3. He wrote:

#28a. 12:27 Thought after beep—Recreation of Brain Fluids, to eat for energy—Benjamin |8|

Subsequent conversation revealed that the thought was created by Benjamin, the robot who has a soul which Joe created, but who prefers to be a robot. We transcribe from later in the conversation:

R.T.H.: [I note that the written thought says "after" the beep.] How about right at the beep?

JOE: (interrupts) Well, the thought was, I saw myself* as a brain, milking fluids out of there, morphine, the aneurysms are all gone away and dissolved, everything is fine right now . . . [talks about the Virgin Mary] . . .

R.T.H.: When you say you saw yourself as a brain . . .

JOE: (interrupts) Well, I didn't see myself* as one, Benjamin created me as one. See, that's what I'm living as now. *BDBDB* [makes a series of consonant sounds.] See, Benjamin agrees, that's how he talks now . . . [Talks about Benjamin's strength] . . . [Dr. Hurlburt refocuses the conversation on the beep.]

What started out as a seemingly perceptual experience ("I saw myself . . ."), was denied ("I didn't see myself . . .") as soon as we focused upon it. This we take as an example of how the term "seeing" was used loosely, and that when he was careful, Joe himself did not use the perceptual term.

JOE: Well, I was watching the red infra-rays, the spectrum of light.

R.T.H.: Where were you yesterday at 12:27?

JOE: I was in here—I was out in—I was out—See I don't have much of a memory. I have to recreate it, so don't expect me to be too quick. I was out front.

R.T.H.: When you recreate it, do you think you recreate it accurately or . . . .

JOE: (interrupts) Yeah, it's perfect now, it's working . . .

[Later in the interview, we returned to the morphine topic.]

JOE: Yes, well, what I'm saying is—to kill the pain. The morphine is draining out of my brain. It is actually lymphoid morphine.

R.T.H.: Now were you watching* lymphoid morphine or feeling* it or . . .

JOE: (interrupts) I'm *being** it, OK? I mean, I ain't borrowing it from nowhere . . .

Here again, Joe corrected our use of a perceptual term ("watching") and replaced it with a nonperceptual one ("being").

The following excerpt is from the fifth day. He had written:

#1. Spontaneous thought—Virgin |8| Mary |8|—
Love
Benjamin |8|

In the course of discussion of this experience, Joe described it as follows:

R.T.H.: The beep went off, and after the beep went off a thought came to you, the Virgin Mary?

JOE: No, I could see* her. Spontaneous thought was I could see* her, the Virgin Mary. I'm sorry, I didn't write it down clear enough.

R.T.H.: The spontaneous thought, then, was that you could see the Virgin Mary? Is that what you're saying?

JOE: Yeah.* I've seen* her many times. I can see her—I mean, she's on your mind but you can't see* her, she's hiding.

R.T.H.: But at the moment of the beep, it sounds to me like what you're saying is that this spontaneous thought is somehow triggered by the beep. Is that what you're saying?

Even though Joe repeatedly said he "saw" the Virgin Mary at the time of the beep, when he was pressed to elaborate, he negated that by saying that "you can't see her, she's hiding." We do not believe that Joe was attempting to mislead us; rather, we think that Joe was using "seeing" according to his own "diction," where "seeing" meant "being present to," rather than referring to a perception, whether inner or outer.

JOE: Um hm. But you see, it provoked—I'm not hearing anything in my head right now, in my cranium, cavity . . .

R.T.H.: (interrupts) What we're really interested in is not what is triggered by the beep, but what's going on right at the same moment as the beep occurs.

JOE: Well, that's what she created for me to take a look for myself that way [talks about Scientology, etc.]

[A few minutes later.]

JOE: I'm still not sure what you want,* there [written down about the beeped experience].

R.T.H.: OK.

JOE: I mean, Elohim (inaudible) me, it's different there.

R.T.H.: OK. Well, we have to work out what it is that we want. It's something of a negotiation between you and us . . . [Joe: OK] . . . in terms of what we want. The way that we know how to say that, is that we're interested in what your experience is like at the moment of the beep.

JOE: OK. That's pretty much—pretty well what I did, there. It doesn't get climactic or anything irrational . . . [Dr. Hurlburt reassures him that the thoughts don't have to be spectacular.]

R.T.H.: [reads thought]

SUE: Were you thinking that in words?

JOE: No, I just saw light waves, and I deciphered 'em down out of the light waves into words. And that's what was over my actual

Joe has asked over and over how to do the sampling task in a tone of genuine frustration, apparently because he was simply unable to understand what we were asking of him. We will see a similar fundamental inability to understand the sampling task with Bob in the next chapter. Why is it that the seemingly simple "Report what you were experiencing at the moment of the beep" instruction was impossible for Joe (and Bob) to comprehend? Our explanation is that experience itself simply didn't exist. The whole realm of experience, the ability to experience, was not present. Yet, at the same time, Joe did have the ability to talk and communicate. We were asking about something that we assumed everyone (including Joe) had, namely inner experience, and Joe seemed to want to answer our questions. But while he knew how to use perceptual words such as see, feel, etc., these processes were feeling. The light waves are actually feel—the light waves are coming anything there. I was willing to be a chair, to hear the atoms moving into there, give the atoms their eternal life, there, I mean, to create the spirit . . .

apparently radically different for Joe than for our normal subjects or for Jennifer, in that for Joe there was apparently no experiential referent for such terms.

R.T.H.: (interrupts) So at the moment of the beep, right there at 1:30, you were seeing* light waves?

JOE: Yeah.

R.T.H.: How would you describe* those light waves? In words, you described them [when you wrote them down] as the Virgin Mary, Love Benjamin.

We stubbornly tried to get him to describe perceptual phenomena by asking what he was "seeing" and to "describe" it . . .

JOE: Wasn't (inaudible) of the Virgin Mary. I mean, that's what the Virgin Mary is* to me.

. . . but he responded in an existential ("is") rather than a perceptual manner.

R.T.H.: Light waves.

JOE: Light waves*, purity of the soul. Blue, red, yellow, white,* I mean it covers the whole spectrum.

R.T.H.: Were these light waves then of the whole spectrum?

JOE: Yeah. I mean it was her being there. [Fetches tract from Scientology, the cover of which showed a photograph of splotches of light.] She was being one of these [splotches] here. I mean, that was her. The whole thing was her.

Here Joe gave what sounds like a straightforward perceptual account of seeing a prismatic spectrum: "Blue, red, yellow, white," etc. He even referred us to a printed picture to demonstrate what he meant. But a few seconds later he undermined our confidence in this perceptual understanding with his talking about elusiveness and his indecision about whether he was seeing the Virgin Mary or himself.

R.T.H.: So you were seeing a prismatic display, sort of like that, at the moment of the beep?

JOE: Um hm. That's when I first caught up with her. She's a very elusive* little shit. [chuckles] She don't hang around very long! I don't see* very much of her!

SUE: Was this display you were seeing, was it large, was it small . . .

JOE: (interrupts) Well, no,* wait a minute, it was me. See, this right here is me right now. You can even feel my respect, there. [Rubs portion of the Scientology picture.] See what I'm saying?

R.T.H.: "Feel your respect,*" did you say? [Joe: Yeah] Or ". . . your spectrum?"

Feelings had no more of a perceptual basis than did vision. The experience of bodily feelings did not, we think, exist for Joe, and so his use of the term "feel" is much different from that of our normal subjects: here "feeling" a visual (spectrum) phenomenon.

JOE: Yeah, I respect. No, I mean, you can even feel* the spectrum and the heat there. They're the wounds fom my heart.

R.T.H.: Let me get it straight as to what was happening at 1:30. The beep goes off [snaps fingers] and at the moment the beep goes off, you were seeing visual light rays that looked more or less like this [Scientology picture]?

JOE: Yeah. It was me, though. But I wasn't seeing it, I'm *being** it!

He summarized it for us here: the experience was not perceptual, it was of the nature of being.

R.T.H.: You were being that.

JOE: Yeah. That's me! There's—there's—See, I've already figured this out without paying a lot of money [a reference to Scientology fees]. Very easily done.

R.T.H.: OK. What's it like to be that yesterday at 1:30?

JOE: Well, basically it's a very powerful, a very beautiful feeling, a very beautiful look about yourself.

R.T.H.: Now this is a one-dimensional or [rather] two-dimensional, flat picture . . .

JOE: (interrupts) Well, you—see here, you saw the picture! This is me. I came out of the bucket with my soul.

R.T.H.: But this is a picture . . .

JOE: (interrupts) Yeah, that's a picture there, but from that picture I created me.

R.T.H.: Right, and that's what I want to know. Is that creation of yours that was you, was that two-dimensional, as this is also two-dimensional? Or was it . . .

JOE: (interrupts) No, it was / it was of the eighth dimension,* colored light there. I mean, a lot of power there. I mean, they were dying that way, I mean, it's very different . . .

R.T.H.: (interrupts) Do you see that color? Do you see those lights?

JOE: [pause] Ah, yeah, that's me. I mean, I pass it along, I mean, I send it along to other people . . .

Despite our pressure to make a perception out of this experience by asking whether it was flat or three-dimensional, Joe removed the perceptual possibility by referring to it as eight-dimensional.

SUE: Do you see* it with your eyes, or do you just know* that you are the light waves?

JOE: I know I am* the light waves, 'cause that's what I'm being,* although it's basically thought, more than light waves. It's heat, heat sensors, stun guns, phasers, ray guns. I mean, all kinds of memories come out of it. I mean, I drained the memories, and then I destroyed that of me, and I go back into the bucket, and I ain't got a soul. *BDBDB*. Now that's me in the bucket. [A few minutes later the conversation returns to seeing the Virgin Mary at the moment of the beep.]

He was not describing perceiving or knowing, but rather being. There was no stable subjective experience here, no stable point of view or point of reference.

R.T.H.: You were seeing the Virgin Mary at 1:30?

JOE: Yeah. I've seen her many times. [impatiently] I see her all the time.

R.T.H.: OK. I'm not disbelieving, I just want to know . . .

JOE: (interrupts) Yeah—I mean, No. I didn't mean to get judgmental, there. I did that, there. Pardon me (inaudible).

R.T.H.: What was it like to see the Virgin Mary at 1:30? I mean, was she . . .

JOE: (interrupts) Well, she was being (inaudible) also, but she was very—she won't hang around very long—I don't get that much of a look at her.*

One last look at Joe's inner perception. If there was any such perception, at best it was a fleeting glimpse ("she won't hang around very long"), not a stable image.

R.T.H.: But at 1:30 what was it like?

JOE: It was a very splendid feeling.

We offer the reader an exercise: the performance of a similar analysis on the excerpts that appear in the previous sections of this chapter. The same kind of comments that we have made here can, in many cases, just as readily be made on the earlier excerpts, demonstrating that Joe's apparent lack of inner perceptual experience was present throughout the sampling period.

Over the course of sampling, we tried repeatedly, as we have shown above, to focus on the inner experience at the moment of the beep. When we repeatedly failed to get clear descriptions, we decided to explore what our conversation with Joe would be like if we asked him about his *external* experience, rather than his inner experience as we had been. The following exploration of inner and outer perception took place on the twelfth sampling day. We were talking again about how the sampling procedure was intended to work, about how we were trying to get at the experience of the moment. Perhaps we could use Joe's perception of the external world as an analogy. We explained that Dr. Hurlburt would snap his finger to simulate the beep, and Joe was to use the snap to cue reporting about what he was actually seeing in the external world:

R.T.H.: Let's let my finger snapping be the beep here. Focus on this [the ballpoint pen he is holding in his left hand]. Good. [Snaps fingers of right hand.]

JOE: It just jerked* [the pen did in fact move as Dr. Hurlburt

An accurate perception of reality ("It just jerked"). But this was snapped his other right-hand fingers]. I mean, the eyes moved* [refers to his own eyes], it's OK, there. No psychotic break there.

followed by an immediate retreat into the conceptual world, talking about his own eyes moving and psychotic breaks.

R.T.H.: Sure enough. So what did you see at the moment of the snap?

JOE: I saw the pen move. I saw your finger—out of the corner of my eye—my peripheral vision—snap a little bit.*

R.T.H.: Now that is exactly the kind of a report that I'm looking for, except . . .

JOE: (interrupts) Is that what you want? I thought maybe—I got off the track—[becomes slightly agitated] I wound up in the box, being in the box—got a little hallucinary there. I don't . . .

R.T.H.: (interrupts) OK, except what I want, instead of focusing on the *real* world . . .

JOE: (interrupts) You want a prophecy there, is what you're saying there?

R.T.H.: Well, if you were prophesying to yourself at that moment, I mean, if you're thinking, "Well, I'm having a prophecy here . . ."

JOE: (interrupts) well, I'm not thinking it, sometimes it seems compared to it. I ain't hallucinating it . . .

Under our close supervision, Joe was able to give an adequately complete description of an external perception. That he did not do so for inner experience may be due either to the lack of inner experience or the lack of supervision. We had an occasion during sampling where the real beep occurred in our presence, that is, with our adequate supervision. In this case, he provided the same kind of nonperceptual description that we have been previously describing. Thus we are led to reject the hypothesis that it was lack of supervision that allowed Joe's reports to look as if there was no inner experience.

Two sampling days later, we asked Joe to describe a perception again. This excerpt provides an example of the difficulty that Joe had in staying with perception even of the external world:

R.T.H.: When you look at me, what do you see?

JOE: I see you.

R.T.H.: What's that like?

JOE: You're very stern.*	"Stern" is a conception, not a perception.
R.T.H.: No, when you're *looking* at me [Joe had been looking down].	
JOE: When I'm looking at you? [He looks at Dr. Hurlburt] Well, you have blue eyes.* That's as far as I go. I don't touch you. Blue eyes, very nice blue eyes. Very quiet, modified somewhat as you go through your memories,* there. Your education is—quite right, I like your boots there, you basically dress to fit your own you, there, OK? I like that.	He describes a perception, but immediately withdraws to conceptualize about it.
You have hair on your chest.* I ain't got much. I'm a little envious there—loan me a few strands and I'll grow myself some [they laugh] . . . [talks about worry, disconnection, etc.]	He returns to perceptions, but it is colored by his evaluation of it.

Two days later, the final day of sampling, we summarized our observations from the past weeks, saying, "We never did get to something that looked like what I would say would be a sort of standard inner experience—the kind of thing that our other subjects have done. Either your inner experiences are different from all the rest of my subjects and my own, or for some reason we haven't been able to figure out how to talk about it." Joe responded by talking about schizophrenia in general, Benjamin, girl robots, etc. We continued the summary, saying that Joe spends more time with his concepts than he does with perceptions. This triggered the following dialogue:

JOE: Give me a definition* of a perception—I don't know what it is.	Joe himself had difficulty with the *notion* of perception. It is our understanding that Joe, like most of us, took his mode of awareness for granted, and so did not comprehend that his lack of perception was unusual.
R.T.H.: Well, when I asked you a little bit ago what you saw when you saw me, when you looked at me . . .	
JOE: (interrupts) Well, you're an attractive man, OK? I mean there's no himahaoo junction [Joe's term for homosexuality] there . . .	

R.T.H.: (interrupts) . . . If I asked any of my other subjects what they saw when they looked at me, they would say, "I see a guy with brown hair, and green eyes . . . a yellow shirt, blue jeans . . .

JOE: (interrupts) I look at you as a man.

R.T.H.: (interrupts) And this is the difference. While somebody else would see the perceptions, you see or become involved in or wrapped up in the concepts, of not homosexual, good-looking, smart . . .

JOE: (interrupts) Well, I'm sure you're charming and pleasant with your wife . . .

[A few minutes later Dr. Hurlburt continued with his summary.]

R.T.H.: It looks to me like when you get wrapped up in that concept, a couple of things happen. One is when you get wrapped up in a concept, you sort of lose visualness—you don't really see *me* anymore, you get . . .

JOE: No, I'm seeing you different now*. In my thoughts you're still a light beam, or someone that's going to live forever. If I sketch it trekkin' or if I'm being you, or something happens to you, I'll haul you out if I can . . .

R.T.H.: (interrupts) and as you get wrapped up into that concept, and pretty soon a new concept comes, and it's not out of that concept, but it seems to be coming from a different direction . . .

JOE: Well, that could be basically schizophrenia. The idea as I look at it there, is the idea of me being perhaps a little inventive,* and so a little misunderstood. I have to go through these things in order to get the proper concept, as they are concepts in my perceptions.

R.T.H.: And *that* concept, as it seems to me, starts out and winds itself up in sort of a different direction and gets tighter and tighter . . .

JOE: It does get tighter,* and I use the androids or the robots to unwind it . . .

Joe basically agreed with our summary of his experience, and added details and clarifications ("I'm seeing you different now," "me being a little inventive," and "It does get tighter") which are consonant with our understanding. This gives us some confidence that we have at least a partial understanding of Joe's experience.

DISCUSSION

We have tried to provide sufficient excerpts for the reader to draw conclusions for him- or herself as to the nature of Joe's inner experience. For our part, we believe it to be the case that Joe's inner experience was rather dramatically different from that of any of our other subjects to date. For all of our other subjects, both inner and outer perceptions were the wellsprings of experience. They were replete with a seemingly endless source of detail, in the sense that if we focused our subjects on any small, randomly chosen part of an image they had reported, they could supply many additional details about that small aspect. Thus, our conversations with other subjects ended not when we had exhausted all details of an experience, but rather when we had covered enough details to feel as if we had an understanding of the experience. With Joe, however, we conclude that neither reality-based perceptions nor inner perceptions were experienced with anything like this wealth of detail; in fact, it appears as if almost no perceptual details at all were present to Joe during the sampling period.

Our conclusion, then, is that Joe's experience simply did not include seeing or hearing during the sampled moments. This does not mean that Joe was blind and/or deaf during those moments; on the contrary, he moved meaningfully and without incident through his environment at those times, proof that he was in fact seeing his surroundings and interacting with them. The important qualifier is that there were no seeing or hearing or other perceptual aspects *present to experience* at the sampled times.

In the literature on schizophrenia there are several accounts by schizophrenics in remission that describe their experience during their psychotic episodes. This literature has not, to our knowledge, described this no-experience phenomenon that we claim characterized Joe. Why is our account so different from theirs? The present study differs from the others in two ways: Joe was not in remission at the time that he was describing his events; and we were not focusing on experience in general or experience as recalled from a distance, but rather on a few mundane, randomly selected moments.

We advance the hypothesis that the experience of schizophrenics when psychotic is dramatically different (in fact, absent) from their experience when in remission, and that this difference makes it very difficult, if not impossible, for a schizophrenic in remission to recall accurately what his or her moment-by-moment experiences were like when psychotic.

We will follow in the next chapter the case of Bob, a schizophrenic who decompensated during his sampling period. We will note that as he became more psychotic, he lost the ability to report about his experience, despite the fact that he had been an accurate reporter about inner experience previously. We will further note that Bob had no comprehension of the fact that he had lost this skill, which underscores the discontinuity in experience between his psychotic and remission state. This kind of discontinuity would perhaps make accurate recollections of psychotic momentary experiences impossible from the remission state. This is not to say that the retrospective accounts are entirely erroneous; in fact, most are quite credible and convincing. However, we believe that they may systematically overlook the kind of moment-by-moment absence of experience which we found with Joe.

Having inner experience as our previous subjects knew it necessitates some relatively stable locus of perspective, which serves as the point of view for visual and other sensory experiences. Joe apparently had no such stable platform; he could be himself, and then one of the investigators, and then the box, and then himself again, in as rapid a succession as it can be written. But it was also apparently not the case that what those alternations of self entailed was a looking at the world first from his own perspective, then from ours, then from the box's, etc. Rather, he did not look at the world from any perspective at any time—in fact, he did not look at the world at all.

We have characterized Joe's reports as reflecting an absence of inner experience. Perhaps a simpler explanation would be that Joe had inner experience but his use of language made it impossible to communicate his experience to us. To rule out this possibility we would need to sample a schizophrenic who was competent to describe inner experience while in a period of relative remission, but who then decompensates, and observe what happens to his reports while psychotic. That is the topic of the next chapter.

13

A Decompensating Schizophrenic

with Leny Meertens

Bob J. H. W. Zeus was a 19-year-old inpatient at a Dutch psychiatric facility. He had been admitted a week earlier when delusions of persecution and grandeur became overwhelming. He had been diagnosed as paranoid schizophrenic several years earlier, and had received frequent psychotherapy and antipsychotic medication since his diagnosis. He volunteered to participate in the sampling research. Bob was bilingual in Dutch (his native tongue) and English, and the sampling conversations took place predominantly in English, although discussion of nuances took place in Dutch with the Dutch second author who was present at all the interviews.

The sampling period included ten sampling days spread over a three-week period. During the first half of the sampling period, Bob did not manifest during our conversations any easily observable characteristics typical of schizophrenics—that is, his speech patterns and content were quite within normal limits. During the second half of sampling, however, his verbalizations included frequent loose or clang associations and frequent delusional content both of grandeur and persecution. This deterioration in behavior was apparently the result of the psychiatric team's decision to reduce his antipsychotic medication. For convenience, we will refer to the first part of the sampling period as the Symptom-Free Period (up to about Sample #20), and the last part as the Decompensating Period (from about Sample #21 on).

This study was performed while the author was a visiting professor at Rijksuniversiteit Limburg, Maastricht, The Netherlands.

We met with Bob daily (excluding weekends) for three weeks, except for a two-day period during which he requested a "vacation" from the procedure because it was "too intense" for him at that time. On two days he did not respond to the sampling beeps, even though we expected that he would do so. There were thus ten days on which sampling took place, plus the first day when the procedure was explained to him. During the Symptom-Free Period sampling, we found that we could discuss three or four samples during an hour-long conversation, or 20 beeps in 6 sampling days. Of these, about 9 of the first of these samples had to be considered training beeps, because Bob had not yet learned to take sufficient notice of his inner experience to make full description possible. There were thus 11 beeps in the Symptom-Free Period that were adequately described. During the last half of the sampling period, the Decompensating Period, he provided only one sample per day, even though we requested that he provide at least three or four. The reasons for his providing only one sample were never perfectly clear, but were stated in terms of the intensity of the conversations about the beeps.

We do not have enough samples to provide a complete description of Bob's inner experience, a frequent occurrence when sampling with schizophrenics. Nonetheless, we can describe three characteristics of his inner experience that were salient during the Symptom-Free Period sampling discussions: These were Feelings, which were clearly experienced, well-defined, powerful events taking place in particular parts of his body; Visual Experiences, which included both the experience of detailed, colorful, and vivid Images and of Blackness, which was a perceptual experience of nothingness; and Inner Verbalization, which included groups of words that were heard to fly through, around, and past his head, and also inner verbalizations which were more spoken than heard. We will then provide a discussion of the sampling during the Decompensating Period, showing how the sampling task became at times difficult if not impossible to perform and speculating on its significance in understanding inner experience when decompensating.

THE SYMPTOM-FREE PERIOD

Feelings

Five of Bob's samples during the Symptom-Free Period included some clear emotional experience which was a central feature of the sample. Most of Bob's samples involved some feeling aspect; but in these five the Feeling was a salient part. In general, Bob could give a clear description of the subjective aspect of the Feeling, saying he felt low and desperate, or slightly self-critical, for example. How he knew that a particular Feeling signified, for example, self-criticalness, was not possible for him to explain, a characteristic Bob shared in common with most of our other subjects. However, unlike most of our subjects, Bob experienced his Feelings to reside in precise, clearly demarcated, vivid bodily locations, and these locations could be described in detail.

For example (Sample #10), Bob was sitting in the information center of the hospital. Someone had just asked where the academic center was, and Bob had mentioned a similar center in another city to him. At the moment of the beep, he felt unsure of himself, felt perhaps that what he had said was not quite right. The Feeling was slightly self-critical and was not an extremely strong emotion. The experience had both a bodily and cognitive component. The bodily Feeling was in his chest, in a well-defined teardrop-shaped area extending from the center of his chest, where it was relatively narrow (perhaps 3 inches wide), down to his waist where it was approximately as wide as his body. The region where this Feeling was located existed in depth, also: at the top of his teardrop-shaped region this Feeling of unsureness extended from the surface of his skin to perhaps an inch into the interior of his body, and it gradually increased in depth as it descended, so that at the waist area it extended from the surface to perhaps four inches into his belly. There was also a cognitive aspect of this experience, which was said to be like a groping, as if he was looking away from the person and trying to remember whether he was right. It was difficult for him to describe this groping experience in more specific terms.

In the second example (Sample #13), Bob was listening to music on the radio while hanging curtains in his room. The song playing on the radio was a pop tune called *Final Countdown,* which Bob (mis)interpreted to refer to the end of the world. At the moment of the beep, he was thinking that the words of the song were right, and this thought seemed to be expressed in words, in Dutch, although the exact words could not be specified. These words started in the back of his head and seemed to move somewhat forward, although Bob could not be sure whether they actually moved. The clearest part of the experience was the Feeling of the song having been right. This Feeling was not further expressible in words, but could be localized as at the surface of his body, below his heart, and in and beneath the surface layer of skin. Thus, this location was lower in the body than the self-critical feeling described above.

In another example (Sample #17), Bob was sitting in the dayroom Feeling low because he didn't have any money. He had money in a bank account in town, but his mother was unavailable to get it for him. The Feeling was rather desperate, and while it was difficult to say how he knew that the Feeling was of desperation, it was easy, as had been the case in his previous samples, to say where the Feeling was physically localized. This time, the Feeling was located in a very small space in the middle of his body between the lowest part of his chest and the upper part of his stomach. This region also was extended in depth: its outermost reaches were about an inch below the layer of skin (not extending to the surface of the body, as had the Feelings in the other two examples), and the region extended inside the body about three inches. Thus, the region was more in the front portion of his body than the back.

The last example of Feelings being a salient feature of Bob's experience was a happy Feeling that he was going to win the game of Risk that he was playing (Sample #16). This experience will be described in more detail in the section called Blackness below.

Bob's experiences of Feelings had thus three major features: First, they were very vividly experienced. Second, they were clearly and unambiguously apprehended; that is, Bob had no difficulty in recognizing the subjective significance of a particular emotional experience. However, he could not say how he knew that a particular Feeling resulted in its own particular significance, and so frequently used phrases like, "I don't know how I know the Feeling is of unsureness, but there is no doubt that it is." In this respect, his reports were very similar to those of most of our other subjects. The third characteristic of Bob's Feelings was that they were clearly localized in particular parts of his body. There was nothing vague or general in these descriptions; instead were highly specific. This exactness of bodily description was different from that of most of our earlier subjects, whose reports of bodily Feelings have tended to be rather indistinct.

As with all our subjects, we need to ask whether Bob's reports were reliable; they could be, for example, fabrications of the moment, and have nothing to do with the experience at the moment of the beep. There is no foolproof way of ensuring that reports accurately reflect inner experience; but our discussions did provide several occasions where we could unobtrusively check Bob's reports by asking him to describe the same sampled experience on several different occasions. His descriptions of his Feelings provided such instances, because we could ask him to compare the bodily area where the sampled Feeling had been experienced with the bodily regions where earlier Feelings had taken place. This required him to describe again the experience of Feelings which we had described in previous sessions, and we could crosscheck the reports for consistency. During the relatively Symptom-Free Period, Bob's accounts were very consistent, leading us to confidence in his reports (we will discuss the reliability of reporting during the Decompensating Period below).

Visual Experience

Bob reported vivid visual inner experiences 5 times out of the 11 Symptom-Free samples. These visual experiences can be divided into two groups which we will call Images and Blackness. The Images were bright vivid visual displays which occupied some portion of Bob's inner visual field. They had a limited extent, and thus were experienced more as inner pictures than as inner seeing. The Images were not true to reality: for example, colors were wrong or a person in the Image leaned at a strange angle. The experience of Blackness, on the other hand, was an inner seeing of a vast black extent. This seeing Blackness was not merely failing to see anything, but was a positive perceptual experience of seeing into an inky void.

Images

There were 2 Images among Bob's 11 Symptom-Free samples. The first example occurred at Sample #11, where Bob was sitting in the dayroom near a man who was knitting a sweater for his child. At the moment of the beep, Bob was seeing an Image of that sweater when it would be completed, being worn by a child. The picture was quite clear, in vivid color. The experience was of seeing an interior picture which had the child as a central feature, not just an imaginary seeing of a child. We should elaborate the distinction between seeing an inner picture of a child and an inner seeing of the child. For most of our subjects, having an Image is simply an inner seeing of the imagined subject: the subject usually appears in the center of the visual field and surrounding objects fade off into indistinctness in the periphery. Thus, the normal inner seeing is experienced by our subjects quite as a real external seeing would be. Bob, however, saw the Image of a *picture* of the child wearing a sweater. It was not the child that was the center of this visual experience, but rather a picture of the child.

Furthermore, the imaged picture of the child was not in the center of his inner visual field, but was seen to the left of center, perhaps 30 degrees left of straight ahead. The child in the picture was standing still, but leaning far forward. The child was seen only from the waist up and had blond hair, but the face was not clear, as if not the focus of attention, which was on the sweater. The child was not anyone Bob recognized. The sweater itself was seen in vivid blue and white tweed, like blue yarn and white yarn knitted together. The real sweater, however, that was being knitted beside him, was blue and *green stripes* instead of blue and *white tweed*. Nevertheless, even though the colors were inaccurately represented in Bob's Image and the stripes were transformed into tweed, the sweater was still recognized as the same sweater being knitted by the man beside him.

The other example (Sample #15) of Images in Bob's experience took place while he was watching a television program about wagering. The person on TV was saying that he had bet that he knew someone who could toss up and hit 200 baseballs in 3 minutes. At the moment of the beep, Bob's experience was what he called a "feeling picture," an Image with an associated Feeling that, if represented in words would be, "He could possibly do it," although there were no words present in experience. The Image was of several balls going by, in a straight line, from right to left in his visual field. The balls were white, and they had a white space or trail behind them that extended for 6 or 8 inches behind the ball. The balls were not actually moving in his experience; that is, the Image was rather like a snapshot of balls moving, with a blurred trail behind each ball. There was no color in the Image—just white balls on a black background. The person hitting the balls was not present in the Image. Attached to this Image, somehow present in the picture itself, was the Feeling that "it's possible," but this Feeling could not be further described.

Blackness

The other characteristic of Bob's Visual Experience was the perception of Blackness, and it occurred 3 times (out of 11 samples) in his Symptom-Free Period. The first time it occurred was Sample #10, which we have described previously in the section on Feelings, where Bob felt self-critical after he had mentioned an academic center to a follow patient. In that example, Bob was able to describe rather clearly the Feeling component of the experience, but was relatively inarticulate when it came to describing the more cognitive characteristics, except to say that he was "looking away" from his environment, that he was "trying to remember" what he had said, and that it was like "groping," although not more specifically apprehended. In later samples, apparently as Bob become more skilled at the sampling task, this groping came to be recognized as a seeing of Blackness.

The next time a similar experience occurred (Sample #14), Bob could be more definite. Someone in his hospital ward had a headache, and Bob had just asked him where he got the headache from. At the moment of the beep, Bob was "thinking about" where he could possibly have gotten the headache. Further discussion revealed that this thinking was experienced as being in a totally dark room, surrounded by unlimited darkness in all directions: in front, behind, beside, above, and below him. His eyes searched into the Blackness looking for the answer, but nothing was there except the Blackness. This Blackness was not metaphorical for Bob but, rather, perceptual; that is, he experienced himself as actually seeing an inky Blackness, not merely not seeing anything. Bob was unable to describe how he knew that this seeing Blackness was a thinking about where he could have gotten the headache; he just knew that this was so.

The last example of Blackness occurred while Bob was playing the game "Risk" with some follow patients (Sample #16). His turn to play was just beginning, and he was "thinking about" the empire he was building on the game board. This "thinking about" was a looking at the game board and seeing the pieces of the empire he was constructing; but his focus was a looking through the board, seeing behind and all around the board a great expanse of Blackness. He knew that this Blackness was his empire; he (correctly) felt that he was about to win the game and the Blackness represented the scope of his expanding and conquering empire. The board itself seemed to be suspended, floating, in the Blackness. The board was seen incompletely; the segment of the board that his own pieces occupied was seen, but the rest of the board had disappeared from his experience, replaced by Blackness. The Blackness was a perceptual reality for Bob, not just an absence of seeing. It extended in all directions behind and around the board, and seemed to go on and on in all directions, that is, it had no edges. Bob took the Blackness to represent not only his expanding empire, but also the happy Feeling—the great Feeling of being about to win the game.

Verbal Inner Experience

Two (of 11) Symptom-Free Period experiences included some kind of inner verbal experience. In one of these experiences, the impression was of hearing a phrase that seemed to follow a well-defined trajectory or path through Bob's head (Sample #12). Bob was pushing the doorbell to gain admission to the hospital ward where he was currently placed, and was wondering who would open the door for him. This wondering was verbal, and the sentence "Who will open the door?" (in Dutch) was present, as if Bob was hearing himself speak the words. The sensation was more like hearing the words being spoken than of producing them himself, and the words themselves, all as a group (not one at a time), seemed to be produced in the interior of the back of his head, near his neck, and to move rather rapidly up through the interior of his head. The sounds of this sentence started out at a single point near the base, inside the back of his head, then divided into two equal tracks separated by about two inches at its point of widest separation, and then gradually rejoined by the time it reached the top of his head. The experience of this separation was that each lateral track was heard only by the ear on the same side of his head. When the sound of the words, after rejoining each other, reached the top of his head, they exited through the top of his head and disappeared by flying into the indeterminate distance above him.

To recapitulate this rather complicated trajectory, the voice seemed to start at one unitary point at the inside his head. As it traveled, it split into two channels, like stereo tracks whose separation became greater as they moved upwards. Each track of this stereo display was heard only by the ipsilateral ear. The two tracks were perceived to be identical; that is, each ear heard exactly the same thing, except that it seemed to come from a slightly different direction. As the sounds proceeded upward, the channel separation became less and less, until the channels once again merged as they exited the top of his head. After exit, Bob lost track of these sensations and they disappeared.

The other example of inner verbal experience was more of speaking than of hearing. Sample #13 occurred during the song *Final Countdown* by the pop group *Europe,* and was described above in the section on Feelings. The words in this example were not clearly available to Bob, at least on recollection, and yet the experience did include a sense of verbalization. This verbalization was more a sense of speaking than of hearing, as was the case in the previous sample, and the movement in this example was much less well-defined than in the previous sample. Here, the verbalization conveyed the idea that the song's message was right, but the words that conveyed this message were not clear, or could not be remembered. The verbalization was formed in the back of his head, and it seemed to move somewhat forward, but Bob could not be confident about whether it had in fact moved.

THE DECOMPENSATING PERIOD

During the last half of the sampling period, Bob began to manifest many of the symptoms characteristic of schizophrenia; pressure of speech, rambling, loose associations, delusions of persecution and grandeur, etc. During this time, which we are calling the Decompensating Period, he was occasionally unwilling to sample at all, saying that it was too difficult for him, that the experience was too intense. When he did sample, he recorded only one sample on any given day, despite our requests that he respond to the beep more frequently. There were, however, four samples during the Decompensating Period that were discussed completely enough to be useful. In general it became more problematic to discern the characteristics of Bob's inner experience, and when it could be apprehended, his inner experience became less focused and more rapid or chaotic than in the Symptom-Free Period.

His responses to the first two samples in the Decompensating Period were similar to each other in that he seemed to have lost cognizance of what he was supposed to do when the beep sounded. In Sample #21, for example, he had just left the office after one of our sessions where we had discussed beeps in detail. He was walking down the hall when beeped, and he wrote in his sampling notebook that the world was too big for him, which meant that the pressures on him at the moment seemed too great. When we discussed the sample the following day, he greeted our questions about the beeped experience with surprise, and simply couldn't remember what took place at the moment of the beep. It seemed as if he simply didn't know that we wanted him to focus on what was happening at the moment of the beep, even though he had been doing just that for us for six sampling days already, and had just finished discussing such samples with us only minutes before the beep sounded.

The next sample (#22) took place in occupational therapy, where he was blowing away sandpaper dust from the wood he was working on. A follow patient had called to him, and Bob was turning his attention toward him while still blowing away the dust. That was all that Bob could say about this beep. We have seen, in other subjects, examples where a beep caught the subject "just doing" something, and where inner experience was "empty." In those examples, the subject could confidently say that he or she was simply "not thinking anything" in particular. In Bob's Sample #22, however, it did not seem that he was "not thinking" anything; instead, it seemed either that he had failed to notice his inner experience, whatever it was, or alternatively that the concept "inner experience" was no longer a meaningful concept when applied to Bob.

In the next sample (#23), the ability to perform the sampling task seemed to have returned. Bob was in the living room watching a talk show on television. Author Jackie Collins was being interviewed, and Ms. Collins was stating (in English) that people are intimidated by her books. At the moment of the beep a rapid sequence of experiences flashed by in a very short time. First, the Dutch words *"Zij heeft gelijk"* ("She was right"), which indicated that Bob agreed with what Ms. Collins was saying, were heard seemingly coming from very far away, from the far front left of his head. These words, as a group, came toward him very fast and entered inside his head at a spot between and slightly above his eyes, a spot that he called his "third eye." The words "stayed with him for a minute," which meant that they traversed a looping path that exited his head above the left temple, circled around the back just outside the base of his head, reentered his head at about the right temple, and passed out through his right forehead into the distance in the front right direction. This whole trajectory took place very quickly, "like a flash of lightning."

However, Bob was not so confident about the perceptual nature of this experience. He could not be sure, for example, of the particular characteristics of the voice he heard: he could not specify whether it was his own or someone else's. In fact, he could not even be sure if it was the sound of words at all: it could have been like a thunder that came rolling down and around. Perhaps the experience was not even auditory: it might have been a light that followed the same trajectory. In short, he vacillated in his description, first saying he heard it, then that he was not really sure he heard it, then again becoming more confident that he had heard it, etc.

Then, still part of this rapid sequence of experiences, Bob heard Jackie Collins say the word "Right" on TV, as if she were answering a question from the interviewer, even though Bob could not remember if a question had been asked.

Then, in quick succession, Bob "thought about" a guitar trio that had performed in the hospital lobby the day before, then about a Simon and Garfunkel song that included the words ". . . architects may come and go . . ." (a song that Bob said refers to the architect Frank Lloyd Wright), and then about Frank Lloyd Wright and his work. These "thinkings" could not be further elucidated. We can compare and contrast this sample with a rather similar one from the Symptom-Free Period, Sample #12, where the words "Who will open the door?" were heard moving up and through his head. In the "Who will open the door?" sample, however, these words had clear perceptual characteristics: it was Bob's own voice, being heard rather than spoken. In the present sample, however, Bob could not be sure of the perceptual details of the experience; he could not say whether it was his own voice or someone else's, or whether it was like thunder—perhaps it wasn't auditory at all and was a light that followed that trajectory. His ability to report perceptions had vanished during the Decompensating Period.

The final sample from Bob's Decompensating Period was Sample #24. This experience had three parts that seemed to occur rapidly, so quickly that Bob could not distinguish whether they were in rapid succession or overlapped. The three parts, which we will describe in detail, were the Mt. Everest part, the Jupiter part, and the Very Beautiful part. He was sitting in the hospital ward and was "busy with" his life: the question of his being or not being, and the fact that he did not want to be kept in the hospital. The Mt. Everest part involved a visual Image of Mt.

Everest as seen from the Chinese side. He could see the snow, a small building, and a part of the mountainside that was so steep that the snow had slipped off and thus was bare. He saw some rocks falling down this mountainside, and the rocks disappeared either into the mountain itself or into the snow when they reached the snow-covered part of the mountain. This Image was clearly seen, in accurate color and orientation. Bob could hear no noise associated with the falling rocks.

The Jupiter part of the experience followed immediately, and was itself a simultaneous three-part experience. First, he saw a dim, unclear Image of the planet Jupiter. This visualization was rather vague and without detail; he did not know much about the planet and so could not visualize it accurately, he said. This portion of the Jupiter part of this experience extended in time longer than the other two portions. Second, he heard the word "Jupiter." This experience was a hearing without any particular sensory characteristics; he described it by saying "Like I'm deaf and I can hear the vibrations of the air," and could not give further characteristics of the hearing. The last portion of the Jupiter part was a clear, quick visualization of the word "Jupiter." The individual letters of the word were seen three-dimensionally, as if drawn in perspective, and from slightly above, so that the perspective lines for each letter seemed to recede into the distance as if being looked down upon. However, these perspective lines, instead of being straight, were straight for only what seemed to be a few inches, and then bent downward to the left and disappeared. The whole word, perspective lines and all, was seen as if it was moving toward Bob, coming from the low front left, with the perspective lines trailing behind it marking its trajectory. Then the word, perspective lines and all, passed around the outside of his head and receded into the distance at the front right. Bob experienced himself as playing an active role in this trajectory, as if he had to hold the word away at a safe distance. At the same time that this word was seen flying by, the Image of the planet itself was continuing to be seen directly in front of him.

The last part of the experience of this sample we call the Very Beautiful part. The Very Beautiful aspect of the experience was the two-part sentence, "It would be a long time for people before they travel this way, / but it would be very beautiful," where the two parts are separated here by the slash. The general meaning of this thought was that Bob was thinking that his own way of experiencing ("traveling") was a more sublime way of experiencing than normal people are capable of. The first part of this sentence was experienced as just words coming from Bob's own brain, which was equivalent to saying that it came from "outside," since for Bob there was no clear distinction between inside and outside his brain at this moment. The words were thought, one word at a time, and were experienced not as being either said or heard, but merely as thought.

The second part represented Bob's feelings, which were described to be visual, like a picture that could not be seen but was experienced visually anyway—rather like viewing a television test pattern with the color and brightness turned all the way down so you cannot see it at all. This Very Beautiful aspect was understood to be something of a conclusion to the Mt. Everest and Jupiter parts of the experience, although it was not clear why this constituted a conclusion, and to what. Thus, the Very Beautiful aspect of this experience was described in sensory terms (words, images, feelings, etc.); but these terms were devoid of direct sensory (real or imagined) experience—the words were "just thought," or "seen" on a screen that had no illumination.

On the basis of these four samples, we can now sketch two general characteristics of the experiences in Bob's Decompensating Period. First, the sampling task itself became problematic: Bob seemed at first to forget that he was to focus on his inner experience at the moment of the beep, even though he had been successfully doing so for six sampling days. Second, Bob's descriptions in the Decompensating Period were never clearly tied to perceptual experience, for example, when in Sample #23 he could not ascertain whether the *"Zij heeft gelijk"* sentence was heard or seen as a path of light.

The fact that Bob did not clearly identify the perceptual basis of his experiences could be due to a communication failure, a failure to pay attention to his experience at the moment of the beep, or a lack of perceptual experience itself; and we must consider all three alternatives in turn. We raised the question of lack of communication in the previous chapter, and note that Bob quite clearly had the communication skills as evidenced by the adequacy of his reports in the Symptom-Free Period. Furthermore, he did provide some adequately described perceptual details in the Decompensating Period—his description of the Jupiter part of Sample #24 was of the word seen in three-dimensional block letters with trails going down and to the left, etc. We conclude, therefore, that he had adequate communication skills available to him during the Decompensating Period. A simple failure to pay attention does not seem an adequate explanation of his inability to report perceptual details, either, as the Jupiter sample shows. He could apparently pay adequate attention to the perceptual details of that sample. That leaves the alternative that there were no inner perceptual details to report during the Decompensating Period for all except the Jupiter block letters.

Even though the perceptual basis of these experiences had become less available to him, we should note that his *talk* about these experiences used just as many overtly perceptual terms as he had used in earlier descriptions. He continued to use "seen," "felt," and "heard"; but now these terms did not have reference to any confidently perceived experience.

DISCUSSION

Our conclusion is that Bob's inner experience was much different during the Symptom-Free Period and the Decompensating Period. During the Symptom-Free Period, he had vivid, detailed Images, in which details (colors and patterns) were represented incorrectly and in which a character in an Image was tilted at an odd angle. Thus, his Images were quite similar to Jennifer's goofed-up Images described in Chapter 11 (and also similar to Sally's Images, to be discussed in Chapter 14). During the Decompensating Period, on the other hand, he had great difficulty understanding what the sampling task involved, and asked repeatedly for us to explain it to him; and most of the time could not describe perceptual details that were ongoing at the moment of the beep. In these regards, he was quite similar to Joe in Chapter 12, and for both subjects we concluded that inner experience was absent when decompensated.

There are three other aspects of Bob's sample that deserve comment. First, Bob's perceptual experience of Blackness during the Symptom-Free Period was unique in our sample. The most similar experiences in our collection were Jennifer's, when she reported yellow "clouds" surrounding part of her Images, or black blotches that obliterated part of an Image. This is another point of similarity between Bob's Symptom-Free Period and Jennifer's sample.

Second, while most of our subjects' salient characteristics turned out to be relevant to the *process* of inner experience, we note here a salient *content* pattern in Bob's thinking: a repetitive concern with himself and others "being right." Samples #10 (feeling self-critical because what he said was not quite right); #13 (thinking that the words to "Final Countdown" were right); #15 (feeling that "he could do it" (that is, that the claim was right) referring to a claim that 200 baseballs could be hit); and #23 (thinking that author Jackie Collins was right) all explicitly have in common this characteristic of considering whether something is right. Sample #24 (thinking his own way of experiencing was better than normal people are capable of) seems quite similar in that it could be interpreted to mean that Bob's way is *right*. We have not seen in any of our other subjects such an emphasis on considering the *correctness* of events in the environment.

The last point to be discussed in Bob's sample reminds us of Jennifer's computing-the-beep characteristic, where we observed that accurate observations of the timing of inner events might be problematic for Jennifer because the apprehension of the beep was a rather prolonged active process rather than being a sudden, received-from-outside one, characteristic of our normal subjects. Here we speculate that Bob, too, had at least occasionally inaccurate observations of the timing of his inner events.

To make this speculation, we must deviate from the descriptive procedure we have used throughout Chapters 4 through 14, which, with few exceptions, focused consistently on the task of simply describing the inner experience of an individual. In the paragraphs that follow, we will make an exception to that rule and engage in an exercise of interpretation, rather than description. There are several points to keep in mind while reading the following discussion. First, it will hypothesize a process that is itself hidden, rather than describe experiences that are directly available, which has been the main task of this book. Thus, the following discussion should be observed to be sharply different from the descriptions in the remainder of this book. Second, the hypothesis generated is speculative and based on only one of Bob's samples, and so, despite its similarity to Jennifer, should be regarded as merely tentative.

We invite the reader to reconsider Sample #23, which involved Bob saying to himself, "She is right," in reference to Jackie Collins being interviewed on a television talk show (originally described in the Decompensating Period). When we try to understand that complex experience, we speculate that the sequence of events as experienced by Bob is not the same as the sequence that can reasonably be inferred to have taken place in reality. In order to understand this difference, we will review the sequence of events in Bob's experience and then provide our reconstruction of what might have happened in reality.

The sequence of events as Bob experienced them is as follows: (1) Jackie Collins (on TV) talks about intimidation; (2) Bob thinks, *"Zij heeft gelijk"* ("She is right"); (3) Collins responds to a question Bob had not heard by saying "Right"; (4) Bob thinks about a guitar trio that had played at the hospital; (5) Bob thinks about the Simon and Garfunkel song about architect Frank Lloyd Wright; and (6) Bob thinks about Frank Lloyd Wright. When we try to understand how this process began with Jackie Collins and ended with Frank Lloyd Wright, it seems to us to be a reasonable supposition that the word "Right" said by Collins at step (3) gave rise to the thinking about Frank Lloyd *Wright* at step (6). If that is the case, then how are we to explain the thinking about the guitar trio at step (4)?

Our speculation is that processes (4), (5), and (6) actually *began* in the order (6), (5), (4). That is, thinking about Frank Lloyd Wright (6) triggered the thought about the Simon and Garfunkel song about architects (5), and that song reminded Bob about the guitar trio (4). Yet Bob was adamant: the events were sequenced (4), (5), (6), not (6), (5), (4).

Our explanation of this reversal of sequence is that there was for Bob a time lapse between the *beginning* of a thought process and its *occurrence in awareness*, and this time lapse (during which some form of cognitive processing takes place outside of awareness) is of variable length but can be quite long. In this particular sample, the lapse between the beginning of thought (4) and its appearance in awareness was longer than the lapse between the beginning of thought (6) and its appearance in awareness. Thus, while the processes were *initiated* in the sequence (4), (5), (6), they *appeared in awareness* in the order (6), (5), (4).

We have seen in Jennifer's account (Chapter 11) that the timing of her mental events was apparently different from our previous subjects. In particular, we saw that the beep was not experienced as having a sudden onset, but instead took some time "to register"—a process that Jennifer called "computing the beep," and that may have had a duration on the order of a half second. Our explanation of Bob's sample seems entirely analogous; except that we are considering more than one cognitive process at a time (the three thoughts (4), (5), and (6)), and we are assuming it is possible for one thought process to give rise to another *before* the first registers in awareness.

Our hypothesized sequence of events is as follows; Collins's word "Right" begins a process of thinking about Frank Lloyd *Wright* (*process 6 begins*); this process spawns (outside of awareness) another thought process about the Simon and Garfunkel song about architects (process 5 begins); this song process spawns (again outside of awareness) yet another process of thinking about the guitar concert (process 4 begins); the guitar concern thinking process (having, for whatever reason, a short lapse between its inception and its occurrence to awareness) reaches awareness (process 4 reaches awareness); the song process reaches awareness (process 5 reaches awareness); and the Frank Lloyd Wright thinking (having, for whatever reason, a long lapse between its inception and appearance in awareness) reaches awareness (process 6 reaches awareness).

We reiterate that this explanation is speculative and based on only one beep, and does not correspond to Bob's account. Nonetheless, it does, in concert with Jennifer's computing-the-beep phenomenon, lead to the speculation that the timing of inner processes may be an important aspect of schizophrenia. We might note that one of Bob's general (not sampled) characteristics was that he was proud of his ability to know things before they happened, and was fascinated with the synchronicity of his thoughts and the universe—observations that we feel may be consonant with this relatively long delay between the beginning of a thought process and its awareness. Bob's thinking as he knew it may very well have appeared to him to be coincidentally synchronous with events around him if those events triggered (outside of awareness) a thought process that reached awareness *before* the perception of the external event itself (because of a long time lapse) reached awareness. This would be experienced by Bob as a thought that occurs and is then closely followed by a related event in the environment, in what seems to be a remarkable precognition. Bob's everyday experience was populated by these remarkable coincidences; our hypothesis explains them simply in terms of a long lapse between the beginning of a perceptual process and its occurrence in awareness.

It seems to us that Jennifer's computing the beep, Joe's being the beeper, and Bob's hypothesized time lapse are quite similar phenomena. All show a disjunction between the perceptual beginnings of a thought process and its appearance in awareness. All make what is for normals a passive, received-from-the-outside experience into an active, seemingly self-initiated process. All interfere with the ability to report accurately when a particular even occurred. All posit a process that is extended in time much longer than most normal thought processes.

Overall, we would observe that the process of decompensating seemed to turn experiences that were quite similar to Jennifer's into experiences that were similar to Joe's. Decompensation seems to involve a radical disruption of the ability to organize and perceive inner experience.

14

A Schizophrenic Woman Who Heard Voices of the Gods

Sally Cremer was 31 years old at the time of sampling. The sampling experience had been suggested to her by her psychiatrist, whom she had been seeing regularly for two and a half years. She had been diagnosed as schizophrenic four years earlier, primarily due to the fact that she frequently heard voices. The voices did occur frequently during sampling, but there were no other overt linguistic characteristics of schizophrenia (no pressure of speech, no flight of ideas, etc.) during our conversations. She was a native Dutch speaker but, as her English was fluent, the sampling conversations were carried out entirely in English.

This sampling study took place on three days. On the first day the introduction to the sampling experience was carried out essentially identically to that of our other subjects, and she was given the sampling apparatus with instructions to use it until she had collected about ten samples. The second day she sampled for five hours, resulting in 14 beeps being recorded. She wrote down her experiences at the moment of the beep in Dutch and translated them into English before coming to the sampling meeting the third day. During the course of this third-day discussion of her experiences, she stated that she would prefer not to continue the sampling process, because voices that she called gods would be likely to punish her for continuing; in fact, she had probably already gone too far in the sampling process. She would, however, be willing to complete the descriptions of the samples that she had already

This study was performed while the author was a visiting professor at Rijksuniversiteit Limburg, Maastricht, The Netherlands.

collected. Of course we honored this request, and no additional sampling took place. There were two sampling conversations held on the third day, one in the morning and one in the afternoon, each lasting approximately one and a half hours. A total of seven beeps were discussed thoroughly and, as a result, this report will be based on these seven beeps.

Because of the relatively small number of beeps being considered, it will not be possible to give a general description of Sally's inner experience. However, it will be useful to describe some of the characteristics of the samples that we did collect, which we will first do in general terms, then more specifically. First, Sally's samples always had a salient emotional content; there was always a relatively clear, frequently quite strong, affect such as aggression, uncertainty, irritation, or vagueness present at the moment of the beep.

Second, nearly all of her samples involved hearing voices that were understood to be the voices of beings whom she called gods. These voices were located inside or quite near her head and were heard clearly and vividly, more clearly than hearing in her shared external reality. (Sally experienced three different realms where experience could take place: the "shared external reality," which was the world as experienced by herself and others; a "special reality," which was for Sally an objective reality that was not shared with other people; and "inner experience," a region experienced to be inside or near her head, where Sally could see imaginal Images and hear voices.) The gods' voices occurred either singly or in groups of up to about 20 separate voices, speaking to each other conversationally, speaking in unison, or issuing direct commands to Sally.

Third, Sally experienced visualizations of things not present in the shared external reality. These visualizations included seeing inner Images, and also actual, clear seeing into an external special reality, even though Sally knew that this world was not a part of the shared external reality. Fourth, Sally also experienced internal verbalizations related to external reality, an Inner Hearing of words that a friend had said, and Inner Speech, spoken by herself in her own, naturally inflected voice.

THE VOICES OF THE GODS

Six of Sally's seven samples involved a direct perceptual awareness of voices or beings whom Sally called "gods." She used the word "gods" to describe these experiences because earlier in her life she had believed that the voices existed before she was born and would continue to exist after her death. At the time of sampling she was no longer convinced of their immortality, but nevertheless continued to refer to them as gods because she still understood them to be powerful entities that could control her internal and external realities. The gods were experienced as voices heard inside or very close to her head. The voices were about 20 in number, some "more important" than others in the sense that those voices were heard more frequently and appeared to be more powerful than the other voices. Occasionally the gods were also seen, appearing as shadowy beings who will be described below in the Visual Experience section.

The first sample included such speaking by the gods. She was at her mother's house talking with her mother about her own financial situation. Her 15-month-old son was playing nearby. At the moment of the beep, her mother was asking her what was wrong, although nothing was particularly wrong as far as Sally was concerned. Sally's attention at that time was focused on the voices of the gods ordering her not to tell anything about what the gods said (this lack of outward attention may have been what prompted her mother's question). The gods were also forbidding her to write down (as part of the sampling study) the exact words that the gods spoke.

The voice of this particular god was experienced as speaking these words, and the words were clearly audible, more clearly than externally spoken words would have been. Sally could easily remember what the words had been, but because she was forbidden to speak them, she would not repeat them for me. She could, however, describe the characteristics of the voice. It was one of the most familiar voices, one that she referred to as important because it spoke frequently to her. The vocal characteristics of the voice were easily recognizable, even though they varied greatly from occasion to occasion and within occasions. The pitch was low, like a masculine bass voice, but Sally said that it was not correct to interpret the voice as being either masculine or feminine. The pitch could change rather dramatically within utterances, rising to soprano and back to bass again. The voice was speaking in Dutch (as were all of Sally's inner experiences of words), and the volume was rather soft. The words were clearly an imperative; if an external observer could have heard the words, the inflection would have been recognized as being a command. Seemingly as a reaction to these words of the gods, Sally was experiencing a Feeling of uncertainty.

In the next sample (#2), Sally was still in conversation with her mother, who was talking about money. She was again paying only slight attention to her mother's words, and was also looking at and idly seeing her mother and her son who was playing nearby. However, most of her attention was occupied with the voices of the gods. In this sample, the gods' earlier prohibition against repeating their words did not for some reason apply, much to Sally's surprise, so she could report that the gods said, repeatedly (in Dutch), "Dollie (Sally's friend who sometimes takes care of Sally's son) is a bitch . . . Dollie is a bitch . . . Dollie is a bitch." These words were said approximately (but not exactly) simultaneously by the 20 separate voices of the gods, rather like a poorly rehearsed chorus speaking in imperfect unison. There was a slight pause between each of the repetitions of the sentence "Dollie is a bitch." The sentence was repeated perhaps ten times. The voices were extremely clearly heard, again as if they were either inside or closely surrounding her head, in front, back, to both sides and above and below. The voices had a range of vocal characteristics from bass to soprano, and the rate of speaking was slightly faster than a human chorus would have pronounced the words.

In the next example where Sally heard the gods' voices (Sample #4), she was again talking with her mother about Sally's taxes. Somewhat more of her attention was on her mother's conversation than in the previous samples, but she still was not paying full attention. Instead, she was attending to the voice of one of the more important gods who was commanding her to look away from her mother. The voice was speaking clearly in words, in Dutch, again in the inside or very near her head. Once again, the words were clearly available to Sally both at the moment of the beep and at the time of our conversation the next day; but she could not report them because the gods had again commanded her not to do so. Again she was allowed to describe vocal characteristics: the sentence the god spoke was incomplete, having been broken off in the middle for some reason that she did not know; the voice told her to look away (which Sally did in fact do), and started off as a low bass voice and rose to the soprano range by the end of the utterance; there was much intonation and inflection modulation in the manner of speaking, even more so than a human voice would have; the rate of speaking was slower than normal; and the words themselves were drawn out in time like an exaggerated drawl. At the same time that this god's voice was heard, the rest of the gods' voices were humming in the background, a sort of buzzing noise with no particular melody which came from somewhere in the back of the inside or near-outside region of her head.

At the same time both the "look-away" and the humming voices were heard, Sally was saying silently to herself (in Dutch) in Inner Speech, "I should take a look at Menno (her son)," to make sure that he was asleep. This Inner Speaking had the same characteristics (intonation, rate of speed, etc.) as her external speech would have had. At the same moment, Sally was also aware of a clear bodily Feeling that she knew was a longing for a cigarette. She described this longing as being like a "hunger in her lungs," quite clearly located deep in her chest.

There was one sample where Sally both heard and saw the gods at the same time (Sample #11). She had left her mother's house to do some errands, and had returned a few hours later and was again sitting in her living room talking with her. Her mother was telling her something, but Sally had no idea what it was because she was quite totally involved with both hearing and seeing the gods. Just before the beep, the gods had instructed Sally to look outside the living room window in a certain direction, and she had done so; at the moment of the beep the gods were "showing themselves to her." She could see the shared external reality outside the window—the garden and the wall beyond—but suspended in space in front of the wall was a clearly defined rectangular region in which the gods could be seen. This was experienced as seeing into reality, except that this rectangular region was a special reality known to be of a different order from the shared external reality. Thus, this seeing was *not* experienced as like looking at an inner Image; rather, the objects being seen were not part of an Image but were instead experienced as entities of an external world discovered by perception.

The rectangular area in which the gods were seen was wider than it was high—perhaps a meter wide and half a meter high—and, although the edges were clearly demarcated, there was no border or frame. Inside this rectangle was a series of vertical bars, white in color and perhaps eight in number, which extended from top to bottom of the rectangle, so that seeing the rectangle was rather like looking at a prison window. Behind the bars were the black or gray shadowy figures of the gods, perhaps 20 in number, which moved back and forth, passing in front and behind each other rather like a group of prisoners milling about inside the prison window, some closer to the window and some farther away, moving around without bumping into each other.

The figures themselves were "slim," that is to say, taller than they were wide, and extended completely to the bottom of the rectangle but not to the top, again like seeing people through the prison window from the waist up and above their heads. The gray, shadowy forms had no explicit features (although Sally reported that on other occasions the figures had armlike structures that seemed to reach out to her), but were seen to alter slightly in shape as they moved, although they always maintained their basic slim form.

The visualization was seen in depth, three-dimensionally, and it seemed to float suspended in space a few centimeters in front of the garden wall. The visualization seemed to undulate toward and away from Sally in waves, with part of the visualization moving somewhat toward her while another part was moving away. This movement was not jerky, but instead was a smoothly flowing oscillation in the visualization. The shadowy figures were seen clearly; that is, the figures were in *fact* shadowy and were not merely seen indistinctly, and there seemed to be a mist or fog behind the bars in between the figures of the gods but not between Sally and the bars. Some of the figures were seen to be closer to the bars (and thus also closer to Sally) than others, but all were seen clearly.

Two of the voices were also speaking to Sally while she was looking at them at the moment of the beep. One voice said, in Dutch, "Do you see us now?" and the other voice said a moment later, "We're there." These voices were heard inside Sally's head, in the upper left back part of her inner head or near it. Thus, the voices were heard to be in a different place from where the gods were seen. Furthermore, the seeing of the gods took place in a fixed part of physical reality, just in front of the garden wall, while the sound of the voices was fixed relative to her head and thus turned in space when Sally turned her head.

There was a slight Feeling of reassurance that was associated with this experience. It was not at all frightening, and Sally was calm throughout.

VISUAL EXPERIENCES

Three of the seven samples that we examined included some kind of visualization that was different from Sally's perception of the shared external reality. We have described one of these above, the seeing of the gods in the special reality suspended in front of the garden wall. The other two visualizations involved seeing inner Images, that is, visual displays that Sally described as being like "pictures in her mind."

Images

The first of these (Sample #5) took place while Sally was in conversation with her mother about Dollie and Dollie's husband, who were in the process of getting a divorce. At the moment of the beep, Sally herself was talking aloud to her mother, and at the same time the gods were talking in her inner head or nearby. Sally's impression was that the gods were talking to each other in a conversation that Sally could overhear, and that their general tone of voice was cynical at the moment. She could not remember the exact words of the voices, but the general sense of their conversation was that they were critical of people of the world in general. This critical conversation seemed to trigger in Sally a clear, strong Feeling of anger or aggression, like "of taking a machine gun and shooting everybody down that I see," which had both a bodily and an Image aspect. The bodily aspect was characterized by tension in her hands and stomach. The Image aspect of this aggressive Feeling involved seeing an inner moving picture of approximately ten people riddled with machine-gun bullets, covered with blood and falling down and screaming. The Image was like a moving picture, in color, of the people in various stages of falling while being gunned down. The color was accurate, with red blood, etc., except that the people's skin was very, very pale, almost white.

I asked whether the people in the Image were recognizable to her, and she replied in the negative, but then interrupted herself, as if taken herself by surprise, and said that in fact one of the people was recognizable, an old boyfriend of hers. This boyfriend was not a central or important person in the Image, just another of the gunned-down and falling bodies.

The Image itself was clearly recognized to be a part of her imagination, a picture known to be created by herself in her own inner experience, and was thus experienced much differently from the seeing of the gods in Sample #11. The seeing of the gods was experienced as a seeing into some world that was not created by herself.

The Image occupied the entire vertical extent of her inner visual field, but was seen only in the right half of her inner field. That is, she felt that she had to turn her eyes (or her head) slightly to the right to see the Image. The screaming in the Image was seen, not heard; in fact, there was no sound accompanying the Image. The aggressive Feeling seemed to precede the Image in Sally's experience, and to become stronger while the Image was displayed. The Image did *not* arouse Feelings of compassion or sorrow for the people, etc., but rather was seen as purely aggressive.

The second Image in Sally's samples occurred while Sally was sitting alone on her couch (Sample #7). She was thinking about the irritatingly slow way in which her boyfriend Maarten does things. This thinking was a "visual thought," that is, she was looking at an inner picture of Maarten putting on his coat. Maarten was viewed from the left side, and the full extent of his body could be seen, in motion as he extended his arm to begin putting on his coat. The movement was very slow, exaggeratedly slowed over Maarten's usual slow manner of movement. The Image was in accurate color, and the coat Maarten was putting on was his own accurately represented coat.

The Image included a portion of Sally's living room: the walls and carpet behind where Maarten was standing. The walls and carpet were accurately portrayed in the Image, but the remainder of the room was altered from the way it actually existed. For example, the shelf behind where Maarten was standing could be seen clearly, but it was empty instead of having the books and papers on it as it usually did. Furthermore, the plants, chairs, and piano that were really in the room were absent in the Image, even though the floor and walls where these articles stood were clearly visible in the Image. (As an aside, after the description of the sample was complete, I asked her if she could recreate this image now, as we were speaking about it, and she said she could, and did so. I inquired whether the plants, chairs, etc. were still missing, and she said that they were in fact still missing. I then asked whether she could "correct" the Image, that is, to put the plants, etc. back into the scene. She tried to do so, but reported with surprise that she was unable.)

The Image itself was seen straight ahead in the visual field and, as she watched it, it seemed to bend from the top, to curl over away from her. The Image continued thus to roll away from her until the last (bottom) part rotated, when it disappeared completely from her view. While the Image was thus bending, the visualization of Maarten also bent; that is, his body curved to the side along with the Image as a whole.

Concurrent with this visualization was a Feeling of irritation with Maarten, and while this irritation was said to exist in her body, she could not say exactly how it was experienced.

At the same time that this Feeling and visualization were going on, the voices of the gods could also be heard, asking Sally if she could remember having made love (with Maarten) last night. The exact words the voices used were forbidden to be repeated, but it could be said that the voices occurred one after the other, or sometimes at the same time, asking the same question repeatedly. These voices, as usual, were clearly heard in her inner head or nearby, and when they weren't talking, they were laughing at her. She was embarrassed at not being able to remember having made love, and didn't like the game the gods were playing with her; but those emotions seemed to occur slightly after the beep.

VERBAL INNER EXPERIENCE

We have seen that the inner apprehension of the voices of the gods occurred at nearly every sample that we examined. There were two samples (out of seven) where inner verbalizations were experienced that were not the voices of the gods. One of those has been described above (Sample #4), in which Sally was saying to herself in Dutch in Inner Speech, "I should take a look at Menno." These words were experienced as being said in her own voice with the same vocal characteristics as if she were speaking aloud. In the other sample (#3), Sally was Inner

Hearing Maarten's voice as he had spoken the day before. At the moment of the beep, Sally was eating a sandwich with her mother, who was talking about Sally's sister Monique, who had a new job. Sally was not paying attention at all to the eating, and was only half listening to the conversation over Monique, since she was more focused on thinking about Maarten. Maarten had told her that he would marry her if that would be a help in keeping her son with her, that perhaps then no one would be able to take him away from her. This thinking about what Maarten had said was experienced as a replay of his exact words. Maarten's voice was heard, not very distinctly, saying the words that he had used the previous day, with the same inflection, rate, etc. as in the original. However, the remembered hearing itself was not as clear as the original hearing had been, and even less clear than the hearing of the gods' voices had been in other samples. At the same time, Sally was Feeling a bit "vague," as if she was not really there while she was eating her sandwich.

FEELINGS

In all of the samples we have described except one (Sample #2, where we may have had an incomplete conversation about the experience), Sally experienced a clearly defined emotion at the moment of the beep. We will not repeat those samples here, but instead will draw notice to the general characteristics of Sally's Feeling experiences. First, her Feelings were always clearly identifiable: uncertainty in Sample #1, vagueness in Sample #3, longing (for a cigarette) in Sample #4, anger/aggressiveness in Sample #5, irritation in Sample #7, and reassurance in Sample #11. Even though the Feelings themselves were easily identifiable, it was difficult or impossible for Sally to explain exactly how she knew that that was precisely that Feeling and no other. She could say that particular portions of the body were involved with each emotion, but these portions were not as clearly defined as in some of our other subjects (Bob, for example). The overall observation, then, is that in almost all of the experiences some emotional event took place, was clearly recognized, and had a rather clear bodily expression.

DISCUSSION

We should say at the outset that we believed that Sally's reports were accurate descriptions of her inner experience. Her reports were consistent when on occasion she described the same event in each of two sampling conversations, and she presented what was to us a believable pattern of recollections—for example, at times she said she couldn't remember a particular detail without seeming to be particularly stressed at her inability to recall and without succumbing to any perceived pressure from us. Furthermore, she expressed genuine surprise about some characteristics of her experience when we focused her on them.

Sally was a schizophrenic whom an external observer would describe as being relatively symptom-free during the sampling period. Thus, we should compare her inner experience to that of Jennifer, and to that of Bob in his Symptom-Free Period. Because of the prohibitions of the gods, we do not have enough samples to make a complete comparison, but we can still note some striking similarities.

First, Sally's Images were experienced as inner pictures, rather than inner viewings, occupying abruptly less than her entire inner visual field, characteristics that typified both Jennifer's and Bob's Images.

Second, one of her Images had the striking tilt also observed by both Jennifer and Bob but by none of our normal subjects (or of our depressed subjects; see Chapter 17 and the sequel).

Third, Sally's Image of her friend Maarten was arbitrarily inaccurate in details—a shelf without its usual books and a room seen without its plants and furniture, also similar to reports by Jennifer and Bob, but different from our nonschizophrenic subjects.

Fourth, Sally's seeing into a special reality was a unique characteristic. She was clearly able to distinguish seeing in her shared external reality from the seeing of inner Images, and also from the seeing into the special reality which in the sample housed the gods.

Fifth, Feelings were clearly apprehended by Sally on almost every beep, similarly as with both Jennifer and Bob, and more frequently than many (but not all) of our normal subjects.

Sixth, she repeatedly heard voices she took to be gods talking to her or to each other and giving her commands. The hearing of these voices was quite similar to hearing in reality, except that it was even clearer, and that the voices were heard either inside or quite close to her head, even when the gods themselves were seen in the exterior special reality some distance in front of her.

15

Implications for Understanding Schizophrenia

It is not the purpose of this book to provide a theory of the schizophrenic process, nor even to describe some of the essential characteristics of schizophrenia. Such tasks would require a more consistent focus on schizophrenia as well as data from many more subjects. However, while we do not have complete data, we do nonetheless have sufficient carefully collected data to make some general observations on the inner experience of schizophrenics, to raise some questions regarding our present understanding of schizophrenia, and to speculate on the answers to some of those questions. With this caveat, however, we feel justified in speculating, since we have already provided a fairly complete description of the individuals whose experiences led to the speculations, so that the critical reader can judge the adequacy of the speculations for him- or herself.

Before we begin, we might note that the number of observations in our schizophrenics' samples is generally smaller than in our samples of normal subjects. This reflects the fact that it is generally more difficult to sample with schizophrenics than with normals. While the typical normal subject finds the prospect of sampling interesting, a little exciting, and perhaps slightly threatening, a schizophrenic may view the prospect as intrusive and therefore decline to participate. Once sampling is under way, our typical normal subject finds our reassurances adequate to allay any threat, and the procedure itself to be relatively unobtrusive.

This is not the case with our schizophrenics, who frequently find that the procedure becomes more intrusive rather than less, or requires too much energy, or is not possible for some other reason. Thus, schizophrenics are more likely to discontinue before adequate sampling has occurred (as did several who are not reported in this book), or to discontinue after providing some usable reports but not as many as we would like (as did our subjects Bob and Sally). Furthermore, Joe's discontinuance was an example of what is generally observed to be the typical instability of schizophrenic existence: against medical advice, he left the halfway house program where we met with him and disappeared.

Thus our schizophrenics' reports are based on as many samples as we could get, not (except with Jennifer) as many as we might have liked. We included their descriptions in this book because we believed that they were more or less accurately describing their experience, based on the reliability checks that we have described with each subject; and excluded other schizophrenics who failed to meet this criterion. We clearly need more cases and more complete cases if we are to speak definitively about schizophrenia; nonetheless, for the reasons stated above we feel justified in calling attention to the following generalizations.

Schizophrenics, when not decompensating, may have extremely clear emotional experiences; inner emotional experience is not blunted. It is frequently said that schizophrenics have "blunted" affect, that most of the time their emotional experiences are shallow or nonexistent until sudden emotional outbursts occur. Our samples force us to make the distinction more clearly between the inner experience and the outward expression of emotion. Our schizophrenic subjects simply did *not* have blunted inner emotional experience. On the contrary, their emotional experiences were quite clear to them; they were easily capable of describing nuances and discriminations of their inner emotional experiences; and the range of such emotions was quite varied.

At the same time, however, some of our subjects outwardly appeared to have the characteristic affective blunting; this was perhaps most evident in Sally. Since the inner emotional experience was clear at the same time that the outer expression of emotion was blunted, our interpretation is that what is identified as blunting of affect is at least sometimes the result of *hiding* clear inner emotional experience from expression in the external world, not the result of flattened inner emotional experience. For example, when Sally experienced the aggressive image of gunning down people all around her, that feeling of aggression was clearly available to her; but an external observer of Sally at that moment would have seen her as emotionally flat and detached.

In fact, inner emotional experience in our schizophrenics sometimes seemed *hyper*-clear. Our schizophrenics were *more* adept than our normal subjects in describing the exact physical location of their emotional experience. Normal subjects typically were at rather a loss to describe the bodily aspects of their emotional experience in detail; they would frequently say that they knew they were experiencing a particular emotion, and knew precisely what that emotion was, but could not be more detailed in describing exactly how they knew that. Our schizophrenics, by contrast, could provide complete physical detail, as for example Bob's descriptions of the exact shape of the bodily regions involved in his emotional experience. Thus we are led to speculate that *the externally observed blunting of affect in schizophrenics is the result of hiding extra-clear inner emotional experience rather than deficient emotional experiencing.*

Color is experientially important to schizophrenics. In all of our schizophrenics who had periods of relative remission, color played a very strong role in both imaginal and external perception. Colors were noted for their own sake, as when Jennifer attended to the particular green of the 7-Up machine, and were also sometimes distorted, as when Bob's sweater image should have been blue and green stripes but blue and white tweed instead, or when the faces in Sally's gunned-down-people image were "too white."

In general, colors seemed to have more prominence for our schizophrenics than for our normal subjects. Normal subjects frequently reported that images, for example, were in color, and identified the color of particular features of the image. Color was seen and described as an aspect of the thing being described. But for our schizophrenics, the colors seemed to be more than just an incidental feature of the object being imagined. For example, when Jennifer described the yellow smoke that she saw surrounding her head, it was not described as smoke that happened to be yellow but, rather, it was the *yellow smoke*, as if the yellowness were an inherently important, constituting feature of the smoke. Colors were also seen in apparent exaggerated clarity, as when Bob's blackness seemed to be "blacker than black," or Jennifer's noting of the extremely clear electric blue of an RC Cola can. (We will discuss the theory of color perception in schizophrenia at the end of this chapter.)

Inner visual experience is more frequent in schizophrenics than in normals. We saw in Chapter 10 that the frequency of inner visual experience in our normal subjects ranged from about 6 to 46 percent. Our three nondecompensated schizophrenics (Jennifer, Bob, and Sally) each reported the occurrence of images in about half of their samples. That is, schizophrenics may spend more time attending to their inner images than do normals.

Images exist more concretely for schizophrenics than for normals. Our normal subjects, as we have seen, frequently reported seeing inner images. With a few exceptions, these experiences were essentially like inner seeing: the center of attention is more distinctly seen, the periphery of the experience fades out into indeterminacy, the central focus is usually in the center of the inner visual field, etc. With our schizophrenics, however, the images themselves were seen as concrete realities of inner experience, rather than merely the place where imaginary things are seen. That is, the image itself, not just the objects in the image, had seemingly real characteristics. For example, the image might occupy a clearly delineated particular portion of the visual field, as when Sally's Image of her friend Maarten occupied only the right half of her inner visual field. Furthermore, images could be seen as if viewed obliquely, as when Jennifer reported frequent experiences where the entire image was rotated 45 degrees, or the entire image was seen "leaning away" from her. Sally reported an image that rolled away from her, curling over from the top until it disappeared from view altogether.

Images of schizophrenics were frequently "goofed up." All three of our subjects who had non-decompensation periods described images that were somehow factually incorrect. For example, Bob described an image of a sweater that was in reality being knitted by the person next to him, except that the imagined sweater was blue and white tweed while the real sweater was blue and green stripes; Sally described an image where the books and papers were missing from a clearly seen shelf, etc.

Goofed-up images were most frequent in Jennifer's sample. She described images where a glass of iced tea was seen suspended at an angle above her table, while the table itself was straight up and down; where the garbage bag in her room was seen to be full while in fact it was empty; where the imaged bottle of cream had a splotch of red on it; where the imagined Ping-Pong player was playing left- instead of right-handed and was wearing the wrong colored shirt; where the living room shelf was seen having books on it instead of games, as was actually the case; where the word "Sugar" appeared almost entirely obliterated by lines scratched through it; where the black fuzzy rim appeared in front of the podium of an imagined game show host; etc. When we recall that Jennifer was actively focused on her images in half of her samples, we are forced to speculate that she must never be able to take for granted or be confident of the visual characteristics of her world, particularly when we note that this sample was taken during a time when her schizophrenia was in relative remission.

The timing of inner experience was experienced differently by schizophrenics. This characteristic was most clearly exemplified by Jennifer in her description of "computing the beep." Whereas our normal subjects found the beep to be a clear, distinct, precise, fast-rise-time phenomenon, Jennifer reported that it seemed to take some time for the beep to enter her experience, and that the end result of the gradual rise in awareness was an almost-verbal acknowledgment that, "Yes, that's the beep." The difference here is that Jennifer experienced her own process of recognition as being extended in time, while normal subjects apprehend the process as immediate. We also speculated that Bob's inner processes were of varying speed, allowing inner experience to occur in different sequence from that of external reality.

Words appeared as visual/spatial presences for schizophrenics. As we have seen, words figured prominently in the inner experience of our normal subjects. In almost all normal examples, these words were experienced as if they either were being spoken or being heard. Two of our schizophrenics, however, frequently reported inner visualizations of words, and furthermore saw these words as possessing particular peculiar spatial characteristics. For example, Bob saw the word "Jupiter" as if it had come toward him from the distance leaving a curved solid trail behind it. Jennifer saw the word "Wonder" suspended at an angle, from her forehead off into the distance. At another time, Jennifer saw a whole sentence, "I hope my hair won't fall down," as a jumbled heap of words piled disorganizedly on top of each other. For our normal subjects, words were almost always vehicles for the expression of semantic meaning. For our schizophrenics, they were sometimes objects that existed on their own, stripped of their meaningful connections, thus allowing the words of a sentence to be seen in jumbled order.

Words frequently move in schizophrenics' inner experience. This is an extension of the concrete existence of words described in the previous paragraph. Words, even sentences as an intact unit, were seen or heard to fly by or circle around the subject's head. For example, Jennifer heard in her inner experience the words, "I should get up and change the channel but I don't want to" move swiftly by her head from back to front, and Bob heard the words, "Who will open the door?" start behind him, split into two stereo tracks, and move up through his head and out into the distance.

We have noted that our normal subjects make a clear distinction between the experience of Inner Hearing and Inner Speech, the first being passive and the second creative or active in the doing of the talking.It is noteworthy that our schizophrenic subjects' moving sentences were experienced on some occasions as being heard and on other occasions as being spoken. That is to say, the place where schizophrenics occasionally experience themselves to be actively Inner-Speaking can be a rapidly moving point either inside or outside the head. While our normal subjects had frequently distinguished between Inner Hearings of their own voice and Inner Speech, none of them ever reported the rapid movement of such experiences.

Schizophrenia seems to be more a disorder of perception than of association.

Even in periods of relative remission of symptoms, our schizophrenics' perceptions were different from normals' in the ways that we have just discussed: more frequent images, too-intense colors, goofed-up images, visual words, moving experiences, etc. On the other hand, we never saw anything in any of our schizophrenics' samples that resembled a loose association; for example, the inner sentences reported by our schizophrenics never began on one topic and ended on another, as is frequently the case in schizophrenics' external verbal communication.

Thus we are led to the conclusion that perceptual distortions are probably a fundamental part of schizophrenia; but that loose associations may not be essential features. This is contrary to some views of schizophrenia that see loose association as one of the central features of schizophrenia. We account for this by noting that our philosophic tradition, for thousands of years, has more or less accepted the notion that ideas are verbal and that ideas are the precursors of speech. The disconnected speech of schizophrenics must therefore be the result of disconnected verbal ideas. However, we have in Chapter 10 and elsewhere come to question the associationistic doctrine: inner experience is frequently nonverbal, speech frequently occurs with no experienced ideas, and ideas are frequently experienced with no speech intended.

Furthermore, our schizophrenics have *less* inner verbalization than our normal subjects, and *more* inner visualizations, particularly more goofed-up inner visual perceptual experiences. We therefore speculate that the frequently observed loose "associations" in schizophrenics' external speech are quite probably due to a disorganization of *perception,* rather than *association.* Our results indicate that both inner and external words are probably adequately strongly associated to inner images; but the images themselves are rapidly changing, frequently goofed-up visualizations, with the result that external speech changes topic frequently. Since these rapid changes of topic seem more closely related to rapidly changing images than to inadequately linked words, it seems somewhat misleading to label this phenomenon "loose association."

Decompensating schizophrenics may have no inner experience at all. The having of inner experience as we generally understand it necessitates the existence of some relatively stable locus of perspective from which to view visual or other sensory experiences. As we saw, such a locus seemed to be entirely absent throughout Joe's sampling period. We provided transcriptions that we interpreted as showing that, while his words were triggered by events occurring in the outside world (our own questions, for example), these words could not be said to reflect any single real or imaginary perception or series of perceptions. We proposed the possibility that Joe had none of the images or perceptions or spoken inner words or heard inner words or experienced bodily feelings that we commonly call part of inner experience; in fact, it was as if Joe had no inner experience at all.

We became somewhat more convinced of this possibility during Bob's Decompensating Period. We saw that Bob, while functioning relatively well, identified images and feelings characteristics of inner experience. However, when he decompensated, he exhibited a behavior very similar to Joe's: he seemed to forget what the sampling task involved. Even though he had been telling us about his inner experience quite successfully for days, he could now not understand what we wanted of him. Our tentative interpretation was that he could not understand our questions about his inner experience because he no longer *had* any inner experience; that is, he, like Joe, no longer had Images, Feelings, or Inner Verbalizations, etc.

With all these considerations in mind, then, let us turn to a "standard" description of the symptoms of schizophrenia, that in the American Psychiatric Association's *Diagnostic and Statistical Manual, 3rd Edition-Revised* (DSM-III-R) (APA, 1987), and comment on it from our own perspective. DSM-III-R holds that, in schizophrenia, characteristically there are disturbances in several of the following areas: content and form of thought, perception, affect, sense of self, volition, relationship to the external world, and psychomotor behavior. We will discuss each in turn.

> *Content of thought.* The major disturbance in the content of thought involves delusions that are often multiple, fragmented, or bizarre (i.e., involving a phenomenon that in the person's culture would be regarded as totally implausible, e.g., thought broadcasting, or being controlled by a dead person). Simple persecutory delusions involving the belief that others are spying on, spreading false rumors about, or planning harm to the person are common. Delusions of reference, in which events, objects, or other people are given particular and unusual significance, usually of a negative or pejorative nature, are also common. For example, the person may be convinced that a television commentator is mocking him. . . ." (APA, 1987, p. 188)

Our subjects did in fact report this kind of disturbance in thinking. Sally, for example, believed that the voices she heard were voices of the gods, and Bob clearly attributed unusual significance to his own experience, as when he felt that the world would be great if everyone would experience as he did. Thus our observations corroborate the DSM-III-R descriptions.

> *Form of thought.* A disturbance in the form of thought is often present. . . . The most common example of this is loosening of associations, in which ideas shift from one subject to another, completely unrelated or only obliquely related subject, without the speaker's displaying awareness that the topics are unconnected. . . . (APA, 1987, p. 188)

This passage strikes us as confusing an exterior process, i.e., speaking, with an interior process, i.e., thought. As we stated above, this confusion has its origins in our philosophical tradition of accepting as a given that a thought precedes every act and, in particular, that a thought precedes every speech. We did not find evidence in our own subjects of loose interior associations; but we did find many other kinds of disorder of the form of inner experience. Images were much more frequent than in most normal subjects; images were concrete realities that could be viewed off to the side or rotated or leaning over; inner experience seemed to be more rapid; words were experienced as visual/spatial realities; the semantic meanings of words could be removed, allowing words to be seen in a jumbled pile, etc. Thus we also saw great distortion in the form of thought, but none of these distortions are the kind that DSM-III-R describes.

> *Perception.* The major disturbances in perception are various forms of hallucination. Although these occur in all modalities, the most common are auditory hallucinations, which frequently involve many voices the person perceives as coming from outside his or her head. The voices may be familiar, and often make insulting remarks; they may be single or multiple. Voices speaking directly to the person or commenting on his or her ongoing behavior are particularly characteristic. Command hallucinations may be obeyed, which sometimes creates danger for the person or others. . . . (APA, 1987, pp. 188–189)

In our sample, we did see examples of hallucinations, as in the command hallucinations of Sally prohibiting her revealing what the gods had said to her. However, our subjects' experiences are also riddled with perceptual disturbances that are not part of the DSM-III-R description, namely the hypersensitivity to color and the frequent motion of auditory experience.

> *Affect.* The disturbance often involves flat or inappropriate affect. In flat affect, there are virtually no signs of affective expression; the voice is usually monotonous and the face, immobile. The person may complain that he or she no longer responds with normal emotional intensity or, in extreme cases, no longer has feelings. . . . (APA, 1987, p. 189)

This description leaves ambiguous the distinction between the internal experience of affect and its outward expression. We must be clear that it is only the *outward* expression of emotion that is flat in some of our subjects, not its inner apprehension. Our schizophrenic subjects did have clear inner emotional experience.

> *Sense of self.* The sense of self that gives the normal person a feeling of individuality, uniqueness, and self-direction is frequently disturbed in schizophrenia. This is sometimes referred to as a loss of ego boundaries, frequently is evidenced by extreme perplexity about one's own identity and the meaning of existence. . . . (APA, 1987, p. 189)

This was certainly a characteristic of all of our schizophrenic subjects except Jennifer. For our subjects, however, the term "sense of self" seems far too shallow, as if sense of self is merely one concept among others, and the self-sense is deficient merely because it fails to provide a reasonable ordering to the progression of events in the individual's experience. For our subjects, it was not the *sense* of self that was disordered, but the *self* itself. Our subjects, particularly Joe and Bob when decompensating, had no organized locus of experiencing and therefore no experiences that may or may not be congruent with some sense of self. Our understanding is that they had no self at all.

We recognize that the concept of self is fraught with abuse and confusion in the history of psychology. We need, therefore, to be explicitly clear that we do not mean that the self is some "man within the man," as it has sometimes been seen. Our understanding of "self" is that it is a term best applied to the organization or coordination of processes that make perception possible and, in our view, that organization was deficient or nonexistent in our decompensated schizophrenics. Thus, whatever it is that is disturbed in schizophrenia (which we are here calling *self* for lack of a better term) is *more* than a "sense . . . that gives the normal person a feeling of individuality, uniqueness, and self-direction." What it is that is disturbed in schizophrenia is the organization that makes experience possible at all.

> *Volition.* The characteristic disturbances in volition are most readily observed in the residual phase. There is nearly always some disturbance in self-initiated, goal-directed activity, which may grossly impair work or other role functioning. . . . (APA, 1987, p. 187)

Our samples did not illuminate this characteristic one way or the other.

> *Impaired interpersonal functioning and relationship to the external world.* Difficulty in interpersonal relationships is almost invariably present. Often this takes the form of social withdrawal and emotional detachment. When the person is severely preoccupied with egocentric and illogical ideas and fantasies and distorts or excludes the external world, the condition has been referred to as "autism." Some with the disorder, during a phase of the illness, cling to other people, intrude upon strangers, and fail to recognize that excessive closeness makes other people uncomfortable and likely to pull away. (APA, 1987, p. 189)

It was clearly true that our subjects withdrew from involvement with the external world to become preoccupied with their own ideas. There was even one example of family members commenting on such preoccupation: In Sally's first sample, her mother was asking her what was wrong at a moment that Sally was attending to the voices of the gods. Our observation was that this inner preoccupation with images in general, illogical or not, was accompanied by a simultaneous reflecting of external (interpersonal) events. In our sample of nondecompensated schizophrenics, images were the focus of attention approximately half the time, so that impaired interpersonal functioning may be the result of preoccupation with images, as well as the strong inner experience of affect.

> *Psychomotor behavior*. Various disturbances in psychomotor behavior are observed, particularly in the chronically severe and acutely florid forms of the disorder. . . . (APA, 1987, p. 189)

Our samples did not provide clear examples of this phenomenon.

Thus we see that our observations lead us to rethink nearly all of the characteristic symptoms of schizophrenia. Several comments are in order.

First, our observations are based on only four schizophrenics; it may prove to be the case that some of the observations may be the exception rather than the rule when more schizophrenics' inner experience is examined in detail.

Second, even if only half of our observations prove to be replicable, or, for that matter, even if only *one* of them is replicable, then the detailed descriptive sampling method has something important to offer to the understanding of schizophrenia.

Third, it is reasonable to inquire how it is possible that our observations could differ so greatly from the DSM-III-R standard diagnostic symptoms of schizophrenia. The answer seems to be that the DSM-III-R symptoms are either of directly observable behavior (Volition and Psychomotor Behavior), or are characteristics of inner experience which can be inferred from a relatively gross observation of external behavior. Thus, disorders of thinking are identified when delusions are reported or associations become loose, and disordered perception is identified when the patient reports hallucinations. Our own analysis seems to us to be much more fine-grained, attempting to examine inner experience itself to gain an understanding of its disturbances. Thus, we are not criticizing DSM-III-R—it adequately describes the eternal symptoms of schizophrenia. We are, however, noting that understanding the *inner* characteristics of schizophrenia, which DSM-III-R for the most part (not explicitly) declines to mention, may be at least as important in understanding the nature of schizophrenia.

Other characteristics may have been noticed common to the descriptions of Jennifer, Joe, Bob, and Sally; characteristics that we have not discussed. This chapter is clearly not exhaustive; readers are invited to take their understanding of schizophrenia back to the descriptions themselves to see whether that understanding can be illuminated or amplified.

REFERENCES

American Psychiatric Association (1987). *Diagnostic and statistical manual, 3rd edition-Revised*. Washington, D.C.: Author.

16

Discussion

We have considered the inner experience of ten individuals, and drawn some conclusions and speculations about normal and schizophrenic experience. It is now time to step back and ask ourselves some pertinent questions about the ground that we have covered.

What were our goals in this project? To try to get an accurate glimpse into the thinking of other individuals; to explore the similarities and differences in people's inner experience; to see if everyone else's inner experience is the same as our own; to get some sense of the range of experiences that people have.

Are the descriptions we have presented believably basically accurate? While I can assure you that we have tried to make all of our descriptions accurate, my assurance does not make them accurate, nor make you believe them. There are no external criteria against which you can test these descriptions for accuracy; so whether you find these descriptions compelling comes down to whether you trust our descriptions. There is no way around it: You need to establish for yourself whether we are believable describers. There are doubtless many considerations that you might weigh: Did the steps of the method seem likely to minimize the kinds of distortions that are possible in descriptions of thinking? Did our implementations actually follow the proposed method? Were you convinced that the characteristics that were described in each chapter emerged from each individual's own sampled inner experience, rather than resulting from preexisting expectations of the author or subject? Because these are important questions in seriously considering any description, and especially important in evaluating a description of inner experience where there is no external criterion, our task in this work necessarily consisted of providing enough evidence for you to determine for yourself whether we were trustworthy describers, as well as providing the descriptions themselves.

You may have noticed that some of the descriptive chapters (particularly those by Smith and Melancon, which were completed before the others) provided more of this kind of evidence than did later chapters. For example, Smith and Melancon each wrote Pre-Sampling Retrospective General Accounts, which allowed you to ponder whether the emerging categories merely recapitulated Smith or Melancon's expectations; furthermore, they gave examples of how categories emerged and were modified over the course of sampling.

Why did we not continue to provide such data in our succeeding chapters? Primarily, because we had gained confidence in our own ability to use the method as relatively free from the distortions of preconception. As we gained confidence, we could dispense with the more step-by-step procedures of the method.

Assuming that you found the accounts we have provided to be believable, *Should you believe others who might attempt to use this method?* No and Yes. No, because use of this method does not guarantee trustworthy reports. I do not believe that there is a single feature of the method we have used here that assures that the resulting descriptions will be basically accurate. If you believed our reports, it was not because we used "The Descriptive Sampling Method," but because we presented enough information for you to decide whether to trust us. Should other individuals use the method, then they also would have to present some evidence of their believability to win your trust. Accordingly, yes, you should believe other describers, but only if they somehow convince you that their descriptions are trustworthy. The point is that this trust is not a characteristic of the *method,* but rather a characteristic of the relationship between you and *its users.*

Why this emphasis on trust? Isn't science supposed to present facts that are free of such personal characteristics? I don't know the answer to this general question. Perhaps that is the goal of science. At the moment, it seems to me that the period of sterility of method in which I believe psychology finds itself is at least in part due to a mistaken view that trust can be dispensed with, replaced by adequate scientific method. Please notice that I am not recommending any general, across-the-board increase in trust. This is not a statement in support of a "trust your psychologist" movement analogous to the "trust your feelings" movement of the 1960s. Rather, I simply note that we have rather blindly accepted the so-called "scientific" method with increasingly barren results in psychology; and I suggest that other kinds of data should be accepted *if, and only if* those data are presented in such a way as to be trusted.

We have seen that there are rather big differences among normal individuals in their inner experience, for example, that images appeared in Jason's thinking 42 percent of the time, but only 7 percent of the time in Helen's. *Could it be true that these differences are merely differences in the words used to describe essentially the same kinds of inner experience, rather than differences in the thinking process itself?* That is, could it be true that Jason's and Helen's inner experience are actually the same, but that Helen chose to *call* an experience an image less frequently than did Jason? Perhaps there are some ambiguous experiences, rather like images but not quite, which Jason decided to call images and which Helen did not. As far as I know, there is no possible way to answer this question definitively. There is no way to disentangle the thought from its description, since we have no direct access to the thought itself.

However, the hypothesis of merely a language difference does not seem plausible to me, and I advance the following analogy to explain why. Imagine that Jason and Helen have each (separately) just returned from a visit to the American West, a region where we ourselves have never been. We ask Helen what she saw there, and she reports that she saw "the biggest hole in the ground that I have ever seen! It seemed to extend for hundreds of miles." Separately, we inquire of Jason what he saw, and he says, "What a canyon! It was absolutely the most incredible excavation I have ever seen." Our method encourages us to probe further—to attempt to recreate the experience being described, so we ask Helen for more details. "I couldn't believe the changing grandeur! I got up at sunrise and saw the shadows falling from the rim, moving at what seemed like a hundred miles an hour down the wall toward the river. Then I walked nonstop (well, almost nonstop since I did pause when overtaken by the mule riders) until noon, when I came out onto a grassy plain which from above had seemed the size of a football field but now was actually over a mile across." We also ask Jason for additional details: "I was truly amazed when I saw it for the first time. I came around the corner, and there it was. I walked up to the safety fence and peered through one of those viewing holes that they cut for you and peered through. The cranes and the bulldozers at the bottom of that chasm looked like Tonka Toys. I watched as a cement truck made its way to the bottom—it took fully ten minutes of switchback roads to arrive at the bottom. I learned later that there would be nineteen stories underground in that building. What a site!"

If we were casual, uncritical observers, we were likely to have concluded initially that both Helen and Jason had visited the Grand Canyon and were impressed by its awesome magnificence. But the details make it clear that while Helen was describing the canyon, Jason was describing a construction site. The task of describing the inner experience of thinking seems, to the participants, to be very much like describing landscapes: "Tell me what you saw at a particular moment." Just as in listening to descriptions about landscapes, we tried to keep in mind that the same words could refer to different views, or that different words could refer to the same view; and so we would need to press for the experiential details to help us understand accurately. It seems to us that the differences in inner experience are in fact as distinguishable as are differences in external experiences, and the evidence comes from the meanings transmitted in the experiential details. I don't believe the hypothesis of merely a language difference, because the details our subjects provide about their inner experience are every bit as complete, detailed, consistent, and compelling as are any external descriptions.

How could it have been easy for the subjects in this study to focus on their inner experience at the moment of the beep? You may have asked yourself the question, "What am I thinking about right now?" several times while reading this book, and found answering the question quite difficult. Shouldn't the subjects described herein have had the same difficulty? First, this doubting of your own ability to apply this method is a very frequent reaction among prospective samplers in our research. With very few exceptions, however, subjects discover that it is *much* easier than they had thought it would be to report their immediate experience, and that ambiguities about what to report at each beep are much more the exception than the rule.

Why, then, is the self-questioning, "What am I thinking right now?" so difficult? The answer is that at the moment you are asking yourself "What am I thinking?", your thought is precisely that question itself. However, your intention is to find something in ongoing thought, so it seems that you must *exclude* precisely that question from whatever you might report as your current thought. Thus you are intent on excluding the very thought that is presently occurring, with the result that *nothing* seems to be ongoing in thinking. This is the same kind of problem that historically has plagued any reflective attempt at describing thinking. However, it turns out that non-schizophrenic thought samplers unanimously report that, once they have a little practice, they can respond to the external event of the beep by "freezing" the current thought before the thought "What am I thinking" obliterates it.

Perhaps you went further in your own informal sampling trial, and used some event in your own environment, such as the occurrence of the next TV commercial or the next telephone ring, to trigger your own sampling. Now you have sampling triggered by some external event, which we have just seen is necessary, but still you may have found sampling to be difficult or impossible. The explanation here is that the signal that cues sampling must have a sudden onset and be totally unambiguous so that it has a clear, crisp, undeniable, meaning of "Sample now!" Neither the TV commercial nor the telephone ring meets those requirements. When the TV show action pauses and the moment of silence or music between TV events occurs, you have time to ask yourself (in words or images or however you might do so) whether this pause signals a commercial, so you can be ready to sample. When you then recognize the presence of the commercial, you attempt sampling, with the (unstated) intention of excluding any thoughts that may have been preparations to thought sampling. These, of course, are exactly your current thoughts, so it seems, by erroneous exclusion, that there is nothing being thought at that moment.

The telephone ring, when used as a cue for sampling, has, unfortunately for the sampling, an ambiguous meaning, both as a sampling cue and in its normal function as a cue for answering. Thus, if you used it in this way, the ring likely triggered a series of internal events that carried the meaning (whether in words or however), "I must now suspend my usual answering response to this signal until I first sample my thoughts." This, of course, is again the kind of thought that you would exclude from any thought report, so again, it may seem (erroneously) that there is no thought at the moment.

The point is that these unsuccessful attempts at thought sampling should not lead you to conclude that thought sampling as we have described it is impossible; but rather should lead you to an appreciation of the relative delicacy of the method. The signal, in order for sampling to be possible, must at least be sudden and mean "Sample now!" and nothing else. Other characteristics of the signal are desirable also (see Chapter 3).

At a rather technical level, we note that some experience samplers have used as a signalling device the beep from a programmable wristwatch or electronic pager rather than the earphone beeper that we have used here. While further research is clearly needed on this point, we believe that the earphone signal is much preferable to any externally audible signal for sampling inner experience. When sampling external behavior, which does not fluctuate as rapidly as inner experience, the audible beepers are adequate. But sampling inner experience is a much more delicate matter, and the earphone beep is preferable because it is absolutely unambiguous and because it does not disturb the external environment. Some of our subjects find it difficult to freeze their ongoing thought when they have, at the same moment, some internal "competition" from the embarrassment caused by others being present and possibly disturbed, or wondering what others think about their involvement in the research project, etc.

What should we make of a book that only provides descriptions of inner experience? We want a good theory that explains the thinking process, not merely good data waiting to be explained. To this question I counsel patience. *A theory is not likely to be better than the data it purports to explain,* and the data about human inner experience will take some time to amass carefully. Theories about thinking would be in fact valuable, but only *after* the general landscape of individuals' thinking is very familiar. As far as I know, for example, no existing theories of thinking have pointed to the *existence* of something like Smith's corrupted word repetitions; much less explained issues such as their frequency in the general population or their significance to individual behavior. Why not? Because the theorists didn't even know that such phenomena existed. We are in the midst of a cognitive revolution, and theories about thinking are again becoming abundant. Unfortunately, it seems to me, these theories are fabricated with almost no careful understanding of the basic nature of inner experience. I believe we should take our ignorance about thinking seriously, and refrain from theorizing until inner experience is more familiar.

Wouldn't that mean that we would need books with hundreds of chapters, each as detailed as Chapters 4 through 14? No one could be expected to master that amount of material. Yes, it might mean precisely that; or that some other way of access to real inner experience would be devised. However, the reluctance to master that volume of material is merely a prejudice of modern theoretical psychology. By contrast, the student of music is required to be familiar with hundreds of different symphonies, overtures, sonatas, concerti, etc., and then, beyond that, to be familiar with the generalizations and theories about this sonata-form or that variation treatment. We would be justly critical of a musician who could accurately cite the several theories of counterpoint but who could not recognize the themes from the Second Brandenburg Concerto. We should be equally critical of the psychologist who can cite the several theories of cognitive processes but who is not familiar with the inner experience of any individual living being. Familiarity with a collection of several hundred descriptions as detailed as those of Chapters 4 through 14 is not an overwhelming obstacle, once we decide that the effort is worthwhile.

What is the significance of this project? First, it demonstrates that believable (assuming you found them so) descriptions of inner experience are possible, which is in itself no trivial demonstration, given the several-thousand-year Western failure to provide such descriptions. Second, it sketches the size of the differences in thinking that can be expected in normal individuals. We do *not* all think alike. Third, it opens the inner experience of schizophrenia to our view, and suggests some rather radical perspectives on the understanding of this disorder. Finally, it makes a clear call for many additional such descriptions, so that we may become knowledgeable about the range and significance of normal thinking and the difference between normalcy, schizophrenia, and other disorders that should be examined with equal care.

Isn't the last chapter a series of generalizations about schizophrenia, and haven't I advised you to avoid such generalizations? Yes and no. It *is* difficult to curtail the urge to generalize, for me as well as for others, but there are two characteristics of these generalizations that deserve note. First, they are stated extremely tentatively: the conclusions *suggest* that schizophrenia *may* be related. . . . Second, the generalizations follow from the careful observation of a number of individuals—ten, to be exact, including four schizophrenics. The generalizations are true at least for them. Although a data set of only ten subjects is not enough to make confident generalizations, it is enough to make tentative speculations, especially when that tentativeness is explicitly acknowledged.

Our aim in this entire book has been simply to describe the experiences of our subjects, and in so doing, we have made it a rule to avoid for the most part such distractions as comparisons of our data with that found by nondescriptive measures. We have made one exception to that general rule, namely, our discussion of the differences between our own results and the DSM-III symptoms. We allowed ourselves that exception because we thought it wise to demonstrate how our *results* differ from mainstream psychology. To highlight how our descriptive sampling *method* differs from mainstream psychology, we will use the case of color perception in schizophrenia. Our goal will be to show that the descriptive sampling technique is a much more direct investigative procedure than that typically used in psychology. We have refrained earlier from such contrasts because we have not wished to be involved in a debate over psychological method. We have decided instead that the best way to demonstrate the fertility of our method was simply to *show* its results, not to *argue* for them. The method can then stand or fall on its own merits, not on the adequacy or inadequacy of some supporting arguments. However, we should highlight the differences in method between our own descriptions and experimental psychology in general.

Psychology has been interested in how different people respond to color for at least 65 years, when Rorschach (1921) noted a relationship between a person's affective responses and his frequency of color response to the Rorschach ink blots (a Rorschach percept is a "color response" if the subject indicates that the color of the ink blot or portion thereof was influential in determining what the person saw in the ink blot, as for example, if the subject says, "It's blood *because* it's red"). Rorschach himself attempted to explain this phenomenon by noting that emotional phrases were often colorful, as in "rose-colored glasses" and "green with envy"; but his explanation was, for a variety of reasons, inadequate. Weiner (1966) summarized the subsequent research as follows:

> . . . It remained for later writers to pursue a more sophisticated explanation of the basic processes of Rorschach color use. The three major themes that have emerged from subsequent formulations of the interpretive significance of Rorschach color responses are (a) that color perception is a passive phenomenon resembling affective experience, (b) that color complicates the perceptual task and initiates emotional reactions in the perceiver, and (c) that color is a specific case of the general class of strong stimulations that require the perceiver to exercise his available resources and preferred style for integrating strong stimuli. (pp. 183–184)

These are three conflicting theoretical explanations of the relationship between color perception and affective style. Our concern here is not to decide which, if any, of the three statements is correct; but, rather, to discuss the logic that led to the advancing of the three theories, because it will serve to exemplify why we find the present work important.

Let us use as an example the theory of Rapaport, Gill, and Schafer (1946), which may be understood as an exemplification of Weiner's theory type (a), the similarity between color and affective response. Rapaport advanced a theory about inner experience in general, starting from observations of subjects engaged in one particular activity, namely, responding to the Rorschach inkblots. It seems to me that Rapaport used what may be schematized as a three-stage process in developing his theory: (1) the collection of the basic data (the Rorschach responses); (2) the inference from the basic data to inner experience in general; and (3) the explanation of the processes underlying that inner experience. Rapaport's Stage 1 basic data were observations of individuals and their responses to the Rorschach inkblots, for example, that a person who gives frequent pure color Rorschach responses is either impulsive and wildly affective, or is extremely controlled in his or her emotionality (see Rapaport, 1946, p. 242).

On the basis of these and similar observations, Rapaport seems to have inferred (Stage 2) a characteristic style of inner experience: "Persons prone to quick and violent emotional outbursts bring also to the testing situation a make-up which has its characteristic associative processes: these processes are such that they will be greatly stimulated by, and will cling to, the colored areas of the inkblots. More generally, the subject's characteristic organization of his associative processes will exercise a selective effect over the stimulations emanating from each inkblot" (Rapaport, 1946, p. 238).

Then, in Stage (3), this inferred inner experience is explained: Normal affective experience is the result of acquiring the skill of delaying the rapid gratification that is associated with color until the slower associations coming from the form of objects can be adequately integrated. The reason, then, that affectively unstable individuals give Rorschach color responses is that these individuals have not acquired a smooth, reliable system of delaying gratification either of color or affect. "The smoother the control of the delay and satisfaction of the instinctual impulses [of color or affect], the more varied and rich their derivatives become" (p. 239). Variability and richness of emotional experience are the desirable characteristics of healthy individuals, according to Rapaport.

Our concern is not particularly with the adequacy of the theory (Stage 3), but rather with the accuracy of the Stage 2 *inferences* on which the theory rests. If my understanding of Rapaport is correct, then he viewed inner experience as existing along a continuum of domination by color: sometimes color overtakes us and obliterates all formal aspects, and sometimes the effects of color are suspended so that the shape of the environment can be viewed accurately.

There is a subtle but important difference between Rapaport's understanding of the inner experience of color and that provided by our Jennifer or Bob. For Jennifer and Bob, there was a continuum of hyper-clarity of color; but this continuum always occurred alongside, parallel to, or within their apprehension of the form or shape of the environment. We did not see evidence for a continuum of the domination of inner experience by color, as Rapaport apparently did when he concluded that color perception had to be delayed so that formal aspects could be attended to. That is, we saw that some *portions* of visual experience were sometimes hyper-colorful, but we did not see that the *whole* of visual experience was sometimes color-dominated.

While other explanations are possible, the differences between Rapaport's understanding and Jennifer and Bob's experience is likely due to the fact that Rapaport's view of inner experience was mistaken. We recall that Rapaport's view of inner experience was an inference based on what his subjects said about *inkblots* (where by contrast our own view of inner experience is an inference based on what our subjects said about *inner experience* itself). In the Rorschach situation, the subject must *talk about* the blot, and in so doing, must either talk about the aspects that are hyper-colorful or not. Because the *talk* is thus either about the color-dominated aspects or not, it is possible to conclude erroneously that *perception* must be either color-dominated or not, when the actual case is that the subject is forced to talk either about a color-dominated *aspect* of perception or about a non-color dominated aspect. Thus, Rapaport may have mistaken a part of inner experience for the whole. We believe that hyper-colored portions of inner experience exist embedded in or alongside normally colored well-formed regions of experience.

Thus we see that Rapaport was theorizing about an inferred version of inner experience that was itself a misconception. Our rather extended consideration of color perception theory has not been intended to criticize Rapaport in particular; on the contrary, we see his method of theorizing as being rather typical of psychology. Instead, we wish to highlight our belief that the science of psychology has handicapped itself by failing to look directly at the phenomenon it seeks to understand. Rapaport (1) looked at Rorschach responses and on that basis (2) inferred what the corresponding inner experiences must be, and then (3) offered a theoretical explanation of that inferred inner experience. The present analysis suggests that inferential leaps should be kept as short as possible, in this case by beginning with subjects' own descriptions of their inner experience, and then inferring what their experience must really be like. Then it would be appropriate to offer theoretical explanations of that experience.

Should these descriptions be called "phenomenological"? I would prefer not. The term "phenomenological" has two rather distinct meanings in modern usage, what we might call the philosophical and the vernacular. In philosophical usage, phenomenology is an attempt to arrive at essential natures, truths laid bare without human distortion. Our own project is much *less* ambitious: we merely tried to describe things the way they were seen to be, with no attempt to elucidate essential characteristics. In vernacular usage, phenomenological refers to anything subjective, including just about anyone's opinions about anything. Our project is much *more* ambitious than that: we tried to eliminate our own opinions because they could distort the things we were trying to describe. Thus the term "phenomenological" usually means either much more or much less than deserves to be applied to this project. If "phenomenological" meant "We took rather great pains to describe phenomena carefully," then we could say, yes, our project is phenomenological. But that is not what the term generally means, so we prefer not to apply it to these descriptions.

Should this project then be called "ethological"? That is a much better term, especially if what is meant by "ethological" is any attempt to observe behavior in its natural habitat. However, the term ethological in modern usage is usually reserved for the observation of animal behavior, so we would need to widen its scope to apply it to the present project. In passing, we might note that the animal ethologists *have* avoided the rush to generalization that we have described, and have instead provided painstaking descriptions of actual behavior that has slowly but inexorably shaped comparative psychology.

Suppose you found yourself "rushing to generalization" as you read the descriptions. What should you do about it? First, you should recognize that you already have done something about it, because the first step towards changing behavior is to recognize the behavior that might need changing. Second, you might examine within yourself why you generalize so quickly. The chances are that honest answers to that question will not be flattering: to be able to impress my friends/colleagues; to feel as if I actually know something; to gain an advantage over others not quite so facile; to meet the publication demands of promotion or tenure; to avoid facing my own ignorance; to keep a conversation going so that I don't feel awkward/stupid/alone/unwanted/ignorant; etc. Any of those motives that are also true for you, or any other such statements that apply, are part of the basic data about yourself. The third step is to practice resisting whichever pressures apply to you.

Only time will tell whether these descriptions are believable, whether additional descriptions accumulate, and whether such an accumulation seems useful. However, the actual or projected results of a method are only one measure of the method; another perhaps equally important measure is the effect the application of the method has on the applier. Thus it might be reasonable to inquire *What have I learned or how have I changed as a result of ten years' involvement, on and off, with the intensive attempt to provide careful, accurate descriptions of other people's inner experience?* This is, of course, an impossible question to answer objectively, since I have had many experiences unrelated to sampling that have had significant impact on me over the past ten years. Nonetheless, a few of my personal musings on the subject may prove informative.

Before we begin, we might note that besides the kind of intensive, qualitative descriptions provided here, I have conducted and published univariate hypothesis-testing experiments, multivariate quantitative studies on thinking and emotion across large numbers of subjects, intensive quantitative analyses of individuals, etc. In short, I have worked in a rather broad range of the methods of modern psychology. My overall conclusion at the moment, however, is that there is more to be gained from intensive, qualitative descriptions than from any of the other quantitative or experimental methods.

Perhaps an example will make it clear why I believe that there is presently more value in qualitative descriptions than in quantitative studies. In 1984, an article appeared that I authored with Brian Lech and Sonja Saltman. That article described two large quantitative thought and mood sampling studies, a total of nearly half a million data points. The main findings of that article were that the thoughts of groups of individuals in widely different settings can be clustered into six replicable descriptive categories or "factors," namely, Aggressive/Bad Mood,

Pleasant/Sexual, Daydreaming/Past Sexual, Clear Thought, Thought and Mood Duration, and Self-Critical.

This finding was important because hitherto there had been no direct evidence that regularities in inner experience could be found that were stable across a variety of settings. (Sue Melancon, Steve Reise, and I have since published four more articles relating to the stability and generalizability of those factors.) Contrast that result with any one of the findings of the present study, for example, the existence of the decaying Word Repetitions in a normal subject. The simple observation that words are frequently "just there" in inner experience opens a window on thinking that we had never before even imagined, and this should have profound impact on our understanding of thinking. For example, it significantly undermines whatever credence we put in the popular notion that all thinking is subvocal speech. In my view, the quantitative findings take what seems to be a blind step forward when compared to the descriptions, and do not get at the question that motivates all this research, namely, What is thinking *like?*

In another example, as I was nearing completion of this book, an issue of the *Schizophrenia Bulletin* (Holzman, 1986) was published which was entirely devoted to the thinking of schizophrenics. I do not wish to be unduly critical of that edition, because the papers reported there are probably neither worse nor better than my own quantitative studies. These sophisticated analyses found significant, but not really large, differences between schizophrenic and normal thinking! I was struck by the fact that if we can't find huge qualitative differences between normal and schizophrenic thinking, when we firmly believe that schizophrenia is the most disordered form of thinking that exists, then our research must be profoundly misguided. Anyone reading that issue of *Schizophrenia Bulletin* may be interested in comparing it to Chapters 11–15 of this volume with regard to how much may be learned about schizophrenia.

For what it may be worth, I will list a few of what I would cite as changes in my perspective due at least in part to involvement in writing careful descriptions. First is a much deeper awareness of the difference between the way things *are* and the way things might plausibly be *said* to be. This is obviously not a new distinction; what *was* new for me was the vastness of the distinction and my sense of the insensitivity of modern psychology (and modern society) to it. This theme has recurred frequently in the previous chapters of this book, usually as some form of what I referred to as the "rush to generalization." We get a half-clear glimpse of a fact and rush to classify it or explain it, and in so doing create a theory that is merely *plausible* rather than *true,* with two results: First, we lose what half-clarity we had and, second, we become enamored of our classifications or explanations. This was the tendency of individual samplers as described in Chapter 3; this is also the tendency of the science of psychology as a whole: we spend much more time, energy, and emotion revising and defending our plausibilities than we do developing our expertise in observing actualities.

The second, third, and fourth observations are related to the first. Second, I have gained an appreciation for the fact that those actual experiences that we call "thought" seem to be undisturbed and untouched by any clamorous theorizing about them. Despite theoretical claims that, for example, "self-downing" thoughts lead to irrational emotional consequences, or that thoughts of loss lead to depression, our thinking itself continues unchanged and little understood, as if still awaiting discovery. *Our theories about thinking do not seem to have affected how we think at all.*

A similar, third observation is that while ten years ago the theories in psychology fascinated me, they do not hold much interest for me anymore, whether they be behavioristic, psychoanalytic, humanistic, cognitive, etc. All these explanations seem to be immediate steps *away* from the facts. A half-clear observation is followed by a half-true explanation, and then subsequent efforts, sometimes monumental and lasting for generations (as in attempts to prove or disprove psychoanalytic theory), are focused on the *explanation,* not on the quality of the original or subsequent *observations.* The point here is that I have acquired the taste of noticing that *our theories tend to take on a life of their own,* which, while initially fascinating, is ultimately disappointingly shallow compared to the individual facts themselves.

The fourth observation is also related to the first three: I have become increasingly aware of a ubiquitous tendency to avoid the personal in favor of the general. In our sampling experiences, this was evidenced by our having to learn to resist the tendency to drift into general statements about thinking, rather than to describe the particular momentary thought under consideration. In psychology in general it is evidenced by our overwhelming lack of information about what real, existing people do or think. For example, there is only one attempt that I know of to describe in detail what any individual person really does for any extended period of time, Barker's *One Boy's Day* (1951). In everyday life, it is characterized by the inclination of most people most of the time to describe themselves in general terms ("I usually do . . .") and to respond to others in stereotypes.

The fifth change is my deepening awareness of what it means to speak or write or be truthful. My earlier understanding was that "true" meant something like "conforming to the known facts"; but I have come to view that as a very shallow understanding of truth. The deeper meaning of true is something like "straightforward" or "uncovering without misleading." I see my earlier understanding as a personal shortcoming, but one that is shared by many people, including many psychologists. It is the shallower "fact-conforming" understanding of truth that allows, for example, psychoanalysts authoritatively to interpret according to their theory, and behaviorists to scorn the understandings of others because they do not conform to the behaviorist's view of the facts.

What I have come to believe about both these examples, and about dogmatic statements in general, is that they frequently are true in the shallower sense (true in conformity with the facts that the theory holds to be important), but false in that they mislead about some important but not stated related issue, typically the insecurity of the speaker. "True" has come to mean for me "not misleading on any level or from any perspective." That is an exacting standard, one that I am sure I myself do not meet, and am not entirely sure is humanly attainable (although I have come to believe that it is attainable). Even so, the recognition that truth-as-fact-conformity is a shallow or derived form of truth-as-uncovering-without-misleading is a significant change for a psychologist, it seems to me, since plausible theories form the foundation of modern psychology, but plausibility itself rests on the shallower truth standard. It should be noted that the entire descriptive sampling procedure is from start to finish an exercise in uncovering without misleading, applied to communicating with each other about inner experience.

Sixth, the intensive-descriptive experience-sampling experience has been seen as "therapeutic" or "growth-promoting" by all participants in both the present study and the previous attempts. This does not mean that we ever explicitly attempted to make favorable changes; we did not. Nor does it mean that we always constructively actualized the opportunities that we had; in fact, we did not. Nonetheless, the kinds of activities we describe here were experienced as powerfully, personally influential.

We have considered and reconsidered the results of this study and the range of possible effects on the participants. *What, then, is our overall evaluation of the method itself?* Given that we hold an understanding of inner experience to be important, and the descriptions we provided to be accurate, it may come as a surprise that we do not consider the method itself to be especially significant. There are two reasons for this. First, as we stated earlier in this chapter, we do not believe that using the method guarantees in any sense the adequacy of the resulting descriptions. That is, we can conceive of individuals (perhaps narrow-minded or dogmatic individuals) who could apply all the steps of the descriptive sampling method in sequence and still write descriptions that would not be believable. Secondly, not using the method does not necessarily mean that descriptions of inner experience will be inadequate. We can conceive of other individuals (particularly perspicacious observers) who could skip all the steps entirely and yet write highly believable descriptions. Thus, there is nothing either necessary or sufficient about this method as a vehicle for providing good descriptions of inner experience.

Does that mean that the method is not useful? Not at all. The method does have its usefulness, even though it does not provide guarantees. Its value is as a vehicle to allow the *evaluation* of the believability of our descriptions, not to guarantee it. We have laid open a particular procedure to allow you to see what we value in terms of observations, and to allow you to observe the proceedings by which we transformed those values into verbal descriptions. If you considered the values and our exposition and transformation of them, and then were led either to credit or not the accuracy of the descriptions, then the method was successful in its way. That another unrelated method might have produced the same results is not a criticism of either method, any more than the fact that I can drive to New York on either Interstate 40 or 90 is a criticism of either road. The important point is that if you believed the descriptions presented here, it is *not* because we used the method of Chapter 3, but because in so generating and using that method, you came to see us as believable describers.

Are there risks in the application of this method? Yes; and the major hazards are related to what is called transference and countertransference in psychotherapy. Descriptive sampling, as we have done it here, places the participants in an extremely powerful psychological situation, where the subject is providing intimate details of his or her own private experience while the observer listens interestedly but reveals nothing of his or her own. This is similar to the transference situation which Freud and subsequent psychotherapists have described, except that the transferences and countertransferences during sampling are faster and more powerful than those I myself have encountered in my psychotherapy practice. My recommendation is simple: If you are not ready to deal with strong, sudden, positive and negative emotions directed both towards others and yourself, or are not ready to accept the risks and responsibilities of putting another person in what may be an extremely vulnerable situation where you yourself have an inordinate amount of power, then put off sampling until the risk of abusing or being abused by the transference-type emotions lessens.

What, then, is our general conclusion about this project? We believe that we heightened our own sense of the desirability of describing things as they are without misleading the reader, and learned that a good description does not have to be complete, but should not be misleading about (neither understating nor overstating) its completeness. Furthermore, we believe that such descriptions are within the range of human capability, and even if the present descriptions fall somewhat short of this ideal, they may serve to illuminate the possibility of creating good descriptions. The results themselves were informative in their own right, which led us to believe that a series of such studies are needed if we are ever to understand inner experience adequately.

REFERENCES

Barker, R. G. (1951/1966). *One boy's day*. Hamden, CN: Archon Books.
Holzman, P. S. (1986). *Schizophrenia Bulletin, 12*.
Hurlburt, R. T., Lech, B., & Saltman, S. (1984). Random sampling of thought and mood. *Cognitive Therapy and Research, 8*, 263–275.
Rapaport, D., Gill, M., & Schafer, R. (1946). *Diagnostic psychological testing*, vol. II. Chicago: Year Book Publishers.
Rorschach, H. (1921/1942). *Psychodiagnostics* (5th ed.). Bern: Hans Huber.
Weiner, I. B. (1966). *Psychodiagnosis in schizophrenia*. New York: Wiley.

17

A Look at Depression and Beyond

We have shown, we think, what we have set out to show: that descriptive sampling can demonstrate individual differences between subjects and can find dramatic differences between individuals who are identified as being members of dramatically different groups: the inner experiences of our schizophrenic subjects were in fact much different from those of our normal subjects.

However, is it possible that the characteristics that we identified in Chapter 15 as being features of schizophrenic experience are characteristics not of schizophrenia alone but of some larger class, perhaps of mental illness in general? Further research with a variety of groups will be necessary to delineate precisely the boundaries of the phenomena we have identified; but we can cite some preliminary results from a study of depression that will appear as a sequel to this book. That project is not yet complete, but we have sampled enough depressed individuals to be relatively confident of the following generalities about depression, which we provide without presenting the evidence (the interested reader will have to await our forthcoming book on depression).

Our purpose, then, in presenting the following brief sketch of depressed inner experience is to show that the descriptive sampling method can dramatically differentiate not only schizophrenics from normals, but also just as dramatically differentiate schizophrenics from depressed individuals.

The fact is that the inner experiences of our depressed subjects are markedly different from that of our schizophrenics. While our schizophrenics (when not decompensated) report frequent Images in inner experience, our depressed subjects have Images only rarely or never. We have never seen a "goofed-up" Image in any of our depressed subjects. While our normal subjects report frequent Inner Speech and Inner Hearing samples, our depressed subjects have such experiences only rarely.

The main characteristic of depressed inner experience is the predominance of the kind of thinking we call Unsymbolized Thinking: well-differentiated thinking that occurs without words, Images, etc. While such thinking is relatively rare in normal and schizophrenic subjects, it is extremely frequent in the depressed individuals we have sampled, occurring perhaps 75 percent of the time or more. We have described Unsymbolized Thinking in the present book; but unless further sampling with depressed individuals turns up some major surprises for us, the sequel will focus on the distinction between Unsymbolized Thinking and other kinds of thinking.

There are other characteristics of depressed inner experience, but they will have to await the more adequate treatment in the forthcoming book. For the moment, we have given enough of the depressive results to be able to say that *none* of the characteristics that we have discussed in Chapter 15 apply to depressed individuals. Therefore we can conclude that those characteristics are *not* relevant to all mental illness (although they still may be relevant to a class somewhat larger than schizophrenia alone).

Our preliminary results suggest that the inner experience of depressives (including manic depressives) is extremely different from that of schizophrenics, and the descriptive sampling technique can clearly differentiate individuals from the two diagnostic categories. If our completed results and those of other relicators uphold that conclusion, then the descriptive sampling method should be able to contribute to the sometimes problematic differential diagnosis between depression and schizophrenia. The method may be particularly useful because it can reliably identify *individuals,* not groups of individuals. If it is true that depressed individuals have 75 percent or more Unsymbolized Thinking while normals and schizophrenics have very few; and if it is also true that schizophrenics have goofed-up Images while depressed individuals do not, then those large differences seen in individuals should make differential diagnosis extremely reliable.

However, those are speculations based on an incomplete project. We will attempt to be more definitive in the sequel on depression.

Index

Alcohol, 89, 94
Altered States, 89
American Psychiatric Association, 259, 263
Antrobus, J., vi
Aristotle, 11
Association, 259
Assumed experience, 78
Auditorium voice, 51, 60, 146

Barker, R. G., 277, 280
Beep, experience of, 196
Beeper, being the, 201
Bellow, S., vi
Bem, D. J., 2, 7
Ben's samples
  angry at requested change, 79, 81, 94
  collage of three friends, too close, 91, 94
  cover of Judas Priest album, 88
  eating coleslaw, 90
  embracing girl in bar, 82
  fear girlfriend would come in, 82
  folding aluminum foil, 86
  friend is asleep, 79
  frustration over finding pen, 83
  guessing age of actor, 92
  happiness as a family, 90
  hearing Andy Partridge and himself, 86, 147
  I have to make this appointment, 85
  I have to teach Chris, 79
  I'm talking on the phone, 83
Ben's samples (*Cont.*)
  I would say no, 81
  Image of girl and M&Ms, 87, 89
  Image of shoplifter, 88
  inner hearing of friend singing, 85
  leafing through 45 rpm records, 91
  more than two dollars, 80
  ninety-four seventy-two, 85
  noticing the sung word "Never", 83
  rubbing a hickey, 84
  scanning computerized inventory, 78
  singing *Maybelline*, 80
  singing "We're the Monkees," 86
  twenty-six East Charleston, 85
  where'd we lose a buck?, 87
Blackness, 230, 231, 232, 239, 255
Bob's samples
  academic center/teardrop feeling, 229, 232, 239
  blowing away sandpaper dust, 235
  didn't have money/small feeling, 230
  end of the world/surface feeling, 229, 239
  headache/blackness, 232
  Jackie Collins was right, 234, 235, 239, 240
  knitted sweater, wrong color, 231, 255, 256
  moving baseballs, 232, 239
  Mt. Everest/Jupiter/very beautiful, 236, 239

Bob's samples (*Cont.*)
open the door, moving words, 233
win at Risk/blackness, 230, 232
world is too big, 235
Body Sense, 72

Collins, J., 234, 235, 239, 240, 241
Color, 171, 255, 271
Computing the beep, 184, 190, 207, 256
Cornell, v
Countertransference, 279
Csikszentmihalyi, M., vi

Daydreaming, 42, 163
Decompensation, 234
Depression, 281
Diagnostic and Statistical Manual, 259, 263
Dialect, 99, 102
Diener, D., ix

Ericsson, K. A., 1, 3, 4, 5, 6, 7
Ethology, 274

Faulkner, W., vi
Feelings, 55, 58, 59, 62, 81, 104, 179, 228, 254, 260
Follow-up sample, 28, 122, 141
Foreign language, 99
Freud, S., v, 11, 279

Gill, M., 272, 280
Glossolalia, 130, 145
Gods, voices of, 244, 252
Grand Canyon, 266
Grover, S. C., 1, 7

Harvard, v
Helen's samples
Alfons, Alfons, Alfons, 103
Big Two-Hearted River: I, 97, 104, 146
brothers in arms, 107
continual back pain, 101
deeply unhappy, 103
dissatisfaction watching TV, 105
escape from jail, 105
everyone is a social scientist, 105
funny situation, 102
going home, 98, 100
how cold your paws are, 99, 100, 146
Image of the *Hoofdgebouw*, 107
inner speech directed to author, 97, 146

Helen's samples (*Cont.*)
just a quick cleaning up, 97
must be in the week of, 103
Napoleon's hat, 101, 144
radio announcement of pop group, 104
relationship, 98, 99, 101
six characteristics, 108
street fair, 103, 107
talking about a professor, 104
they didn't spell it right, 106, 108
three incomplete verbalizations, 100, 108
violas too green, 97, 106, 108
watching *Lou Grant*, 104, 150
Holzman, P. S., 276, 280
Hurlburt, R. T., 280

Imageless Seeing, 56, 60, 108
Imageless thought, 11
Images, 41, 59, 63, 65, 88, 107, 116, 132, 147, 162, 166, 248, 255
Images, distortions in, 168, 191, 249, 252
Images, problem-solving, 45
Images of External Reality, 160
Images of written words, 166
Implied experience, 78
Information processing, 3
Inner Hearing, 51, 59, 85, 99, 127, 146, 176, 178
Inner Speech, 51, 53, 58, 84, 96, 125, 146, 176
Introspection, 1

James, W., v
Jason's samples
auditorium voice, 51, 60, 146
calculator, 46
classroom, 50
clichés, 57
commissaries, 56, 148
concentrating on remembering, 57
conjugating a phrase in French, 56
feeling hungry, 59
fish tanks, 47, 148
holding prices of ovens in mind, 57
I despise my French class, 55, 144
I hate traffic lights, 53, 58
I'm sleepy, 52
it is too cold, 53
jangling keys, 58
McDonald's, 48

Jason's samples (*Cont.*)
morning news, 58
neuron schematic, 50, 148
Olympics, 44, 58, 149
peanut butter, 52
playing tennis, 44, 148
Russians are evil, 55, 56, 58
ski resort, 42
Socrates, 42
Swedish market, 43
teacher, 52, 60
television credits, 49
tennis ball trajectory, 46, 47, 149
that is absurd, 53
twelve noon in French, 55
watching a horror movie, 57
weather in hometown, 43
what a stupid comic, 52, 54
what is on TV?, 52
wrong homework assignment, 58
yellow spectrum, 48
Jennifer's samples
aunt with beady eyes/yellow smoke, 171, 173
aware of melting ice, 182
balls on pool table, 172
Bill from the back, over shoulder, 172
Bill on couch, tilted, 169
brilliant blue can, moving words, 171, 178, 255
coleslaw and carrots, 181
colorful word JOHNNY, 174, 189
figure-8 shape, 174
garbage sack, 161, 256
hairdresser/red and white shirt, 165
hearing "I should change channel," 178
hearing "She's going home," 178
Image of Joe/blue iced tea, 161
Image of Rod Stewart, 162
John on couch/rubbing mascara, 163
looking at cigarette box, 183
makeup case/words moving, 161, 169, 172, 177
messy counter top, 160, 166
midget, 164
moving image of skirt and legs, 175, 185
Ping-Pong/red and white shirt, 163, 256
pinning hair/mixed up words, 168, 171
RC Cola can, disconnected arm, 170
reading sampling notebook, 178
Jennifer's samples (*Cont.*)
rice and pork chops, 162, 172
room inspection, 179
Sally's blue dress/sugar, 167, 171, 184, 256
Seven-Eleven store, 177
sexual song, 180
tan telephone/red and white shirt, 165, 172
The Gong Show, tilted, graffiti, 169, 256
thinking about being inspector, 183
tilted color TV, 169
waiting to brush off ants, 181
walking into foyer/Virginia Slims, 164, 166
warm positive feeling for Gary, 180
WONDER/Pepsi can/yellow cloud, 166, 175, 181
wondering if Joe would catch up, 181
wristwatch, yellow word THOUGHT, 173, 188
yellow patches/word YELLOW, 173
Jim's samples
all it's cracked up to be, 72
art gallery ramp, 69
attaching a handle, 65, 70
bereavement, 69, 70, 73, 145
brick eaten away by fire, 69, 150
bus tour, 64, 66
cardboard box in trash, 69, 71
CAUTION, 64, 66, 69, 70, 73
clay and body swelling, 63, 72
closing the door, 71
comparing bricks and vase, 70, 71
forcing clay down on wheel, 62, 72
glaze splash, 66, 149
heard a boom, 71
himself in tree, 67, 148
how people use initials, 73
Image of dune buggy, 67
Image of judge, 67
Image of Julie's teacher, 68
Image of section of pot wall, 66
Image of telephone caller, 63, 68
observing colors of slip, 70
observing shape of the pots, 70
observing the word "Interest," 70, 73
orange peel, 65
pain in finger, 68, 72
pot with side flattened, 63, 149
pouring Diet Coke, 64, 70

Jim's samples (*Cont.*)
  rock in the clay, 64
  rushing to unload bisque pots, 62, 71
  saying words to a song, 73
  shorting connections in radio, 71
  taking radio apart, 64
  throwing pot at ISOMATA, 62, 68
  turning a bucket of clay, 71
Joe's samples
  Marilyn Monroe, 197
  recreation of brain fluids, 214
  SS Golden Crescent, 208
  Virgin Mary, 215
Joyce, J., vi
Just Doing, 71

Klinger, E., vi, ix

Lech, B., 275, 280
Leipzig, v
Listening, 138

Mantras, 130
Marijuana, 89, 94
McAdams, D., vi
McConnell, H. K., 2, 7
Method, 17, 31, 268, 278
Multiple Experiences, 108

Nisbett, R. E., 1, 2, 3, 6, 7
No Thought, 92, 139, 182
Noticing Characteristics, 69, 136

Partially Wordless Speech, 100
Paying Particular Attention, 56, 103, 118
Phenomenology, 11, 20, 31, 274
Preconceptions, 20, 36, 265
Pre-sampling account, 19, 119, 139, 266
Psychoanalysis, v

Rapaport, D., 272, 273, 280
Reading, 102
Reflective thinking, 11
Reise, S., 276
Retrospective account, 19
Reverie, 116
Reviewing samples, 28
Revisualizations, 50
Richardson, D., vi
Rorschach, H., 271, 272, 273, 274, 280
Rorschach Ink Blots, 136, 271, 273, 274
Rush to generalization, 12, 14, 15, 32, 39, 271, 275, 276, 277

Sally's samples
  boyfriend putting on his coat, 249, 251
  gods ordering her not to tell, 245, 251
  gunning down everyone, 248, 251, 255
  hearing Maarten say I'll marry, 251
  I should take a look at Menno, 250
  money/gods: Dollie is a bitch, 245
  seeing the gods, 247, 249, 251
  taxes/gods: look away, 246, 251
Saltman, S., 275, 280
Sampling instructions, 21
Schafer, R., 272, 280
Schizophrenia Bulletin, 276, 280
Self, 260
Self-aware thoughts, 113, 151
Short-term memory, 5
Signal detection, vi
Simon, H. A., 1, 3, 4, 5, 6, 7
Singer, J. L., vi vii, ix
Sonja's samples
  aware of exaggerated speaking, 115
  aware of friend's expression, 114
  aware of her interaction, 114
  aware of impatience in voice, 114
  aware of moving very fast, 113
  aware of own forced smile, 115
  aware of own gestures, 114
  aware of own polite smile, 114
  big sleek tiger, 117
  boy screaming, 116
  buttering toast/I'm nervous, 112
  eighty-eight, 112
  farm basket, 112
  hard when you have to perform, 117
  his usual good time, 116
  how serious we must seem, 114
  I am too heavy, 118
  I should not be so critical, 115
  Jacqueline Bisset with man, 116
  lunch bag/tea bag, 113, 122, 145
  observing forming an opinion, 114
  question during basketball on TV, 115
  reading "Otanez," 117
  red Duplo cube, 119, 149
  saying "No it isn't," 119
  self-critical, 115
  sell it for a few hundred bucks, 117
  talking to family/feeling good, 114

Sonja's samples (*Cont.*)
telephoning a friend not home, 116
Thursday, Friday, Saturday, 113
typewritten pages, 116
Speaking Aloud, 86, 103, 137
Speaking in tongues, 130, 145
Storms, M. D., 2, 7
Sue's samples
always reality-based, 130
aware she was smiling, 137
bartender and waitress, 128
buyers' reluctance, 133
clients, 129
data table/PESTAN runs, 127
don't panic, 126
driving through traffic, 139
dying 14-year-old girl, 133, 149
fill up on number ten, 126
first edition has an index, 128, 131
flames at Auschwitz, 134, 138, 148
God, who are you/collage image, 135, 148
hands cold during glossolalia, 130
I got a pebble in my shoe, 126
if I were to die today, 133
if you'll be my valentine, 138
I'm at the pivotal time, 126, 146
I'm really going to "stuff," 138
Image of previous sample, 132
Imaging yellow notebook paper, 138
intelligence tests, 127
it wasn't that dirty, 139
Jesus, mercy, 130
Jill has a new job too, 127
keep your humor/balloon image, 134, 149
looking in phone book, 128
looking through crafts catalog, 139
looking through kitchen spices, 131
Lucien curve, 128, 131, 150
man in hospice, 132, 148
my God, what does this mean, 126
observing co-worker and coffeepot, 138
observing élan and lipstick color, 137
observing friend's pressure, 137
observing head tilt of co-worker, 136, 150
pick up your stretcher and walk, 127
positioning pens/glossolalia, 130
Sue's samples (*Cont.*)
positively, totally great, 126, 146
pouring bacteria into toilet, 129, 148
precipitation data, 137
reaching for phone book, 129
reading legal document, 127
Rorschach card collage image, 136, 148
scanning computer printout, 129
speaking in tongues, 130
taking off her sweater, 126
that's OK, 126
the anxiety has been coming, 127
thirty-nine cents a pound, 139
this meat has discolored, 125, 147
tired, 129
walking across kitchen, 134
walking through stadium, 139
watching people mill around, 139
wear your long underwear, 138
who would be teaching aerobics, 129
wondering if co-worker would come, 131

Thematic Apperception Test, vi
Think-aloud studies, 4, 10
Tilted images, 161, 164, 168, 169, 170, 250, 252, 256
Titchener, E. B., v
Transference, 279
Trust, 266
Truth, 277, 278

Unconscious, 11
Unsymbolized Thinking, 78, 90, 102, 106, 131, 150, 151, 181, 282

Watson, J. B., v
Weiner, I. B., 272, 280
Wilson, T. D., 1, 2, 3, 6, 7
Woolf, V., vi
Word Repetition, 103, 111, 147, 270
Wordless Speech, 54, 60, 101
Words, moving, 177, 178, 233, 234, 235, 237, 257
Wright, F. L., 236, 240, 241
Writing descriptions, 26
Würzburg, v

Yellow, 166, 171, 173, 175, 189, 239, 255

MIX
Papier aus verantwortungsvollen Quellen
Paper from responsible sources
FSC® C105338

If you have any concerns about our products,
you can contact us on
ProductSafety@springernature.com

In case Publisher is established outside the EU,
the EU authorized representative is:
Springer Nature Customer Service Center GmbH
Europaplatz 3, 69115 Heidelberg, Germany

Printed by Libri Plureos GmbH
in Hamburg, Germany